BASICS FOR A
Biblical
WORLDVIEW

bju press®

Greenville, South Carolina

Note: The fact that a given writer is cited or quoted in this textbook does not mean that BJU Press endorses that writer from the standpoint of morals, philosophy, or scientific hypotheses. The nature of a worldview book is such that we must cite and quote people with whom we disagree. Part of developing a biblical worldview is cultivating the ability to discern between the good and problematic views of all sorts of people, even Christians.

Basics for a Biblical Worldview, Student Edition

Course Vision and Design
Brian Collins, PhD
Bryan Smith, PhD

Writer
Mark Ward, PhD

Contributing Writer
Daniel Olachea, MDiv

Consultant
L. Michelle Rosier

Academic Oversight
Jeff Heath, EdD
Rachel Santopietro, MEd

Editor
Suzanne Villegas, MA

Cover and Book Designer
Michael Asire

Design Assistant
Katy Labadorf

Cover Illustrator
Karen Schipper

Illustrators
Patrick Mahoney
Kathy Pflug
Rommel Ruiz
Karen Schipper
Dana Thompson
Del Thompson

Page Layout
Lydia Thompson

Digital Content Management
Peggy Hargis

Permissions
Tatiana Bento
Carrie Hanna
Elizabeth Walker

Project Coordinator
Christopher Daniels

Photo credits appear on pages 381–82.

Acknowledgements appear within the notes, which begin on page 363.

Excerpts from MERE CHRISTIANITY by C.S. Lewis copyright © C.S. Lewis Pte. Ltd. 1942, 1943, 1944, 1952. Reprinted by permission. (pp. 17, 23, 331)

Some content taken from pages 64 [first quotation] and 39–40 [second quotation] of *A PROMISE KEPT*, by Robertson McQuilkin. Copyright © 1998. Used by permission of Tyndale House Publishers, a Division of Tyndale House Ministries. All rights reserved. To order book, please visit www.tyndale.com. (p. 240)

The text for this book is set in Adobe Avenir, Adobe Minion Pro, Adobe Myriad Pro, Arial Hebrew by Monotype Typography, Avenir 95, Futura and Futura Condensed by URW, Oswald by Vernon Adams, and Wingdings 3 by Bigelow and Holmes.

ISBN 978-1-62856-627-7

15 14 13 12 11 10 9 8 7 6 5

CONTENTS

UNIT 8: HOW DO I RELATE TO PEOPLE WITH OTHER WORLDVIEWS? 314

FOREWORD

The world you are growing up in has changed. People don't think like they used to. I'm not saying that everything was fine when I was in the sixth grade (back in the early 1980s). We had plenty of problems. But there was a lot more agreement about what was right and what was wrong, especially among Christians.

But now people honestly believe that certain things are right that just a few years ago most people would have said were very wrong. Another way to say this is that we live in a time when there is a lot of confusion.

This is the reason we decided to produce this course. We've learned that Christians need help thinking about all of life in the right way, and this help needs to get started by the sixth grade, at least. You've already run into ideas that are wrong and dangerous. If you're old enough to come across these ideas, you're old enough to try to understand them from God's viewpoint.

This course will challenge you. You're going to have to think about your thinking and why you believe what you believe. Some people may say that this kind of course is too challenging for someone your age. But I don't think so. I've learned that sixth graders are wide open for a course like this. They're hungry to learn and accept the challenge of new ideas.

I wish our world were a better place. But I think I see the wisdom of God in the confusion. It's forcing us to take our Bibles seriously. That's a very good thing. All we ask is that you stay hungry to learn and accept the challenge of every new idea.

Bryan Smith, PhD
Senior Manager, Biblical Worldview Formation
BJU Press

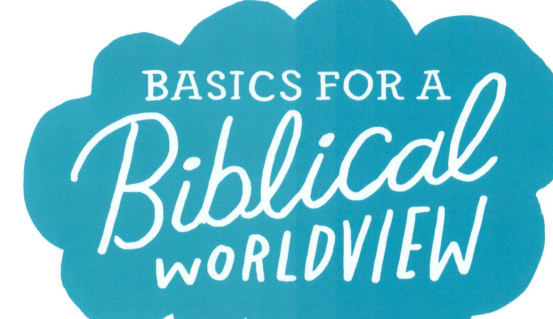

WHAT IS A WORLDVIEW?

1.1 WORLDVIEW LENSES

What is a worldview ?

Have you noticed that people around you don't all see the world the same way?

It's not just that some people are always happy and others aren't. No, it's almost like people wear different kinds of glasses that make them see differently. Two people can look at the same thing and come to opposite conclusions about it.

Take human life for example. Some people see both humans and animals as the result of billions of years of random evolution. Other people see humans as special creations of God, quite different from animals. Same world, different glasses.

Problems are the same way. Everyone can see bullying and poor leadership and family conflict as problems. But where do these problems come from? Some people see poverty or the lack of education as the cause. Other people see the cause as the sinful human heart. Same world, different glasses.

People see different solutions to the world's problems too. Everyone wants a peaceful, fair society. But they can't agree on what counts as "peace" or what counts as "fair."

Why do people disagree so profoundly over such basic things? Well—same world, different glasses. It might sound simplistic, but it's true. They have different **worldviews**.

A worldview is indeed like a pair of glasses. And everybody is wearing them, including you.

Some people have very ineffective worldview glasses. The way they see is all wrong. Things get all bent out of shape from the way they really are. And maybe these people don't even know it. Their worldview is not helping them live well in the world.

Some people, however, have well-made glasses, glasses that help them see the world clearly. Obviously, you want to have good glasses, a correct worldview.

Now's your chance. This book is all about how to put on corrective lenses by listening to the only person who can see the whole thing at once—the person who designed and created it all, including you. The intent of this book is to shape the "glasses" in front of your eyes so that you see the world (as much as a human can) as it truly is, the way God sees it. You should have a *biblical* worldview.

THE PARTS OF A WORLDVIEW

Every worldview out there has three parts.

1. Every worldview tells a **big story** about where the world came from, why it is the way it is, and where it's going.
2. Every worldview includes **basic beliefs and assumptions driven by what a person loves**.
3. Every worldview logically leads to certain **actions** by individuals and groups, and sets of group actions make up what we see in the world as different cultures.

Big story, basic beliefs driven by loves, actions. That's a worldview.

And guess what? You're having a worldview, right now, as you read this book. You are believing a big story about the world. You are using your basic beliefs from that story without even thinking about it. Your beliefs are being driven by your loves: you are either interested or suspicious or bored right now, partly because of the attitude of your heart before you ever picked up this book. And you are living out your worldview with your actions. Whether you're reading intently or whether you're daydreaming is based on your big story and your beliefs and loves.

We'll talk more about what a worldview is and does, but these are the basics. Big story, basic beliefs driven by loves, actions.

Although you might never think much about your worldview, it shows up everywhere in your life, all the time.

THE THING EVERYBODY HAS

And worldviews show up in everyone else's lives too, no exceptions. Let's review the three parts of a worldview and see where they show up in *other* people's lives.

1. BIG STORY

You can't make it to middle school without having an idea about where you came from, why you're here, and what the whole point of the world is. And all the kids around you have ideas about these things too. Even if they're still asking questions, they tend to have a story they're wondering about.

If you're around a bunch of kids from Christian families, hopefully you'll find that they share the same big story that starts with Genesis 1:1, "In the beginning God created the heaven and the earth." Hopefully Jesus is in the middle of this story, dying and rising again. And, hopefully, He's at the end, bringing God's rule to a restored earth. That's the Bible's big story.

But if you're not with Christians, like if you play on a local soccer team or have non-Christian friends, you'll probably find that those kids are telling them-selves a very different big story, one that doesn't include God at all. Their story might start with a big bang and end with a *piff*, as the universe dies out a trillion gazillion years from now. That's the big story believed by most educated people in the West (North America and Europe).

And here's the thing: they *can't not* have a big story. Everybody past the age of five has *some* idea about the big questions in life. Where did I come from? Why am I here? What's wrong with the world? Where are we all headed?

Everybody has a big story.

2. BASIC BELIEFS DRIVEN BY LOVES

Think of how people talk to each other when they disagree. "You *have* to give me some of your orange, because I gave you the biggest piece of cake yesterday!" Have you ever heard someone talk like that? If you have a brother or sister, you know you have.

But notice what the kid who wants the orange is assuming. He has a basic belief or assumption that if he does something good for his brother, his brother now owes him something in return. Share and share alike. But who says so? Well, probably it was Mom—but who told her this rule? Who made a universal law that if one brother shares, then the other brother has to? If there is no God determining fairness, why shouldn't I just try to get as much orange and cake as I can? Fairness is a basic belief, and people have different ideas about what counts as fair.

Or try this one: a kid falls and twists his ankle really badly on the playground. He screams his head off. A bunch of moms look up from their phones, but only one comes running with a scared look on her face. Can you guess which one? Why do mothers lovingly respond to their own children more quickly than to other children? Who says it should be this way? Who made a universal law that people should lovingly respond to their own families more quickly than to other people's? Your duty to your family is a love, or a value, that you grew up having. It's one you probably never think to defend or explain.

Everybody has basic beliefs driven by loves.

BASIC BELIEFS

Basic beliefs are the things that you believe but probably never think about. They are beliefs you can't always prove; instead you use them to prove other things, like the idea that you can believe what you see. If someone says, "How do you know that your sister ate the last piece of candy?," you can say, "I saw her do it ten minutes ago." But how do you know your eyes are trustworthy? People see things that aren't there all the time, like when magicians appear to saw people in half. The belief that you can trust your own eyes is a basic belief.

3. INDIVIDUAL AND GROUP ACTIONS

Think of how boys and girls relate to their friends in Western culture. In the West, boys do not hold hands, even when they've been best friends since age two. But girls and women sometimes do. In the Arabic world, however, grown men hold hands to show friendship. Westerners and Middle Easterners have different assumptions and values that give rise to their different cultures, their different group actions.

Everybody acts based on a worldview.

How many prongs do you think you see in this illustration called a blivet?

7

DIFFERENT GLASSES

If you ever go shopping for glasses, you'll notice that there are a lot of styles available—but not an infinite amount. There might be 493, but not 493 million. So it's possible that if you choose the blue plastic ones, you'll find out the next day that someone you know chose the exact same ones. (And depending on who it was, that might be very cool or very not cool!) There aren't an infinite number of worldviews either.

There are certain major options out there if you're shopping for a worldview. People don't have totally unique worldviews. They tend to share their big story and their basic beliefs and loves with a group. It might be the culture of a large group who speaks the same language and follows the same religion, or even a smaller group within it that has a few differences from the larger culture. For example, Westerners tend to say that they like for people to "think for themselves." But they say this only about people who agree with them. Really, most people tend to hang out with others who think about and love the things they do.

And if you're a Christian, all of this should be really helpful to understand. It means that the people who are criticizing your glasses have glasses of their own. It's not like there are some people out there who don't need or don't have glasses—people who have no big story, no basic beliefs driven by loves, and no culture. No one out there is completely objective or neutral. If someone doesn't love Jesus Christ and doesn't share a basic belief in the truth of the Bible, he loves other things and has other basic beliefs. It's not only religious people who have faith; everyone does. We will talk *a lot* more about this.

YOUR GLASSES

You can't look *at* your glasses and *through* your glasses at the same time. It's one or the other. Either at or through. So if you're a Christian, this book will not ask you to try to be neutral, to take off your biblical glasses in order to prove that they're the right ones to wear. (Remember how it's impossible to be neutral anyway?) This book assumes that God exists, that He created the world, that He has spoken to us in the Bible. It assumes that the biggest love driving you should be your love for Him. It assumes that good cultural actions are those based on the truth of the Bible.

If you're not already wearing biblical glasses, this book will invite you to see through them. When you look at yourself and the world through a biblical worldview, you should see more clearly. A biblical worldview should feel like you finally got the right prescription.

After all, God made your eyes, and He knows how to make you see correctly.

Thinking It Through 1.1

1. Define *worldview* using its three parts.

2. Which of the following statements show a worldview?
   "Tigers are meat eaters."
   "Tigers have strong spirits that connect with the spirit of the earth."
   "Jesus lived in Galilee."
   "Jesus is the Son of God."

3. Why do you think every person has a worldview?

Which big story is in my head ?

Start saying "Once upon a time . . ." and people can't help but want to know what happens next. Toss in an ". . . all of a sudden . . ." and all of a sudden people are captivated. They can hardly wait to get to ". . . The end." Stories are powerful. Humans are built to love and enjoy stories.

It is no accident that every worldview tells a big story about the world. It's the first ingredient. Stories tap into something deep inside every one of us, and for a worldview to gain true believers, it has to tell a satisfying **big story**.

BIG STORIES AT THE MOVIES

Some of the most powerful stories of our time are the big stories told in popular movie series. Think of *Star Wars*. The movies, TV shows, novels, or comic books from this big story are everywhere around you. The *Star Wars* big story has made massive amounts of money by capturing the hearts and minds of people.

People love stories—and they love big stories. The opening lines on the screen in every *Star Wars* movie shout, "BIG STORY."

A long time ago in a galaxy far, far away . . .

And what follows, in multiple films, is a story that sweeps up the whole galaxy, from tiny planets to emperors who seem to be all-powerful. It includes a kind of "religion" that actually tries to explain "god" and the two sides of good and evil as the Force. The Force is powerful: it can teleport someone's image across the universe; it can lift spaceships out of swamps through a person's mental concentration; it can give someone the power to block dozens of laser bullets at once with a swinging lightsaber. (The only thing it can't do is fix the sentences of Yoda®.)

And, very interestingly, this impersonal godlike Force has purposes, even plans. It produces Jedi knights (good) as well as Sith lords (evil). One film actually explains that the Force tries to balance the two.

Big stories don't just provide entertainment. They explain the world for people. Big stories carry powerful ideas. They answer basic worldview questions like these: *Where did we come from? What's wrong with the world? Where are we all headed?*

BIG STORIES PEOPLE TELL

The Bible tells a big story that goes like this (we'll highlight the three big points):

God **created** this world very good. He created humans in His image to rule over the world. But man **fell** into sin and took the world down with him; now the entire creation groans under the weight of human sin. But Christ, through His perfect life and atoning death, is **redeeming** His fallen creation, especially sinful mankind, through the power of the Holy Spirit. All these events are for the glory of God, that all authority, fame, beauty, and perfection be acknowledged as belonging to God.

You could summarize the story with just those three boldfaced words: **Creation**, **Fall**, **Redemption**. We'll talk more about the Christian big story in this book.

Though some people reject the big story the Bible tells about the world, they never go around without a big story. No, they tell a different one. People always have *some* idea of where we came from, what's wrong with our world, and where our world is going.

The most popular big story about the world that's told by Western people is the evolutionary story. If you attend a secular school, you'll hear this story assumed not only in science class but in history and even English class. You'll hear it in popular songs, books, and movies. You'll even hear it in what people *don't* say; God never shows up in this story.

The evolutionary story goes something like this:

In the beginning, stuff just was. (Don't ask why it was or where it came from.) The stuff was all concentrated in a tiny, extremely dense dot. Then, *bang.* (Don't ask why it went *bang.*) Then billions of years went by as the dot expanded to become the universe. At some point, life just was. (Don't ask why or how it was.) Then life evolved into birds, trees, and us. Humans are the most advanced evolutionary beings known to exist. Our problems come from unfinished evolution. Evolution will weed out more and more of our problems until our world becomes an ideal place to live. And then in the distant, distant future, everything will grind to a halt, and all matter and energy will cease to exist. The end.

Not a very inspiring story. But it certainly is big. And here's the key: just as with *Star Wars*, people use it to explain their world.

11

EXPLAINING WHAT YOU SEE
THROUGH THE LENSES OF A STORY

Everybody explains everything through the lenses of a story. Whether that story is true or false makes a big difference in how they see the world.

Are there some people you know who don't like you? They are telling themselves a story about you that (hopefully!) isn't true, and they view all your actions through those twisted lenses. Maybe you memorized all the verses you were given in Sunday school because (1) you love the Lord and want to please Him and (2) your parents offered you a special trip if you learned them all. But kids who don't like you might be telling themselves a story like this: "They're always trying to show off; they only memorized those verses to impress the teacher."

Maybe those kids have a good reason or two to tell that story about you: you *did* show off a few times. But they are forgetting (or don't know) the parts of your story that show that impressing others is not your main motivation. Once they start telling themselves the false story, it's very hard to get them to change it.

It's probably not a big deal if a few people tell an untrue story about you. You can't be friends with everyone in this fallen world.

But sometimes telling or believing the wrong story can cause trouble for you. Like if you are a police officer investigating an apparent burglary.

You see the broken glass door and the overturned potted plant next to the door. The computer bag—with the computer in it—is gone. Another smash-and-grab, just like all the others. The burglar must have broken through the door, grabbed the bag, and overturned the plant trying to get away quickly.

You have your story—so everything you see from then on you try to fit into that story. The footprints outside are the burglar's. The open gate is where he or she ran out.

You're piecing together the entire story when you notice the glass from the door is on the outside of the house as if smashed from the inside. Suddenly, your story doesn't seem to work. Then the victim says, "Wait, what's that?" She picks up a computer bag off the coffee table. "This is my son's bag that's like my stolen one, but he's on his way to school . . . oh . . . wait . . . ."

Then her phone rings. After a "Yes . . . are you OK? . . . I'll be there soon," she ends the phone call and says, "My son grabbed my bag by mistake in his rush to get to school and slammed the door too hard. He made all this mess trying to get to school on time!"

You interpreted what you saw based on the more likely story. But that didn't mean it was correct.

We constantly interpret the things we see by the big story we believe. Like the "crime" scene, if our story is wrong, we will misinterpret the evidence. The only way to correctly understand the evidence—all the stuff in the world you see, hear, touch, learn about—is to get the story right.

WHAT YOU SEE THROUGH YOUR BIG STORY

People explain everything they see in the same way: by fitting it all into a story. You do this too. Everybody does.

Let's look at *you*, now, through the lenses of two big stories currently being told in the West.

EVOLUTIONARY GLASSES

What are you, when you look at yourself through the lenses of the evolutionary story?

You are a very advanced ape. You have the "rights" your group has decided to give you. Your thinking is shaped by your environment and by your evolutionary history. Your height and weight are mostly preprogrammed, and so are your morals and your personality. Many eons ago, your ape-like ancestors were more likely to survive if the group worked together. Religions developed to aid groups in working together. Religion also provided explanations for things the group did not understand, like thunder and lightning. They began to view the seasons as the work of spirits and gods. That is why you are religious today—your religion is a holdover from earlier on the evolutionary timeline.

You are preprogrammed by evolution not only to seek your own happiness but also to look out for ways to protect and promote your group. Your group needs to be on top if the strongest survive and the weakest die. Your survival depends on it.

Soon enough you will die either way, and there is no afterlife. Life is your only chance to have fun. Make the most of it, but don't worry about death. It's natural.

14

BIBLICAL GLASSES

What are you, when you look at yourself through the lenses of the biblical story?

You are made in the image of God. All the worth, privileges, and responsibilities you have are a gift from Him. He made you to glorify Himself by being fruitful, filling the earth, subduing it, and having dominion over it. He made you part of a family, with obligations to honor your parents especially. He has provided salvation through the death and resurrection of His Son, Jesus Christ. If you are indeed a Christian, He has given you His Spirit. He has given you gifts to use for His church, and He calls you to do good works out of love for your neighbor. He has promised that, if you love Him, everything in your life will work together for your good.

Death is unnatural; it is evil. It is the last enemy. When you die as a Christian, you will not really die but will move from one kind of life to a better kind of life. And some day, you will be resurrected in a perfect body and will live forever on a renewed earth.

Look at yourself through the lenses of the Bible's story, and you see something very different from a dying ape. Big stories matter.

Thinking It Through 1.2

1. What kinds of questions must a story answer in order for it to be called a "big story"?

2. Give an example (other than *Star Wars*) of a big story, perhaps from a book or movie.

3. How does a person's big story relate to the way he looks at evidence?

4. Which big story do you think you use to explain your world?

1.3 ASSUMPTIONS

What do I
assume about
the world **?**

Have you ever felt the tug of a powerful ocean wave? It can be scary; suddenly gravity seems to flip in every direction, and you have no control over where your body is.

The apostle Paul, in his letter to the Christians in Ephesus, compares some ideas to waves. He says that the opinions around you can be like water pushing you this way and that (Ephesians 4:13–14). We are all exposed to waves that move through our culture. We all feel pressure to conform to the ideas of the people around us. Maybe the idea is as simple as one you might be thinking right now: *all the cool people have this gadget*. But that's a bad idea—not because having the gadget is necessarily wrong, but because your level of coolness should not be based on the number of gadgets you own.

Little kids are easily persuaded by the ideas around them. If all the other three-year-olds have a Tickle Me Elmo® toy, they have to have one too.

But one way to know whether you're growing in maturity is whether those waves of pressures knock you over. Have you stopped being persuaded by "all the cool people are doing it"? Maturity, Paul says in that letter to the Ephesians, means being able to stand up to the waves in your culture without being moved—like a tall tree with deep roots, one so strong that even a tsunami can't knock it down.

Yet even a small wave can knock you down if you're not paying attention. So maturity also means noticing the more subtle ideas that your culture presses on you.

Are you able to spot the subtle assumptions people make? An **assumption** is an idea people believe without trying to prove, or without even caring to prove. It's often an idea people don't know they have.

We all have assumptions. And that's not necessarily bad—as long as they're good assumptions! Let's talk about some bad assumptions present in Western culture and then a few good ones.

The "Miracle Pine" was the only one out of seventy thousand pines left standing on the shore after a tsunami hit Japan in 2011.

BAD ASSUMPTIONS ON TV

There are bad assumptions all over TV. Shows aimed at middle schoolers sometimes assume this idea: *a truly good life is one in which you have a boyfriend or girlfriend*. They never come out and say it like that; no, it's an assumption baked into the story. All the cool boys in the show are trying to get girlfriends; all the not-cool boys have zero interest in girls. All the cool girls in the show are trying to *become* girlfriends; all the not-cool girls think boys have cooties.

But this is a bad assumption. Do people who are too young to be married need to have boyfriends or girlfriends? Since the Bible says in 1 Corinthians 7 that singleness is an honorable way to live, you can live a truly good life without romance.

BAD ASSUMPTIONS AT SCHOOL

The further you go in school, the deeper you'll get into science and history—and that's a good thing. But the more you study, the more you'll run into the assumption that *only observation counts as proof*. In other words, seeing is believing—and so are smelling, touching, tasting, and hearing.

And this assumption is not so much wrong as it is incomplete. Observation is one good way to know things. It's the best available way to know the properties of an orange, for example. But this assumption says that the many things you can know only by faith can't actually be proven. In fact, saying that only observation counts as proof makes a rule that God can't be the cause of anything (because God can't be observed). In other words, only natural causes count since they can be seen and confirmed in the natural world; supernatural causes don't count.

The truth is that faith is a way to know and even prove things. C. S. Lewis, the author of The Chronicles of Narnia, pointed out in his famous book *Mere Christianity* that he had never seen New York City, but "reliable people" had told him it existed. Thus he knew it was true. We'll talk more about what counts as proof in Section 1.4. For now, realize that if we refuse to believe in anything we can't see (or hear or taste or smell or touch), there will be many things we will never be sure of. *Only observation counts as proof* is a bad assumption.

BAD ASSUMPTIONS ABOUT TECHNOLOGY

When a kid says, "Can I have a phone?," a good parent immediately starts weighing the benefits versus the dangers.

Pro: *It would be good for my child to be able to text me that basketball practice is finished.*

Con: *It would be bad for my child to have access to the internet all day.*

But a wise parent will also think about the assumptions baked into this technology.

Con: *This phone represents an assumption that its owner will always be connected and available.*

Think of that: *always* available. Even when you should be doing homework; even during family dinner; even during church and during school.

If you have a phone, the temptation is to pull it out and look at it every time it buzzes—which is all day and all night. It's designed to distract you, and it's made with the assumption that this is what you should want. This is a bad assumption, even though phones also have positive uses.

BAD ASSUMPTIONS ABOUT SOCIETY

Christians who believe in biblical marriage, one man with one woman until death, have been told recently that they are "on the wrong side of history." They should "get with the times" and accept other definitions of marriage—as if time can change **morality**, what's actually right or wrong. These critics assume that *Western society is progressing through evolution to better forms of morality.* Journalist Andrew Sullivan explains that the progress Westerners typically believe in is "a gradual ascent of mankind toward reason, peace, and prosperity." He even says that this belief in progress has come to replace the West's belief in God.

By saying that Christians are "on the wrong side of history," Westerners are sneaking into their evolutionary story the Christian view of a judgment of right and wrong at the end of time. They're assuming that whoever wins in the end are the good guys—and since they're the ones winning right now, they must be on the right side of history. But how can anyone possibly know that history ends well if there's no God to tell us? And here's another problem: how can we measure "progress" if we don't know what our goal is supposed to be? (How can you win a race if no one has told you where the finish line is?)

18

It's odd that people who believe in evolution should have such firm faith in this kind of progress. In their worldview, the "progress" that they work so hard to gain will ultimately finish with the destruction of all matter and energy. If they took a good look at their worldview, they would have to conclude that we are literally going nowhere. No one will even be there to care when we get there.

Have you noticed yet that Western culture makes a lot of assumptions? Those assumptions can knock you down and pull you under like waves in the ocean.

GOOD ASSUMPTIONS

We've just looked at some bad assumptions. But good and true assumptions run through cultures like waves too. You probably assume it's true that the earth revolves around the sun (rather than the other way around), even though you don't *feel* like you're traveling through space around sixty-eight thousand miles per hour. Reliable scientists have done the calculations and let us know it works this way. You believe them and move on with your life. And your assumption isn't shaken when you learn to recite "the sun rises in the east and sets in the west."

Schools also make good assumptions. They assume that students need human guidance, motivation, and accountability in order to learn. In other words, you can't just hand five-year-olds a big stack of textbooks and expect them to finish all their own schooling by age eighteen. They need teachers.

ASSUMPTIONS AND WORLDVIEWS

We've spent more time on bad assumptions than good ones in this section. This is because you need to be alarmed a little bit. If all assumptions were good, there wouldn't be much reason to examine them. If all riptides at the ocean took you to Happy Candy Island, then there wouldn't be warning signs about riptides at the beach.

But you need to be careful about the assumptions around you. You need to grow in discernment. In other words, you need to learn to recognize assumptions and distinguish between good and bad ones.

This simple point will help. Good assumptions and bad assumptions don't come from nowhere. They grow from someone's worldview. All the bad assumptions we talked

BAD ASSUMPTIONS ABOUT GOD

People have bad assumptions about God too, like this one: it isn't possible for God to be a God of love and yet punish humans for their sins. Or this one: it isn't possible for God to be all-good and all-powerful if evil exists in the world.

about grow out of worldviews in which there is no God or He hasn't spoken in the Bible.

- The idea that *everyone needs a boyfriend or girlfriend to have a truly good life* comes from a worldview in which romantic love has replaced God's love as the highest and best love.
- The idea that *only observation counts as proof* comes from a worldview in which God doesn't exist, so there are no supernatural (and therefore unobservable) causes.
- The idea that *you should always be available* comes from a worldview in which God hasn't explained through the Bible what young people's priorities should be.
- The idea that *everything is progressing toward better morality* comes from a worldview that rejects God's standards of morality and accepts things He does not.

Assumptions don't come from nowhere.

Thinking It Through 1.3

1. What are some assumptions people make about the world?

2. What assumptions might a person who believes in evolution make?

3. How many people make assumptions about the world?

PROOF AND AUTHORITY

Boys like to one-up each other.

"I can jump and touch the basketball net."

"Well, I can touch the rim!"

"Well, I can dunk!"

All the other boys will know just what to say, and they will say it together in chorus: "PROVE IT!"

PROOF BY EXPERIENCE

And there is only one way to prove it to the onlookers. The boy who made the boast cannot argue that, in theory, he *could* dunk if people weren't watching and making him nervous. All the other boys will mock him if he tries any excuses. He has to actually dunk. Or else he hasn't proved it.

What's their proof, and who says so?

It is an extremely rare twelve-year-old who can dunk, but let's imagine that this boy—we'll call him Aiden—actually does it. He leaps up and slams the ball home, shattering the glass backboard, impressing all the girls, and *proving it* to all the boys.

Now imagine further that there is another kid who has watched this whole event. He heard Aiden's claim, he shouted "PROVE IT" with all the others, and now he has shards of glass from the backboard littering his shirt. And yet he says, "I still don't believe you can dunk."

Aiden, the dunker, can't believe his ears. "But I *proved* it!"

"That's not proof," says the skeptic.

All the kids standing around conclude that this other boy is either joking or, well, being a jerk. How could anyone deny the most amazing dunk in the history of twelve-year-olds? The other boy ought to be persuaded! What more proof could he ask for?

AND THAT'S WHAT PROOF IS—WHATEVER REALLY OUGHT TO CONVINCE SOMEONE ELSE OF THE TRUTH OF SOMETHING.

And direct experience, seeing something with your own eyes, is evidence that ought to count as proof.

Now think for a moment—what *ought to be persuasive* changes depending on what you're trying to prove. This is true especially for things beyond what you can see with your eyes, hear with your ears, or touch with your hands. Think of things like the existence of God, or the truth of the Bible, or the existence of right and wrong.

Actually dunking *does prove* you can dunk. But fast-forward ten seconds, and what counts as proof changes. How do you prove that something happened in history?

EXPERIENCE

AUTHORITY

PROOF BY AUTHORITY

Imagine that a teacher comes skidding into the gym after hearing a huge smash (the backboard) and then a huge cheer (the audience). She shouts, "Is everybody okay?"

"Yes," the kids say.

"What in the world happened?" demands the teacher.

One of the kids replies, "Aiden jumped up and dunked the basketball, and he broke the backboard."

"Don't joke," she says. "Tell me what really happened."

Suddenly we're not talking about being convinced by your own eyes: the question is, what ought to persuade someone that an event truly happened in the past?

The most important and obvious answer is this: the authority of reliable eyewitness testimony. You need to hear from someone who saw the evidence and is known for telling the truth. If you get that, you probably ought to believe it, even if it's hard.

Sure enough, all the kids start talking at once, and they all insist that Aiden really dunked. This includes kids who, the teacher knows, don't tell lies or play practical jokes. Every one of them is insisting that Aiden can dunk (except the one skeptic, and he's known for always contradicting everyone else).

The teacher looks at Aiden. He's not super tall. And he's *twelve*. She has no evidence to prove from her own experience that he can dunk, but she's hearing from good authority that he can. All the reliable eyewitnesses say the same thing.

Does the teacher have "proof"? Well . . . *yes*. She has enough proof to make Aiden pay for a new backboard; she also has enough proof to insist that he try out for the school's basketball team!

In *The Lion, the Witch and the Wardrobe*, Lucy's older siblings worry that her stories about a land called Narnia might mean she is going crazy. The old professor zeroes in on the real issue:

> Either your sister is telling lies, or she is mad, or she is telling the truth. You know she doesn't tell lies and it is obvious that she is not mad. For the moment then and unless any further evidence turns up, we must assume that she is telling the truth.

Lucy has something her sneaky brother Edmund lacks: a history of telling the truth. In general, you *ought* to believe the eyewitness accounts of trustworthy people.

TWO MAJOR KINDS OF PROOF

You've just seen two basic ways of proving something: direct experience and authority.

1. If you are one of the kids watching the dunk, you have direct **experience**, visible evidence. Your eyes should persuade you that the boy can dunk. You have proof.
2. If you didn't get to see the dunk, then you will have to be persuaded in a different way. You will have to rely on the **authority** of the eyewitnesses. But you still have proof.

It's tempting to think that only experience counts as proof and that authority is not as good for proving something. But actually, we all rely on both kinds of proof all the time. We couldn't live without the proof that comes from experience or from authority.

Back to C. S. Lewis's example from *Mere Christianity*. He explains how important it is to accept proof by authority:

> Do not be scared by the word authority. Believing things on authority only means believing them because you have been told them by someone you think trustworthy. Ninety-nine per cent of the things you believe are believed on authority. I believe there is such a place as New York. I have not seen it myself. I could not prove by abstract reasoning that there must be such a place. I believe it because reliable people have told me so. . . . A man who [is unwilling to accept] authority in other things as some people do in religion would have to be content to know nothing all his life.

The testimony of an authority is an important kind of proof.

CASE STUDY: WHY YOU SHOULD TRUST US

The company Wirecutter recommends all sorts of products on its website, from computers to blankets to suitcases. Writers prepare articles to compare, for example, computer keyboards from different companies. They tell you which one they think you should get by "proving" that it is the best. Many articles include this heading: "Why you should trust us." Wirecutter explains that their writers are independent researchers, have experience in the topic they're writing about, and do the long, hard work comparing products.

1. Why would Wirecutter want to prove itself as an authority on the products it recommends?

2. What other authorities might people listen to instead of Wirecutter?

3. How does Wirecutter try to prove itself as an authority?

4. Would you take Wirecutter's authority as proof of what is the best product? Explain.

PROOF IN THE BIBLE

Experience and authority are not the only ways to prove something, but all people use at least these two kinds of proof all the time. And so does the Bible.

EXPERIENCE

The book of 1 John opens with this claim: "That which was from the beginning" (in other words, Jesus) is someone "which we have heard, which we have seen with our eyes, which we have looked upon, and our hands have handled" (1:1). John was making a claim to the first kind of proof: evidence from experience. He heard, saw, and touched the Messiah. John told his audience he's persuaded that Jesus and the eternal life He gives are real.

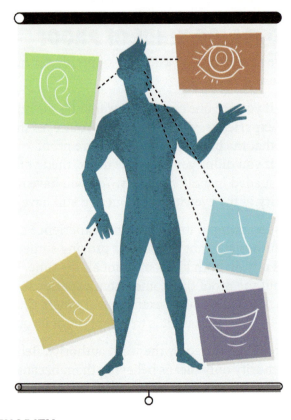

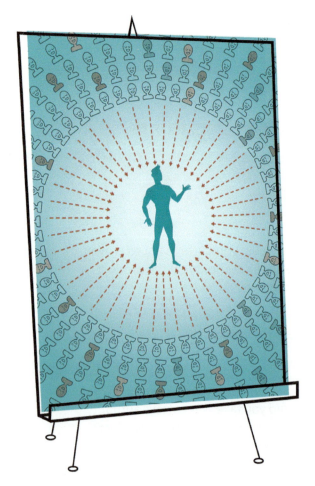

AUTHORITY

When Paul reported that Jesus most certainly rose from the dead, he also commented: "After that, he was seen [by more than] five hundred brethren at once; of whom the greater part remain unto this present" (1 Corinthians 15:6). Why did Paul mention not only that there were eyewitnesses to Jesus' resurrection but also that most of them were still alive? He was appealing to the authority of eyewitnesses. His readers could've actually asked these people for their testimony.

So, proof that comes through the five senses is important, but it is not the only kind of proof. It's possible to rely on someone else's witness of the evidence.

DETERMINING WHAT COUNTS AS PROOF

We've already talked about the common assumption that only observation counts as proof. "Seeing is believing." Many non-Christians talk as though everything they know comes from the direct experience of observation that we call "science." They like to say that they have *sight*: they have "evidence" and "proof." Christians have only *faith*.

Richard Dawkins, the famous atheist, makes this distinction and implies that human reason has already determined what counts as proof. There's no room for revelation from God.

> I have a . . . desire for people to use their own minds and make their own choices, based upon publicly available evidence. [But] religious fanatics want people to switch off their own minds, ignore the evidence, and blindly follow a holy book based upon private "revelation."

Science is indeed a wonderful, God-given tool for finding truth. Science is basically a way of extending our powers of observation. It expands our sight through telescopes and microscopes; it extends our hearing through decibel meters; it extends our other senses through sensors of all kinds. Science is like the kids in the gym watching the boy dunk. It does offer many proofs. But it doesn't own all the proofs in existence.

Richard Dawkins and others who deny that God exists look at the natural world like the skeptical boy looks at the slam-dunker. They fold their arms and say, "Nature doesn't count as proof for God's existence." They do this by shutting their eyes and ears. The Bible says God's eternal power is "clearly seen" through the creation (Romans 1:20). The evidence is there, but atheists can't—they won't—see it. The Bible says that "the heavens declare the glory of God" (Psalm 19:1), but atheists can't—they won't—hear it.

Many non-Christians in the West purposefully tell themselves a big story about the world that includes only natural things and excludes supernatural ones. This big story shapes their worldview lenses so that it becomes impossible for them to see God. The proof is right in front of them. The shards of God's glory are littering their shirts. Still they shake their heads.

THE ULTIMATE AUTHORITY, THE ULTIMATE PROOF

Mere creatures like Dawkins should not be permitted to determine what does and does not count as proof. God, as Creator, is the ultimate authority and the ultimate reliable eyewitness. He was present at Creation, and we were not. And He has spoken in the Bible. God "cannot lie," the Bible says (Titus 1:2). His testimony in Scripture is true. The fact that *God says it* is proof of its truthfulness.

His authority as Creator even extends to telling you how to understand your experiences. Your experience may imply you are worthless, but God says, *No, you are made in My image.* Your experience may imply you are the most perfect kid in town, but God says, *No, the debt you owe because of your sin is infinite, but I have paid it, and you can have forgiveness if you repent.*

Proof is what *ought* to persuade you. Above all other proofs, what your Creator says surely ought to persuade you. When God speaks, that's proof.

Thinking It Through 1.4

1. By what two ways may things be proven?

2. Does the testimony of a trustworthy authority count as proof? Explain.

3. Who do you believe is an authority on truth? Why?

My parents say the
Bible is true because
it is logical.

My church
says the
Bible is true.

WORLDVIEW DILEMMA #16

How do
I know the
Bible is true

?

The Bible
says it is true.

1.5 HEAD AND HEART

Have you ever argued with your friend about the best book or team or TV show or video game? Did either of you actually "win" the argument? Most likely not, because even if you had massive amounts of statistical data behind your argument—like your team's victory in the last championship game—your friend loves his team too much to admit they're not the best. His love for his choice is driving his thinking, not the facts of the matter!

As for you, you might know all the genuine reasons your choice is *not* the best—such as a low number of book sales, conference wins, awards, and appearance on top-ten lists—but you love your choice too much to change your mind. Why do you insist those reasons don't matter?

People choose not to be convinced by reasons disproving their choice *because of their loves*. Ultimately, all the arguments against it as the best won't convince them.

What do
I love ?

HEAD AND HEART FOR ME

Your head and heart are related. They both are involved in virtually every decision you make. The problem is, because we are sinful people, our heads and our hearts are all mixed up in sin.

Have you ever done something you knew was wrong—perhaps hurting someone emotionally or even physically in the process—and then regretted it? You decided you would never ever do that again, and then you found yourself right back at it? Deep down, you loved your sinful choice more than you loved the change in behavior.

We all love things we shouldn't love: we are naturally selfish people. Even though your action may have hurt someone, your heart is selfish enough to want to make that choice again, never mind who gets hurt. We like to think we make levelheaded decisions based on how things should be. The truth of the matter is that we make our decisions based on our loves.

You are a complex mix of head and heart. Your ability to think and your ability to love were both given to you by God. But sin twists your head and your heart in wrong directions. Humans are all born loving wrong things and, therefore, thinking wrong things.

Your loves drive your thinking. If you want to *think* the right things, you'll have to start by *loving* the right things.

LOVE AND "STUFF"

Go to the mall. Look around. What does it want you to love?

Stuff.

Specifically, shopping for *more* stuff.

The pictures of attractive, happy people enjoying stuff, stuff, and stuff are everywhere. They're huge. They're an invitation to you to love stuff too. They're especially trying to train you to love stuff—if you don't already.

The writer of this book has children himself, and every time he goes to the mall he uses the same "joke" with them. Now all his kids catch on. He says, "Look at that advertisement! Wow—if only we had that ear thermometer [or spatula or bike or phone], we would be happy like that person!" And all his kids say, because they're in on the joke now, "No, Dad . . . it doesn't work like that."

But some people, because they love stuff more than they love God, can't see past the posters. The mall is, for them, like a temple of worship. They love stuff, they worship stuff, they dedicate their lives to getting more stuff. They truly believe that having more stuff will make them happy. The one who dies with the most toys wins.

And they don't need to hear a single argument in order to be persuaded. The mall doesn't hire someone to write research papers arguing that, according to the latest scientific studies, stuff makes people happy. The mall doesn't aim at your thinking. It aims at your heart. At your loves.

Jesus aims right back:

> Beware of covetousness: for a man's life consisteth not in the abundance of the things which he possesseth. (Luke 12:15)

It's not wrong to shop at the mall. But it is wrong to love what the mall wants you to love to the point of coveting it, strongly desiring it as the solution to your unfulfilled life. Your loves will drive your thinking and your actions. And if you love the wrong things, you will not have the abundant life God wants you to have. You'll have your reward: a bunch of stuff that ends up cluttering your garage and never satisfying you.

LOVE AND ARGUMENTS

The point here is not that arguments and reasons are useless for persuading people. The Bible uses many arguments. Paul's letter to the Romans is one big bunch of reasoned arguments. The point is that no amount of arguments will change some-one's *mind* if his or her *loves* are pointed in another direction. Arguments and reasons could potentially turn the loves themselves.

BUT UNTIL THEN, THE MIND WILL NOT GO WHERE THE HEART WON'T LET IT.

So if you want to persuade someone—or even yourself—you need to remember that humans are not brains on sticks. God has indeed given us brains; reasons and logic and arguments *do* matter. But at our core, we are lovers. The engine that drives each of us is what the Bible calls the "heart" (Proverbs 4:23).

LOVE AND STORIES

And that's a huge reason every culture tells itself so many stories. Stories have a way of grabbing you by the heart and at the same time managing to get ideas into your head. This works for good loves and for bad ones too, which is why your parents don't let you watch every movie you might want to.

We already talked about bad assumptions that stories can place into your heart—like *a truly good life is one in which you have a boyfriend or girlfriend*. This is a bad love; you were not made to worship romance.

But stories can also demonstrate *good* loves. The Disney movie *Frozen* at first seems to suggest that true love from the princely boyfriend of Anna® will save the day, rescuing the land of Arendelle from danger. But when it turns out that the prince is a manipulative liar, other true love must be found. And it is. Anna loves her sister Elsa® enough to pursue her when she flees. And this love rescues Elsa from her own selfish loves. The story of the movie grabs the heart and teaches it a true lesson: sister love also can be true love.

If the movie were to affect your heart well enough, you might change your mind about what true love is. But you'll need to be careful which stories you let grab your heart. They have the power to persuade your heart and thus direct your thinking about what's right and wrong, true and false.

The Bible tells countless stories, all of which grab the heart and teach it truth. David and Goliath, Noah, Jonah, Rahab, Ruth—these are powerful stories. And as we saw in Section 1.2, the Bible itself is a big story—the most powerful story. It tells us how God glorified Himself by sending His Son, Jesus, to redeem His fallen creation. This big story is supposed to fill your heart and shape your thinking (that's the point of this book).

If you want to love the right things, the things God loves, then read your Bible. Soak in its stories, especially the big one they all tell together.

HEAD AND HEART FOR GOD

You have a head. It should think like God shows us to think in Scripture. The Bible says we should be

> bringing into captivity every thought to the obedience of Christ. (2 Corinthians 10:5)

There are no thoughts you should have that are disobedient to Christ. But how can you make them all obedient? They definitely don't start out that way!

Here's how: you have a heart, and it should love like God does. The Bible says that at the top of our list of loves should be two "items":

> Thou shalt love the Lord thy God with all thy heart, and with all thy soul, and with all thy mind. This is the first and great commandment. And the second is like unto it, Thou shalt love thy neighbour as thyself. (Matthew 22:37–39)

There are no loves you should have that are disobedient to Christ. And if, by God's grace, you do truly love God and neighbor, your thinking will follow.

CASE STUDY: LOVE AND RACISM

Long after Hitler had died at the end of World War II, a young abandoned boy picked up Hitler's racist thinking. Floyd Cochran grew to become a white supremacist, someone dedicated to promoting the white race. He wanted American blacks and Jews to go back where they had come from—or be gotten rid of altogether.

Cochran moved to an Aryan Nations compound in Idaho ("Aryan" is what Hitler called the ideal race). There he could live among those who shared his hateful, racist views. Cochran even became a leader in the group—until his whole racist worldview was shattered. He recounts what happened:

> I had been told by the leadership, the people above me at Aryan Nations, when they found out that my son was born with a cleft palate and a cleft lip that he was a genetic defect and that he would have to be euthanized, which is a polite word for murdered.

When Cochran had the hateful conclusions of his worldview directed against his own son, his love for his son changed his thinking about racism. A worldview that said his precious son should die because of a physical defect just had to be wrong. Cochran now travels around the United States speaking against his former beliefs and helping to identify hate groups.

1. What idea did Floyd Cochran love in the beginning?

2. How did Cochran's love affect his thinking?

3. Why did Cochran's love change?

4. How did Cochran's changed love affect his thinking?

Thinking It Through 1.5

1. What is the relationship between head and heart?

2. How do arguments affect both head and heart?

3. How do stories affect both head and heart?

4. Give an example of how what you love affects what you believe.

Satan's lie to Eve in the Garden of Eden was actually half true. Many lies are. They're more powerful that way.

The half-truth with which Satan tempted Adam and Eve was this promise: *You will be like God* (Genesis 3:5). Adam and Eve were already like God. They were made in the image of God! That was the truth part in Satan's words. But there also was a lie hidden in his words. It was this: that mere creatures could—and should—go sit on God's throne with Him. *Move over—we belong on here too.* And humanity has been falling for this lie ever since.

DUALISM VERSUS THE BIBLE

That's what we call **dualism**: putting something on God's throne with Him. *Dual* just means "two." Dualism, then, is a worldview that imagines two "gods"—God and some other god who is equal in power—fighting against each other.

It's a little like superheroes versus supervillains. Normal bad guys don't stand a chance against the superhero, but along comes a supervillain and he might be as powerful as, or more powerful than, the superhero. We might wonder whether the superhero can actually win. Some people believe God is like a superhero who may or may not beat Satan (or some other person or thing just as powerful as God). Humans betray their Creator like Adam and Eve did by imagining that anyone or anything could be a part of a dualism at the center of the universe.

This dualism, of course, is *not* what the Bible shows. God has no rivals. God has no equal. "I am God, and there is none else," He told the prophet Isaiah; "I am God, and there is none like me" (Isaiah 46:9).

And there is no territory in the universe that God does not rule. So many verses in the Bible say this that it's difficult to know where to start, but there's one that's especially powerful.

It's in the story of Nebuchadnezzar, the king of Babylon during the time of Daniel. Nebuchadnezzar was walking around on the roof of his palace, looking at all the splendor around him, and he began to boast:

Is not this great Babylon, that I have built for the house of the kingdom by the might of my power, and for the honour of my majesty?" (Daniel 4:30)

God's answer was quick. And it boiled down to this: *I'm going to make you eat grass like an animal until you learn the lesson that God rules over all the kings there are, and He gives power to whomever He wants.*

Who's really in charge here?

THE LIMITS OF SATAN'S POWER

One of the ways we know dualism is a lie is that the only other power in the Bible even remotely close to God is still clearly less powerful than God. Two times God told Satan what he could do to Job—and what he couldn't do.

God first told Satan that he could touch anything Job had, but he couldn't touch Job (Job 1:12). Sure enough, Satan touched tons of Job's stuff, but not a hair on Job's head was harmed.

God then told Satan that he could touch Job directly, but he couldn't take Job's life (2:6). Sure enough, Satan gave Job a painful skin condition, but Job remained alive.

Satan is not a power or authority equal to God. And in the end of the story, God showed everyone—including Satan and Job—just how powerful He is.

Sure enough, Nebuchadnezzar went and ate grass—and learned his lesson. And this is what he said right after God put him back into his kingship:

All the inhabitants of the earth are reputed [regarded] as nothing: and he [God] doeth according to his will in the army of heaven, and among the inhabitants of the earth: and none can stay [stop] his hand, or say unto him, What doest thou?" (Daniel 4:35)

Nebuchadnezzar had been imitating Satan who, long before, wanted to act like God and had openly rebelled against Him. Nebuchadnezzar learned his lesson the hard way but left this testimony for others to learn from: *nobody has greater power or authority than God*. But this and the similar testimonies of multitudes of others throughout history haven't stopped many people on this planet from acting as if there are two gods.

THE TWO-STORY VIEW

One of the most common forms of dualism is called the **two-story view** because the concept reminds everyone of a two-story (two-level) house. Take a look at this picture: you can't miss the dualism.

In the two-story view, the lower story actually ends up being sort of like a god—a power separate from and equal to the God of religion in the upper story. That's because there are no stairs connecting the two stories. Religion (in this view) shouldn't touch real life, and real life can get along just fine without religion.

Remember, the two-story view is a half-truth that amounts to a lie. It's true that serving God is more important than anything else in this life. We set aside Sunday each week to show that importance. God ought to be the center of your life, and other things should yield to God.

But the lie is this: the two-story view says that God (if He actually exists) doesn't *really* rule real life. He rules religion, but He doesn't have anything to do with all the stuff you study in school or with most of the stuff you do when you step outside the door of your church.

You are probably a student in some kind of Christian school or homeschool. You probably aren't an atheist, thinking there's no reason even to have an upper story because there's no God up there anyway. But the dualism in the two-story view can still affect you.

While running for president in 1960, John F. Kennedy delivered a speech that provides a good example of the two-story view.

At the time, the United States was mostly "Protestant," a description from the 1500s for people who "protested" the authority and teachings of the Roman Catholic Church. Kennedy, however, was Catholic. His religious views concerned many people when he announced his candidacy for president. They feared that Kennedy would take orders from the pope in Rome. Their fear could have caused them to vote for someone else and cost Kennedy the presidency.

So on September 12, 1960, candidate Kennedy defended himself in a speech to an association of Protestant ministers. This is what he said:

> I believe in an America where the separation of church and state is absolute . . . ; where no public official either requests or accepts instructions on public policy from the Pope . . . .

> I believe in a President whose religious views are his own private affair . . . .

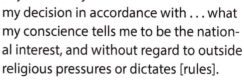

Kennedy got specific about particular issues he would not let his faith touch:

> Whatever issue may come before me as President— on birth control, divorce, censorship, gambling or any other subject—I will make my decision in accordance with . . . what my conscience tells me to be the national interest, and without regard to outside religious pressures or dictates [rules].

1. What was Kennedy's purpose for his speech?

2. Where did some Americans expect Kennedy to get his direction for decisions?

3. Where did Kennedy say he would get his direction for decisions instead?

4. How does Kennedy's speech demonstrate the two-story view?

A REAL-LIFE KID AND THE TWO-STORY VIEW

Think of a middle-school kid who loves science. Classic nerd. (This writer is thinking of real-life examples.) This nerd loves learning about God's world: biology, chemistry, botany, ornithology, astronomy. It's all a good bit more fascinating to him than it is to most of his classmates, and they get a little tired hearing him talk about it. They tease him for his nerdiness. But whenever they have a scientific question, they give him the respect of asking his opinion first.

This science lover has also grown up in a Christian home, and all his life he has been encouraged to pursue his love of science. So even as an eight-year-old he read tons of fact-filled books and memorized lots of science trivia and dinosaur names. Though his parents happily bought him science-rich books, he was taught to skip over all the stuff about "millions of years" and about dinosaurs evolving into birds and, especially, apes evolving into humans.

But about the time he gets into middle school, he starts to realize that the number of people who believe like his parents is small compared to the number who believe like his books. And though he knows there are scientists who are strong Christians and believe the Bible, he starts to wonder whether what the Bible teaches is really contrary to evolution. He also finds out that there are Christians who believe in evolution.

This sets off fireworks in his head. *Why can't I believe in the Bible and also believe that all life comes from a common ancestor? Why can't I hold to the authority of Christ and also the authority of science?*

We'll talk more about these questions later in this book because they are extremely important. But here is one answer that the Bible will not allow our science-nerd Christian boy to give: he cannot say that God and religion give us morality but science gives us facts. He can't take a two-story view.

A REAL-LIFE SCIENTIST AND THE TWO-STORY VIEW

Famous atheistic scientist Stephen Jay Gould tried this: he tried to say that science and religion were like two countries with separate territories or like two teachers who are experts in totally different subjects. Math teachers shouldn't tell spelling teachers how to spell, and spelling teachers shouldn't tell math teachers how to do math. Why should they fight with each other? Why can't they just stay in their separate classrooms and teach only what they know?

This view is really tempting when you're trying to figure out the relationship between science and religion. Maybe a Christian kid who loves science might think, *Science can let religion talk about "souls" and "right and wrong," and religion can let science talk about evolution and the age of the earth.*

But this is a dualistic worldview, a two-story view. It's saying that there's a part of the world that God doesn't rule. It's saying He doesn't get to tell us how to make sense of our scientific data. It's saying that science is not His classroom, that He should stay in Bible class only. And this worldview is wrong. God in His Word claims that His authority is universal, not limited anywhere.

There aren't two stories after all.

STAY ON YOUR SIDE!

Scientist Stephen Jay Gould talked about the soul as an example of something that belonged to religion. He said, "The subject of souls lies outside the magisterium [authority] of science. My [scientific] world cannot prove or disprove such a notion, and the concept of souls cannot threaten or impact my domain." In other words, science and religion should stay on their sides of the back seat and play nice.

Thinking It Through 1.6

1. What is dualism?

2. Describe the two stories in the two-story view.

3. How might an evolutionist describe the upper and lower stories of a two-story view?

4. How can the two-story view affect the thinking of someone who believes in God?

1.7 MAKING SENSE OF THE WORLD

How do I make sense of the world

Everybody sees the world through worldview lenses. And those lenses matter. They either help you see what's really there or they twist your vision so you can't. All worldviews make some kind of sense of the world. If you have the wrong worldview, however, you make the wrong sense.

MAKING SENSE OF THE WORLD THROUGH A BIG STORY

As we saw earlier, big stories either help or hurt—depending on the story—your ability to see the world as it is.

THE GOOD BIG STORY

A good big story will start and end with God. In the beginning God created the heavens and the earth (Genesis 1:1), and in the end all glory will go to Him (1 Corinthians 15:28). It will explain the existence of evil in the world: Adam and Eve brought it into the world by disobeying God (Genesis 3). It will also explain how evil will be eliminated: God is rescuing the world through Christ's sacrificial death, restoring new life with His righteousness. One day He will restore everything to its just relationship to God (Revelation 21:1–8). There's only one big story that actually accomplishes these things: the one told by God Himself.

Believing this big story will make you see the world the way it really is. It's a world in which good is real, because God put it here. It's a world in which evil is real, because humans let it in. It's a world in which good *will* triumph over evil, because God said so.

A TWISTED BIG STORY

A bad big story will *not* help you see the world as it really is. It will make you look through twisted lenses.

For our example we'll go back to the big story about the world that says humans are accidental products of millions of years of evolution. If this is your big story, you will start to see other people, and your own life, in a twisted way. All human behavior will have to be explained in evolutionary terms. Scientists Piet van den Berg and Tim Fawcett wrote an article trying to explain why so many girls date boys their parents don't like. Their parents would end up giving them a lot more money and attention if they married guys who were less capable of supporting them—more than their parents would give to their sisters. Supposedly, this marriage choice helps them and their children survive. But this is a twisted view of the world. It boils down your behavior to what helps you survive.

And this is silly. We know that music and art and beauty and love and the soul and meaning in life cannot be boiled down to their survival value. The evolutionary story distorts your worldview.

GOOD

TWISTED

CREATION

FALL

REDEMPTION

BIG BANG

EMERGENCE OF LIFE

DEVELOPMENT OF HUMANS

MAKING SENSE OF THE WORLD THROUGH LOVE

There's more to love than a survival value. It actually drives the beliefs and actions of *everybody*. This means that love is another aspect of every worldview. Every worldview produces certain loves that will be embraced by those who put on those particular worldview lenses.

GOOD LOVE

The biblical worldview is no different. When some Pharisees asked Jesus what the greatest commandment was, He didn't mention a specific law but instead a standard for the heart itself:

> Thou shalt love the Lord thy God with all thy heart, and with all thy soul, and with all thy mind. This is the first and great commandment. And the second is like unto it, Thou shalt love thy neighbour as thyself. On these two commandments hang [depend] all the law and the prophets. (Matthew 22:37–40)

Jesus explained that all the Scripture they had up to that point—every last thing God had commanded—depended on these two commandments. That means that loving God and neighbor are essential for living in a way that pleases God.

For your worldview lenses to function properly, you have to love God and neighbor as Jesus commanded so that the direction of your heart will be pointed toward them instead of yourself. Only then will you see the world as it really is. The world God made is a place in which God should be the first love. Your neighbor should be next. (Remember Section 1.5?)

The salvation that comes from God reorders your loves. And this reordering will have a major impact on your worldview.

TWISTED LOVE

But if you love primarily yourself, your worldview will be distorted. You won't see the world the right way.

If you play on a sports team with a selfish love, you may ignore God's desire for justice and attempt to cheat to get a victory for yourself. You may play with poor sportsmanship and be a sore loser or an obnoxious winner because you don't love your neighbors—the team on the other side of the field or court—enough to treat them well. These are distorted views of competition that may result from your love being twisted inwardly instead of turned toward God and others.

People's loves shape their views of the world. When they love themselves, their view of the world gets twisted.

GOOD

TWISTED

MAKING SENSE OF THE WORLD THROUGH AUTHORITY

Every worldview has trusted authorities, the people or positions that others with the same worldview trust. Sometimes those authorities do good; they help others see well. Sometimes those authorities blind people, including themselves.

GOOD AUTHORITY

God is the ultimate authority. All good authority flows from Him. He's the one who gave you the authorities over you. Because of sin, none of these authorities are perfect. But each can be good. You have inherited a lot of the ways you see things from your authorities, especially (but not only) your parents. And that is a good thing, even if American culture tells you that you should think for yourself. Nobody really does that; nobody thinks for himself without any influences. Every worldview has trusted authorities that it tells people to turn to.

TWISTED AUTHORITY

But authority can go bad. People can abuse their authority, and they can steal authority that isn't theirs.

Different cultures see various types of people as authorities. Some see witch doctors or elderly people or political leaders or celebrities as authorities. In the West, scientists tend to be seen as authorities and are often used in TV commercials for "proving" that you need certain medical treatments. While scientists *have* helped us all see things that are really there (such as distant galaxies and tiny germs) and we have general reasons to trust them, they *cannot* see all of reality. They *cannot* be authorities about spiritual, supernatural realities because their methods only work for observable things.

> "SCIENTISTS [ARE] TAKING AS THE WHOLE OF REALITY THAT PART OF IT THEIR METHODS CAN REPORT."
>
> —MARILYNNE ROBINSON

For example, the neuroscientist (who studies nerves) might conclude from his studies that the reason behind gift-giving is that it stimulates part of your brain in a positive way. The psychologist, a different kind of scientist, might conclude that the reason behind gift-giving is to increase your popularity. Each scientist is seeing something that is really there. Their methods, however, are blinding them to the biggest reality behind gift-giving: love. They can't measure love scientifically.

In other words, if scientists look through their microscopes and telescopes and proclaim that what they can see is all there is to life, then they are abusing their God-given authority.

GOOD

TWISTED

MAKING SENSE OF THE EVIDENCE IN THE WORLD

Every worldview out there claims to make the best sense of the world. They're all looking at the same world, the same evidence. What's different is their lenses. Have you noticed the pattern yet?

- The most powerful and influential people in Western culture look at the evidence in the world through lenses shaped in part by the authorities they trust. Those authorities assure them that the evidence proves there is no God. So even though the evidence really proves that God is real, they don't and won't see it.
- These powerful people look at the world through lenses shaped also by their loves and values. They don't love God, so they find ways to suppress God's truth around them and interpret the evidence in a godless way.
- They tell themselves a big story about the universe that isn't true. And they twist all the evidence to "prove" that story. They then use their influence to push that story on everyone.

When a group claims, "All the evidence is on our side!" You'd better find out what authorities they are trusting, what they love, and what big story they believe about the world—even if they are powerful people.

TWISTED
STORY

TWISTED
LOVE

TWISTED
AUTHORITY

MAKING SOMETHING OF THE WORLD

Who people trust, who they love, what they believe—these are all inside a person. But they all come out. They turn into actions in the real world. People work and play and fight and buy and write and think the way they do because of their worldviews. And those worldviews, and the resulting actions, are shaped by beliefs, loves, and big stories.

Remember the parts of a worldview:

1. Every worldview tells a **big story** about where the world came from, why it is the way it is, and where it's going.
2. Every worldview includes **basic beliefs and assumptions driven by what a person loves**.
3. Every worldview logically leads to certain **actions** by individuals and groups, and sets of group actions make up what we see in the world as different cultures.

If you have a biblical worldview, your actions will demonstrate right beliefs based on the right big story to those around you who have twisted lenses. Your life may help them understand the biblical worldview and accept it for themselves.

Thinking It Through 1.7

1. What is the role of a big story in understanding the world?

2. What is the role of loves in understanding the world?

3. What is the role of authority in understanding the world?

4. What is the role of evidence in understanding the world?

5. Explain the connection between how someone understands the world and how that person acts.

Scripture Memory

John 3:16
Romans 5:19
John 5:39–40
1 John 1:3
Proverbs 4:23
Isaiah 46:9
1 Timothy 1:15

Recall

1. What are the three parts of a worldview?

2. In the West, what is the most popular big story that people tell about the world?

3. Define *dualism* in your own words.

4. What is the lie of the two-story view?

Understand

5. Why is worldview an important thing to understand?

6. Is it possible to persuade pretty much anyone of the truth of something, as long as you find the right reasons? Explain.

Think Critically

7. Your family comes home from a day trip, and the trash lies scattered all over the garage. Your dog gives a guilty look, and his breath smells like the leftover chicken that was in the trash. Tell one story explaining these facts in which the dog is indeed guilty. Tell a story explaining these facts in which the dog is not guilty.

8. Identify one assumption that most people around you make about the world.

9. How would you respond to a girl in your neighborhood who says, "You can't really know whether the Bible is true or not because science can't prove it."

10. Why is it that some people accept the beautiful creation as proof of God's existence and others don't?

Internalize

11. What is the end of the big story you believe about the world?

12. Summarize some of the basic beliefs and assumptions you make about the world.

13. When was the last time you asked for proof of something? What counted as proof for that question?

14. What could you determine about your loves based on how you spend your free time?

HOW SHOULD THE BIBLE SHAPE MY WORLDVIEW?

Why is this story so important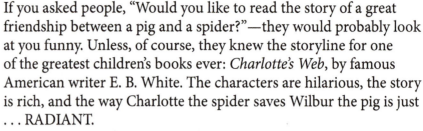

If you asked people, "Would you like to read the story of a great friendship between a pig and a spider?"—they would probably look at you funny. Unless, of course, they knew the storyline for one of the greatest children's books ever: *Charlotte's Web*, by famous American writer E. B. White. The characters are hilarious, the story is rich, and the way Charlotte the spider saves Wilbur the pig is just . . . RADIANT.

Imagine someone who says, "I love *Charlotte's Web*! I read it every day so I can get to know the author better and so I can praise him with my whole heart."

Imagine someone else who says, "I love *Charlotte's Web*! I read it so I can develop a worldview that honors E. B. White."

E. B. White was a truly great writer, and you *do* get to know him through his books. You also learn some real truths about the world through them, like the value of friendship. But it would be odd to read *Charlotte's Web* (or *Stuart Little* or *The Trumpet of the Swan*—have you read those?) with the purpose of getting to know E. B. White. It would be strange to praise E. B. White with your whole heart. It would be peculiar to look to his children's books to develop a worldview. That's not why they were written. They were written to be enjoyable stories. Elwyn Brooks White was a great author, but he was just a man.

The way Christians talk about the Bible, sing about the Bible, honor the Bible, memorize the Bible, think about the Bible, write about the Bible, dig inside the Bible—all this would be weird and wrong *if its author were not God.*

WHERE THE BIBLE CAME FROM

The Bible came from God. It was written by men; God didn't write it with His own hand (except the Ten Commandments). But it still came from God.

What does this mean?

The Bible uses two word pictures to describe how it came to us. First, it says that God the Holy Spirit moved holy men to say what they said (2 Peter 1:21).

The key word is *moved*. Peter says that the Spirit "moved" the writers of the Bible. Another way of saying it is that He "carried them along," like someone might carry a child from the car to the store. The child in his father's arms still has a will of his own and a personality of his own. But when Dad carries the child, they both get to the destination chosen by Dad, not the child.

Likewise, the writers of the Bible—like Moses, Isaiah, Matthew, Paul, and Peter—were carried along in such a way that they arrived at just the destination they were supposed to reach, creating one unified book in spite of coming from different backgrounds and living in very different time periods throughout hundreds of years of history. God didn't drop any of the writers on the way and say, "Oops!" Neither were they like some children, kicking and screaming on their way out of the grocery store. They were willing tools in God's hands.

There's another word picture the Bible uses: breath. You might not see it in the English translation, but it's there. 2 Timothy 3:16 says, "All scripture is given by inspiration of God."

Inspiration of God means that God "breathed it out." Think about what happens when you talk—breath comes out of your mouth. You breathe out your words. In the languages of the Bible, *breath* and *Spirit* are actually the same word. So this word picture is also saying that God gave us the Bible by the working of the Holy Spirit.

We don't know precisely how inspiration worked. We simply know that the words of Scripture are also the words of God. Words that the apostle Paul scratched long ago onto pieces of paper with a pen and ink were, at the same time, being breathed out by God. Words that the prophet Jeremiah scrawled on a scroll during the dark days of his life were also God's words.

The Bible came from God.

WHY GOD GAVE US THE BIBLE

Understanding where the Bible came from should help you see that it isn't strange to go to the Bible looking to get to know the ultimate Author, God Himself. It isn't strange to praise the Author of this one book with your whole heart. It isn't strange to read this one book, and read it every day, with the purpose of getting an accurate worldview. These are some of the reasons God gave us the Bible.

One of the most important ways the Bible gives you an accurate worldview is through something we've already talked about a bit: the big story the Bible tells. Here it is again, in three major points: Creation, Fall, Redemption.

> God **created** this world very good. He created humans in His image to rule over the world. But man **fell** into sin and took the world down with him; now the entire creation groans under the weight of human sin. But Christ, through His perfect life and atoning death, is **redeeming** His fallen creation, especially sinful mankind, through the power of the Holy Spirit. All these events are for the glory of God.

This story is more important than you know. To understand why (on our way to understanding why God gave us the Bible), let's think some more about stories.

KNOWING THINGS THROUGH STORIES

How many stories do you know?

You probably couldn't even count. Perhaps there is *Charlotte's Web*; there are whatever books you've read in the last few years; there are classics like *Goodnight Moon* and *The Very Hungry Caterpillar* and *Green Eggs and Ham*; there is probably a long list of Bible stories you've been learning since you were smaller than the family Bible.

But don't stop there. Think of the stories you know from your life and your family members' lives. You know the story of how your parents met. Maybe you know the story of how your *grand*parents met. You know the story of how you broke your arm behind the couch when you were five. Also the story of how that bully named Randy Beeman tripped your sister on the playground and laughed, and when you saw her bloody knees you got mad and screamed, and that was the one time you didn't get in trouble for screaming. And then there's the one about the cute thing you said when you were three. You know other people *and yourself* through stories.

But don't stop there. Think of how so much of what you know is basically a bunch of little stories. You know what a bike is through stories: Once upon a time you wanted to go somewhere, but you didn't have a driver's license. You got on your two-wheeled conveyance with red paint and pedaled fast enough to remain balanced and make forward progress. Eventually, you made it where you wanted to go. The end. You know what school is through stories too. You know what books are, what courts are, what swords are, what makeup is—all through stories.

If for some crazy reason you couldn't understand stories, you would hardly know *anything*.

KNOWING GOD THROUGH HIS STORY

And what's true about little things like family and bikes is even more true about big things—like God and Creation, Fall, Redemption. If you are going to know who God is and what He is doing, He has to reveal some things to you. He has to tell you the story of His creation of the world. He has to tell you how Adam fell and started the chaos the world is now in. He has to tell you that He is working to redeem it back to Himself—and wants to redeem you back to Himself. He has to tell you, or else you just won't get it.

One of the most important reasons God gave us the Bible was to tell us the big story about our world. And He expects us to listen.

ONLY AS WE UNDERSTAND WHAT HE HAS REVEALED ABOUT HIMSELF AND OUR WORLD CAN WE RESPOND IN A WAY THAT PLEASES HIM.

It really is like we're in a big story written by God (we'll talk about this in the next section!), and God has made the way for us to be reconciled to Him through Christ and be part of His work in His world (2 Corinthians 5:18–21). Jesus came to seek and to save the lost (Luke 19:10), and He sends His followers out to do the same (John 20:21). We learn these truths about God's plan, the part Jesus plays, and the part we can play—*from God's Word* (John 5:39).

WHY WE NEED THE BIBLE TO KNOW GOD

We don't have to wonder what kinds of stories people would make up to explain the world if we didn't have the Bible. We don't have to wonder what would happen if people didn't believe the story the world's Creator tells.

Cultures have already made up many big stories about the world. We looked at some of them in Section 1.2. And somehow, every single one of these stories winds up telling people what they want to hear.

People love to tell themselves big stories in which they are good guys and their enemies are demons with no excuses for their evil. Adolf Hitler told a big story in which the German people—the "Aryan race"—were the good guys and the Jews were the demons. That big story ended very badly with six million dead Jews, most of them killed by ordinary Germans: farmers, drivers, janitors.

People love to tell themselves big stories in which they get to choose what's right and wrong. In fact, one of the popular big stories in the Western world right now includes the idea that people get to create their own meaning by telling their own story about their lives, no matter what anyone else thinks.

We desperately needed God to tell us the *true* big story—found in the Bible. Then we can know God through His revelation of Himself. We can understand His work in the world through His revelation of His redeeming work in Christ. We can really know who we are and what we really should (and shouldn't) do.

We desperately need God to tell us parts of that big story that only He knows, especially the future, so that we can know what good things we can hope for later.

We desperately need to understand the big story so that we can make sense of the parts of the Bible that aren't in story form, like commands and encouragements and explanations and rebukes and songs and prophecies and other things.

The Bible is the God of the universe carrying us onto His lap and saying, "Let me tell you a story."

Or, better: "Let me tell you *the* story."

Thinking It Through 2.1

1. How did we get the Bible?

2. Why did God give us the Bible?

3. What are the three parts of the true big story of the Bible?

4. Why do we need the Bible to know God and His plan?

5. How should you make sense of God's commands in the Bible?

Use scientific evidence to prove that the Bible can be trusted.

Use the Bible as an authority and use other arguments as support.

How do I respond to someone who claims to know God but doesn't believe the Bible

?

Tell him you're glad he's a Christian, even though he doesn't believe the Bible.

Use only the Bible to argue that the Bible can be trusted.

Who is
the author ?

One of the most incredible things about a good story is the way the author can create an entire world for his or her characters. The creativity of good writers is present throughout their stories and in the worlds they create. Some of the writers who are most famous for their creativity are J. R. R. Tolkien (*The Lord of the Rings* trilogy) and C. S. Lewis (The Chronicles of Narnia). And it's very, very hard to put this much creativity into a story. Tolkien even made up *whole languages* and backstories for his world, which he called "Middle-earth."

God is the author of the universe's story, and His creativity is present throughout the story in ways no other author's ever could be. The level of creativity He reached was unbelievable. From the hugest galaxies to the tiniest electrons—and whatever it is (we still don't really know) that goes into electrons—God invented it all from scratch. And He made up whole languages for His world in an instant at the tower of Babel.

GOD—THE ETERNAL AUTHOR

In order for God to create the story of the world, He had to be outside it. This is obvious when you think about it—God can't be trapped by His own creation. He can't be just a character in His story.

The Bible even says that God is outside time. He has no beginning or end. This is impossible for us to really understand. God started the clock at Creation, and it has been ticking all our lives. It will tick, tick, tick until the last moment God has appointed.

But this is how the Bible describes God:

> The eternal God is thy refuge, and underneath are the everlasting arms. (Deuteronomy 33:27)

PRE

PAST   PRESENT

CREATION

God is **eternal**. He's forever in both directions—in all directions. He didn't just exist before the world began; He won't just exist after all time is over; He exists *above* time. He sees all of time all the time.

God's eternal nature might seem to put Him out of reach. If He doesn't exist within time, how can we possibly have a conversation or relationship with Him? Every conversation we've ever had had a beginning and a middle and an end. Every relationship we've ever had began with a meeting and will end some day. How can we relate to an eternal God who is so high above beginnings, middles, and ends?

The Bible sees no contradiction between a God who is lifted up very high above us and yet is also very much present in His own story. Look at the two halves of this one statement from the prophet Isaiah.

> For thus saith the high and lofty One that inhabiteth eternity, whose name is Holy; I dwell in the high and holy place . . .

That's the first half: God is incredibly far above us. He's on a different level of existence. But now look at the second half of the same verse. God dwells

> . . . with him also that is of a contrite [sorry for sin] and humble spirit, to revive the spirit of the humble, and to revive the heart of the contrite ones. (Isaiah 57:15)

God is above His creation and present in it at the same time. The high and almighty God dwells both in a high and holy place and with the lowly sinner who humbly admits his sins. You can relate to this high and holy God by being humble and repentant yourself.

GOD SENT

FUTURE

REVEALED IN SCRIPTURE

MAN

PLANNING THE GOOD END FROM THE VERY BEGINNING

God planned everything in His story of the world, much like an author does for a book. This is what God says:

> Remember the former things of old: for I am God, and there is none [no one] else; I am God, and there is none like me, declaring the end from the beginning, and from ancient times the things that are not yet done, saying, My counsel shall stand, and I will do all my pleasure. (Isaiah 46:9–10)

This is really an incredible claim. God doesn't just "know" the end from the beginning; He "declares" it. He announces it. He informs us all what that end will be. He is not biting His fingernails hoping the story of the world turns out well. He's not in a conflict with Satan that He fears He might lose (remember the false claims of dualism?). In the end, God wins. "I will do all my pleasure."

Throughout the Bible, God makes confident promises that He could make only if He really had planned the world. Jesus discusses in the Sermon on the Mount the things that people worry about: food, drink, and clothing. And then He basically says, *Your heavenly Father knows exactly what you need, so follow Me and don't worry!* (Matthew 6:25–33).

That's right. God says that all God-loving Christians will have all the food and clothing they need. That may sound trivial, but there have been millions, or maybe billions, of Christians living in all parts of the world. Fulfilling this promise requires incredible power.

God has so carefully planned the world that He's able to make an even more astounding promise through the pen of the apostle Paul.

All things work together for good to them that love God, to them who are the called according to his purpose. (Romans 8:28)

We may not be able to always see the good God has planned, but it's there. "All things" are working toward it. There are students reading this book who have serious sicknesses and disabilities. There are some who have divorced parents and dead siblings. There are some, right now, who are being terribly hurt by the sins of other people. But if they love God, *all these things will work together for their good.*

What incredible power and wisdom it will take to fulfill this promise! Stop and think how mind-blowing it is.

ALL THINGS.
TOGETHER.
FOR *GOOD.*

This would be an arrogant and cruel statement if it were not true!

This promise implies not only that God has the power to redirect all the evil in the world toward a good end but also that He knows how to do it. Do you? Can you even think of a way to bring good out of the evil on this planet?

The story of Joseph is one example of how God does this. Twice, evil actions changed the course of Joseph's life—the first to slavery and the next to imprisonment. Yet, Joseph remained faithful. In God's timing and power, these two evil disruptions of Joseph's life resulted in his promotion to second-in-command over Egypt. His position enabled him to save Egypt, much of the world, and especially his own family. God turned the evil plans against Joseph into the salvation of his family, God's chosen people.

God allows all the people in His story to choose good or evil, but their evil does not stop His good plans. Hang on to that thought; we'll come back to it in Section 3.3.

GOD—THE AUTHOR-CREATOR

J. R. R. Tolkien created an amazing world, so detailed that it is quite believable. It is an epic story, but it is still only a story. That world existed in Tolkien's mind and exists in the minds of the readers of his books. God's planned story is more epic than *The Lord of the Rings* and has another major difference—His story is reality.

You are right now living as part of God's story. As the ultimate Author, He did not just plan the story but created the whole reality. We sometimes talk about how an author seems to "bring something to life" with his writing. God literally brought to life every detail in His plan. And He continues to sustain the universe by the word of His power.

In the Bible, God reveals the reality that He brought into existence. From our perspective, that's both the history of our world and our future. He reveals Himself with the Scriptures so that we can know Him as the author and creator of everything. He allows us to choose to be the good guys or the bad guys in the story, but His story still carries on, with our obedience or with our rebellion.

God not only planned all of life's story, He created it all as well.

IMAGINATIVE ENDINGS

Authors often end their stories with hints for the reader to imagine what could happen next to the characters.

Tolkien ends *The Lord of the Rings* with Frodo sailing away to "white shores and beyond them a far green country under a swift sunrise."

When Lewis ends The Chronicles of Narnia, he says that the Pevensies' story had not really ended; it was actually only beginning:

> All their life in this world and all their adventures in Narnia had only been the cover and the title page: now at last they were beginning Chapter One of the Great Story which no one on earth has read: which goes on for ever: in which every chapter is better than the one before.

The Bible's story, the one God planned, created, and then wrote, is even better. It ends with a promise that Christians won't be limited to imagining what it would be like to live with God. They will be able to experience it for themselves!

THE END OF GOD'S STORY

In the big story of reality, God will take the evil plans of men and ultimately turn them into good. Just like He used the evil plans of Joseph's brothers against Joseph to work His good plan for Joseph to save his family from famine. As Joseph said, "Ye thought evil against me; but God meant it unto good" (Genesis 50:20).

God began the story of His world at Creation. But the Bible consistently says that He wrote the end of the story too. The Bible's record of history ends like this (in the words of John in Revelation 21:3–5):

> Behold, the tabernacle [dwelling place] of God is with men, and he will dwell with them, and they shall be his people, and God himself shall be with them, and be their God.

The almighty Creator God, who dwells in unapproachable light, whom no one has seen or can see, will dwell with people. With us! The Author will come permanently into His own story.

> And God shall wipe away all tears from their eyes; and there shall be no more death, neither sorrow, nor crying, neither shall there be any more pain: for the former things are passed away.

There won't even be pain leftover from previous pain. All wrongs will be made right. What humans planned for evil, century after century, God has planned for good to ultimately bring repentant people to Himself for all eternity. What will be an end to the world as we know it will actually be the beginning of everlasting life.

> And he that sat upon the throne said, Behold, I make all things new.

Thinking It Through 2.2

1. How is God different from a human author?

2. What does it mean that God is eternal?

3. How can God tell us the end of the story of His world?

4. List several words that describe God's plan for His world.

5. Explain the ways that God has related to humans since Creation and how He will relate to them in the future.

2.3 THE BEGINNING

How does God begin His story?

Have you ever heard violins sing? Their beautiful music speaks to our hearts. Throughout the 1800s and 1900s, violins were a favorite instrument of Jewish musicians. Their traditional folk music, called klezmer, enlivened weddings and celebrations. Many Jewish families owned violins and often trained their young children to play them.

These were not only beautiful to hear but beautifully made as well. Although Jews were not normally allowed to display pictures of people, violins could be displayed as art. Many were intricately decorated with the six-pointed star of David, a Jewish symbol. They were beautiful creations with the important purpose of enriching the lives of the Jews.

Now think on a much grander scale: God created the world with beauty and purpose for humans to enjoy and use for their needs. How do we know? The Bible says that God's works are perfect. In the beginning, the world worked the way it was supposed to. We see, now, many problems in the world, but they did not come from God's creative work. The problems in this world are not His fault. *God's creation was good. It was very good.*

GOD'S VERY GOOD CREATION

You're in middle school. You've gotten at least as far as page 1 in your Bible reading by now. So you know what that page says about the goodness of God's creation. It says it each day during the Creation week.

And then, He looked back over all the things He had made, and He felt something like you do when you've worked hard and you know you've done a good job. You sneak peeks at your work for the next few days, just admiring it. And you say to yourself what God said to Himself and to whatever angels were listening: *Very good!*

> God saw every thing that he had made, and, behold, it was very good. (Genesis 1:31)

This statement, that God's creation was originally "very good," is a basic truth on which the big story of the Bible rests.

You can't blame creation for the world's problems. Health problems don't come from a bad heart design. Weather disasters don't come from wiring mistakes in the first clouds. Hatred and murder and lust and anger and injustice and all the other wicked things that fill our world—they weren't there to begin with. They entered later. When they twist and bend and even break the good things God made, we cannot point the finger at God.

God made no mistakes in creation. Set this solidly in your mind and heart: what God created was very good.

STRUCTURE

If God's creation was very good, then the way God created the world is the way things ought to be. God's creation worked as it should in agreement with His purpose and plan. We call this **structure**. Though the original design of God's creation has been twisted by human sin, it is still around. We'll be talking more about structure throughout this unit.

CREATED IN THE IMAGE OF GOD

The greatest good thing God made was mankind. Genesis 1:26–27 tells this to us:

> And God said, Let us make man in our image, after our likeness: and let them have dominion . . . over all the earth . . . . So God created man in his own image, in the image of God created he him; male and female created he them.

This is simple language that communicates a profound truth—the most profound truth there is about you. Careful readers of the Bible have had different ideas about what exactly it means to be made in the **image of God**. And the Bible does not give us much detail. But this much is clear: humans were made like God. We are not gods. We never have been, and we never will be. But we are *like* God.

You are a mirror of His glory. If you feel like a loser (and most people do sometimes), remember this. Don't find your ultimate worth in your sports ability or your jokes or your art or your trivia knowledge. Find it in the gift God gave you: His image.

If you feel like a winner, like other people are losers, remember: those people are made in the image of God, just like you. Male and female, young and old, every shade of brown—they all are image-bearers.

God's image in each person is another basic truth in the foundation of a biblical worldview.

HAVE WE LOST THE IMAGE OF GOD BECAUSE OF OUR SIN?

When Adam and Eve sinned, did they lose the image? No. Are you made in the image of God? Yes.

God says in Genesis 9:6 that whoever murders another person must be put to death. Why? It's because "in the image of God made he man."

God says in James 3:9–10 that we shouldn't be blessing God and cursing people with the same tongue. Why? Because people "are made after the similitude [likeness] of God."

Sin messes up the image of God; it makes you far less like God than you would be otherwise. But it doesn't erase that image.

THE CREATION MANDATE

And now we need to look at Genesis 1:28, a verse we'll return to over and over in this book.

> And God blessed them, and God said unto them, Be fruitful, and multiply, and replenish the earth, and subdue it: and have dominion over the fish of the sea, and over the fowl of the air, and over every living thing that moveth upon the earth.

Here God is blessing mankind, but at the same time He's giving us a job. So we call this the **Creation Mandate**. (A mandate is an official command to do something.) What is the blessing-command? There are actually two:

1. God's image-bearers are going to be fruitful and **multiply**. They must replenish, or **fill**, the earth God has given them.

2. God's image-bearers are going to **subdue**, or tame, the earth. They must have **dominion**, or rule, over it.

Let's dig in to some examples to see why it's important to accept the double nature of these blessing-commands.

1. MULTIPLY AND FILL THE EARTH

God expects humans to have baby humans, and we're supposed to have enough of them to fill the earth. Simple enough command, right? But it requires more willful obedience than you might expect.

Right now, the richer a country is, the fewer babies it is having. Take a look at the graph on this page. The higher a country is, the more babies they're having. The further to the right the country is, the richer it is. There is a clear line going from poor countries with lots of babies down to rich countries with far fewer.

Many countries, including the United States and Canada, are below "replacement rate." This means there aren't enough babies to keep the population stable. Instead of growing, these countries will shrink unless people from other countries come in.

The Bible does not tell married couples how many babies to have, but there is something wrong with a culture when its people do not want babies. (There is even something wicked when they kill millions of their babies before they can be born.) "Be fruitful, and multiply" was God's blessing to mankind; babies are not a curse.

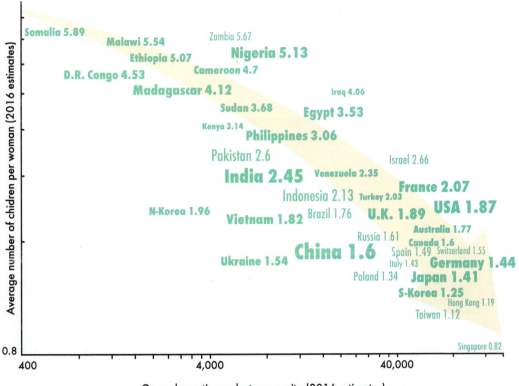

2. SUBDUE THE EARTH AND HAVE DOMINION OVER IT

Babies are a blessing; so is work. And work is what it takes to subdue the earth and have dominion over it.

The earth didn't come with houses and parks and cities and farms and cows willing to be milked. It didn't come with fruit trees all in rows or with the Periodic Table of the elements and a list of what you can make out of them. Humans have had to subdue the earth and rule over it—making it suitable for human use. We have made it more and more useful over time. Ruling over the earth doesn't mean that we get to do whatever we want with it. It means taking care of it like wise rulers.

This subduing has been both the blessing and command of God. And it is the reason that work is a fundamentally good thing. If you are helping to subdue and have dominion, you are doing God's work whether you know it or not.

Billions of non-Christian people do this work too. They are taking part in God's original blessing. But there are also many people who refuse to work. They are disobeying the Creation Mandate.

Austin, Texas, in 1901

REAL VALUE

Big stories that contradict the Bible often see the human race as a cosmic accident with no value or purpose. Be thankful for the biblical worldview, which recognizes *very good structure* in God's creation, *valuable people* made in God's image, *valuable work* in the Creation Mandate—and the *blessings* of that work. The more a culture keeps telling itself a different big story, the more these valuable biblical truths will be ignored—or attacked.

Thinking It Through 2.3

1. How do we know God's original creation was good?

2. What does this goodness prove about the problems in the world now?

3. How was God's creation of humans unique?

4. What does this unique creation mean for human value?

5. What are the two parts of the Creation Mandate?

6. What is creational structure?

Austin, Texas, in 2015

2.4 THE PROBLEM

What's
gone
wrong **?**

In the 1930s, Nazi Germany began a systematic attempt to destroy all the Jews in the world. They built death camps designed to exterminate the Jews by working them to death, starving them, or executing them by bullet or poison gas.

In those camps, many Jews who had brought their beloved violins were forced to play them as their fellow Jews arrived, marched out to forced labor, and worst of all, marched to their deaths in gas chambers. The Nazis, in their sinful hatred and cruelty, bent the good purpose of those violins to the evil purpose of mocking the suffering of the Jews. Because of these memories, many Jews refused to play the violins after the horrors of the Holocaust. With their purpose bent, the violins were silenced, locked away.

Our world, like the violins, was created beautifully for a good purpose. But, also like the violins, it was bent by the Fall in an evil direction against God and His good plan. The glorious beginning of the big story of the Bible was quickly spoiled. And who spoiled it? What went wrong? God points His finger directly at human sin.

THE FALL OF ADAM AND EVE

Adam and Eve were king and queen of creation; they had been given rule over it all. They were called to an amazing, challenging, and downright fun task: multiply, fill the earth, subdue it. They were supposed to make the earth a better place for humans to live in so that humans could fill it.

The commission to rule over the world was part of a covenant that God made with Adam. A **covenant** is an agreement between two or more people with certain requirements and promises. The promises included mankind's rule over the earth.

But King Adam and Queen Eve were not the ultimate rulers of the planet. The covenant required that Adam, Eve, and their descendants obey God by not eating the forbidden fruit. The one who created them and gave them their authority through the covenant—the King of Kings—had a throne far higher than theirs.

And at one tiny spot among all of God's universal dominions, this king and this queen rebelled. Genesis 3 tells the story.

The serpent, the most crafty of all the animals which God had made, asked the woman whether God had really said that they could not eat from any of the trees in the garden. The serpent came to deceive, as he always does. The woman resisted, at first; she knew God's command that she was supposed to obey.

The serpent reinterpreted what God said: "Ye shall not surely die: for God doth know that in the day ye eat thereof, then your eyes shall be opened." *God is hiding something from you*, he implied. "Ye shall be like God," he promised, "knowing good and evil" (3:4–5).

Before their rule could properly begin, Adam and Eve made a terrible choice.

> When the woman saw that the tree was good for food, and that it was pleasant to the eyes, and a tree to be desired to make one wise, she took of the fruit thereof, and did eat, and gave also unto her husband with her; and he did eat. (3:6)

The great poet George Herbert expresses the irony of the situation: "We sold our glorious, gracious God for an apple. Brand it on our foreheads forever: for an apple we lost our God." (Apples aren't actually bad. Whatever the forbidden fruit was, it doesn't exist

anymore.) The point is that God blessed Adam and Eve with good work and authority, and He fellowshiped personally with them. He gave them only one rule, one forbidden fruit in all the garden. For that one fruit, they gave up fellowship with God.

THE CURSE

This is what has gone wrong in our world. We did it. Humans are responsible. And the Lord, the Great King, was ready with both judgment and mercy.

Judgment came quickly on the serpent. God said,

> Because thou hast done this, thou art cursed above all cattle, and above every beast of the field; . . . and I will put enmity [conflict] between thee and the woman, and between thy seed and her seed; it shall bruise thy head, and thou shalt bruise his heel. (3:14–15)

The seed of the serpent and the seed of the woman will have conflict. And then came these mysterious words of God's mercy: the seed of the woman will bruise the serpent's head, while the serpent will only get away with bruising the heel of the seed of the woman. Remember these words about the bruised head and heel. We will talk more about them.

God didn't give more details here. He turned immediately to the king and queen of His creation.

> Unto the woman he said, I will greatly multiply thy sorrow and thy conception [childbearing]; in sorrow thou shalt bring forth children; and thy desire shall be to thy husband, and he shall rule over thee. (3:16)

The woman will suffer in bearing children. Her sin will also negatively affect her relationship to her husband. But the man, king of creation, got even bigger consequences.

> Cursed is the ground for thy sake; in sorrow shalt thou eat of it all the days of thy life; thorns also and thistles shall it bring forth to thee; and thou shalt eat the herb of the field; in the sweat of thy face shalt thou eat bread, till thou return unto the ground; for out of it wast thou taken: for dust thou art, and unto dust shalt thou return. (3:17–19)

Death is the consequence, yes. But look carefully at what God said: even the ground that Adam farms will be cursed. What happens when a king and queen do something terribly, horribly wrong? They suffer—and so do all their subjects. Even the ground! These words in Genesis 3 are absolutely essential parts of a Christian worldview. All creation was under God's covenant with Adam, so when he sinned, it was as if he jumped into a hole and dragged all creation down with him. Here's the thing to remember: the Fall twisted, or bent, *everything* in creation.

Genesis 3 mentions only the ground, but the rest of the Bible shows that all creation groans because of human sin. This is most clear in Romans 8:22–23, where Paul says that "the whole creation groaneth and travaileth in pain together until now." Creation, Paul says, was forced to endure frustration. It was put in slavery to corruption. And, he says, it awaits "redemption," even to this day.

The effects of the Fall are all around you, and inside you.

When people point their finger at God . . .

When people in a land of wealth live on a dollar a day . . .

When cancer strikes someone . . .

When we worship our bodies, riches, intelligence, or power, instead of worshiping God . . .

THAT'S THE FALL

When your own school-work is deeply frustrating . . .

When the most popular music in a culture is wicked and stupid . . .

When a group of friends start fighting and talking behind one another's backs . . .

When the first word out of someone's mouth is a snake-like lie . . .

When a husband and wife grow cold in their love and consider divorce . . .

God made everything very good, but that original structure has been bent far away from its original goodness by the Fall. Sometimes it is bent so far, it's hard to tell how it might have looked originally! But we look around and within and somehow know that this world is not working the way God made it to work. This awful bent is not His good structure. We call it **fallen direction**.

CASE STUDY: "THE SINGLE BEST INVENTION OF LIFE"

You may not know who Steve Jobs was, but you've most likely seen or used something he helped create. He was one of the creative minds behind Apple Inc. He helped develop the Mac®, iPod®, iPhone®, and iPad®—all innovations of their time. He developed Apple into a multibillion-dollar company. In fact, *Forbes* magazine named Apple the most innovative company in the world in 2011. However, it was in that same year that Steve Jobs died.

Six years earlier, in 2005, Steve Jobs had spoken of death in a speech at Stanford University. He said,

Death is the destination we all share. . . . Death is very likely the single best invention of Life. . . . It clears out the old to make way for the new.

His statement demonstrates part of a worldview. The Bible's view of death is foundationally different.

1. Why do people respect Steve Jobs's statement about change and new things?

2. Why did he call death life's "single best invention"?

3. Why is Jobs's first statement true?

4. Was mankind's dominion in the Creation Mandate originally designed to be temporary, only lasting as long as people live? Explain.

5. Why is Jobs's view of death wrong?

THE CURSE AND THE CREATION MANDATE

The very things that God commanded (and blessed) Adam and Eve to do in the Creation Mandate were the focuses of His judgment on them. Did you notice?

God told them to be fruitful and multiply. Now that would be a very painful and dangerous process for Eve and her babies. Even in wealthy countries with shiny hospitals, many women die while giving birth. The wife of the writer of this book very nearly died during the birth of her third child. Her newborn baby came into the world with a knot in his cord. In that hospital room, at the scariest moment of this writer's life, he was witnessing the effects of Eve's long-ago sin.

God also told Adam and Eve to subdue the earth. Because of the Fall, obeying that command would be a very painful and difficult process. The earth would push back against Adam. It would produce thorns and thistles. Work would often be frustrating, as it is to this day.

BLAMING GOD

Our tendency is to blame God when bad things happen. We start to distrust His goodness, to question it. It's crazy to question the goodness of the one who defines what *good* is! But we think we have good reasons. We line up all our complaints about God—all the things He did to us and all the things He failed to do for us.

We're a lot like our too-many-greats-to-count grandfather Adam. When God questioned him, he ended up blaming God. *Yeah, I ate. But it's this woman's fault! No wait, it's your fault, God! You gave me this woman!*

We might like to think we would have done better than Adam and Eve. But we humans keep repeating the sins of our first parents. As George Herbert goes on to say, "For an apple we once lost our God and still we lose him for nothing more. For money. For food."

We listen to lies like Eve did. We tell lies like Adam did. We bend God's structure away from its good purpose. Point the finger at Adam and Eve, yes. They are to blame for the way the world is. But as every little kid likes to say, *when you point, a bunch of fingers are pointing back at you.* You, too, have sinned like Adam and Eve.

You—we—are what's gone wrong with this world.

MANDATE
multiply
&
subdue

CURSE
pain
&
resistance

Thinking It Through 2.4

1. Why did Adam's sin affect all creation?

2. What is the relationship between the blessing-commands of the Creation Mandate and the curses that came because of the Fall?

3. How much of creation was affected by Adam's fall?

4. How do we know that what is wrong with the world is not God's fault?

2.5 THE REAL HERO

Who is the
real hero

We last left the Jewish violins damaged and unused because of the evil of the Holocaust. After the war, people began to bring these instruments to Moshe Weinstein, a violin maker and repairman in Israel, because the painful memories were too strong for these Jews to want to own and play the violins. Moshe purchased them but did nothing with them. He, too, had sickening memories—his own family and entire extended family had died in the Holocaust.

Years later, Amnon Weinstein, Moshe's son and also a master violin maker, decided to restore these violins to show that the Nazis had not succeeded in wiping out the Jews and their culture. It took many years and much careful work to restore them. So many people brought him their violins that he ended up acquiring over sixty throughout the stages of his life.

STAGES IN THE BIBLE

There are stages of the Bible's big story too—stages in which God begins to restore His world, especially people, to it's original structure. Like the work of collecting and repairing the Holocaust violins, this redemption is accomplished in stages.

God made a bold claim at the beginning of the Bible, right after everything went wrong in Adam's sin. He said that the seed of the woman—some descendant of Eve—would bruise the serpent's head.

This claim is bold, but it's also vague. What does it mean? It means that God will take righteous revenge on the serpent who brought sin into His brand-new world. And the rest of the Bible shows (as we'll see) that He won't leave the world cursed and bent. He will redeem the world.

Remember that Adam was given the authority to rule over creation in what we described as a creational covenant? Because he failed to obey God's covenant requirement, he became an imperfect ruler. But God was ready with a plan to fix what Adam broke. God had a new King in store.

God made covenants with men as developing stages in His redemptive plan. (Remember, a covenant is an agreement between two or more people with certain requirements and promises.) Covenants provide the basic outline of the Bible. They prepare for God's new King to rule the whole earth. Everything the Fall touched (which is *everything*!) will be put back under a perfect Ruler—through covenants.

SEED

God says in Genesis 3:15 that the serpent will bruise, or crush, the *heel* of the seed of the woman. But the seed of the woman will bruise, or crush, the *head* of the serpent.

We don't usually think of seeds having heels or being able to crush snake heads. What is this seed?

A **seed** is an offspring. You are the seed of your parents. You are also the seed of your great-great-great-grandparents. *Seed* (and *offspring*) can be either singular or plural. The seed of Abraham are countless people, like the stars of the sky. The seed of the woman, as we'll see in this section, is one person.

GOD'S COVENANT WITH NOAH

The first covenant that begins the process of redemption is God's covenant with Noah. After Adam's sin, people eventually became so rebellious against God that God decided to destroy them with a flood.

But in His wrath, God also remembered mercy by saving Noah and his family. He told Noah,

> I will establish my covenant with you;
> neither [never] shall all flesh be cut off any more
> by the waters of a flood; neither shall there any more be a
> flood to destroy the earth. (Genesis 9:11)

Every three-year-old Sunday-school-attending child knows the symbol God gave as a sign of His covenant: the beautiful rainbow. The rainbow would remind Noah (and us) that God promised to preserve the world from any more worldwide judgment, in order to work out the plan of redemption. This was the first stage in restoring His full rule to the world.

GOD'S COVENANT WITH ABRAHAM

Hundreds of years after Noah, God singled out one person to whom He would show mercy in a special way. His name was Abram (later changed to Abraham). Genesis records the covenant:

- God promised Abraham seed. He would become a great nation (15:5). And, he would be the father of kings (17:6).
- God promised Abraham a land where that seed could live and grow and have dominion (13:14–15).
- God promised Abraham blessing. God would bless him, and God would bless "all families of the earth" through him (12:1–3).

This covenant narrowed it down to one family that redemption would come through, blessing the rest of the people on earth. The seed of Abraham would include the one special seed of the woman that God promised in the Garden of Eden. One of his offspring would be the longed-for King.

GOD'S COVENANT WITH ISRAEL THROUGH MOSES

Abraham had a son, Isaac. Isaac had a son, Jacob. Jacob had *twelve* sons, who all moved to Egypt under the protection of Joseph. After Joseph's death, protection turned into slavery.

But God brought them a deliverer, Moses, and as they escaped Egypt, they became something new: a nation called "Israel." (*Israel* was the name that God gave their ancestor Jacob.) God's mighty hand brought them out of Egypt, and then His mighty finger drew commandments on stone tablets. God made a covenant with Israel, Abraham's seed, through Moses.

The covenant with Abraham focused on promises, things God would do through Abraham's seed no matter what. In contrast, the covenant with Israel through Moses focused on laws, things Israel was required to do to obey the Lord. They had to follow detailed laws and sacrifice animals for their sins. If the nation obeyed God's laws, God would make them into something special:

> If ye will obey my voice . . . and keep my covenant, then ye shall be a peculiar [special] treasure unto me above all people: for all the earth is mine: and ye shall be unto me a kingdom of priests, and an holy nation. (Exodus 19:5–6)

If Abraham's seed obeyed the laws of God, they would be a "kingdom of priests." They would represent God to all the other nations. They would bring God's blessing to all the families of the earth.

GOD'S COVENANT WITH DAVID

But Israel did not obey their Lord. They refused to keep the requirements of the covenant. As soon as the leader after Moses died (Joshua), the Israelites started becoming just as wicked as the nations around them. So God raised up a godly king to rule them, King David.

God made another important covenant, this time with David. He started a new stage in His work to redeem the world. God promised that He would establish the throne of David's seed (there's that word again). What does that mean? God clarified to David,

> Thine house and thy kingdom shall be established for ever before thee: thy throne shall be established for ever. (2 Samuel 7:16)

God was planning to keep His promise to Abraham through David's royal offspring. Do you see the progression? He would raise up the seed of the woman. That seed would bruise the head of the serpent. That seed would be the perfect representative of God and bring blessing. That seed would sit on the throne of Israel forever.

THE PROMISED NEW COVENANT

The story of the Old Testament is not very encouraging. God's grace is evident throughout, but so is His terrible anger against human sin. Even His chosen people, Abraham's seed, rebelled against Him and His law over and over. God cursed them, just as He had promised would be the consequence of not keeping the covenant.

In this dark rebellion, God promised a new covenant. He had explained to Israel through the prophets that their sin problems went all the way to the center of the heart. So through the prophets Jeremiah and Ezekiel, God promised a solution. Ezekiel 36:26 says it this way:

> A new heart also will I give you, and a new spirit will I put within you: and I will take away the stony heart out of your flesh, and I will give you an heart of flesh.

The **New Covenant** that Abraham's seed needed included something no previous covenant did: the promise of heart change. God would write His law on their hearts.

Of course, this just raises a new question: how could God do these things?

THE HERO OF GOD'S NEW COVENANT—JESUS

The answer—and climax of the Bible's story—is Jesus, God's Son. God came to earth as a man, the capital-*S* Seed of the woman. He came to bruise the serpent's head, Satan himself.

Remember why that deceitful serpent's head needed to be bruised? Adam, as the recipient and head of God's original covenant, received God's original blessing, but he failed God's requirement of obedience. As the head of the covenant and its promises, Adam brought down the world with him in his fall. His sin affected the whole world. We are now all sinners. We all die because of his sin—that's the penalty, the curse, of sin.

When Jesus was about to lay down His life on the cross, He sat down to a last supper with His friends and said, "This cup is the new testament [covenant] in my blood" (1 Corinthians 11:25). With His blood, Jesus established the promised New Covenant. Jesus paid the penalty for our sins with His sacrificial death.

In Jesus' death, the serpent bruised the heel of the Seed. But in rising from the dead, Jesus proved that He could not be overcome. Instead, He crushed sin, death, and Satan, effectively bruising the head of the serpent.

Jesus accomplished two things in contrast to Adam. As a result, He's called the **Second Adam**.

1. Jesus kept God's law perfectly instead of giving in to Satan's temptations. Through Him as the Head of the New Covenant, we can receive God's righteousness and a new heart that is able to love God and keep His commandments.
2. When Jesus ascended to the right hand of the Father after His resurrection, He was seated on a throne as the perfect King. Forever.

Now, those who repent and trust Jesus as their Savior enter the New Covenant as His seed. Through Him, believers live eternally. Blessing has come to all the families (nations) of the earth!

God could have snapped His fingers and saved the world ten minutes after Adam and Eve ate the fruit. But He didn't. He executed His plan of redemption in stages, stages that climax in Jesus. Jesus is the real Hero of history, God's big story.

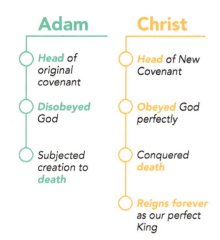

Adam
- *Head* of original covenant
- *Disobeyed* God
- Subjected creation to *death*

Christ
- *Head* of New Covenant
- *Obeyed* God perfectly
- Conquered *death*
- *Reigns forever* as our perfect King

Thinking It Through 2.5

1. List the major stages of God's redemption of the world.

2. Explain how God used the covenants to prepare the way for the coming King.

3. How did Jesus solve mankind's sin problem?

Those Jewish violins are singing once more. Amnon has restored many of them and has named them the Violins of Hope. Instead of displaying them in homes, Amnon lends them to museums and orchestras so that as many people as possible can enjoy them. The Violins of Hope are played in concerts around the world to remember what the Jews endured through the Holocaust. They have been restored to their original beauty and good purpose.

God works through Christ to restore human beings to Himself. The violins were broken and unused, but the master craftsman was able to take what was left and restore their beauty. In spite of all our brokenness, the image of God begins to be restored in us when we repent of our sin—our evil bent—and trust Christ, the Redeemer.

But what about the rest of creation and God's blessing-commands in the Creation Mandate?

How is God making things right?

THE FIRST AND SECOND KINGS

So you've learned that the Creation Mandate both blessed and commanded Adam to rule the earth. He was its first king. When he betrayed his Creator, God set in motion a grand plan to establish a new King with a perfect, eternal kingdom. He sent Jesus, His own Son. Jesus is the *Second* Adam. Thank God we weren't stuck with only the first. *Thank God.*

Hopefully you've trusted Jesus as your Savior and King and received a new heart, the promise of the New Covenant. But you might still be looking around the world wondering, *if Jesus is on the throne ruling, why hasn't the world been redeemed from the corruption of sin yet?*

Great question. The purpose of Jesus' first coming was to provide the solution to the sin problem. He initiated His reign in the hearts of Christians. He conquered the power that sin had held over their lives. These things offer a glimpse of what full restoration will be like in the future.

1. In His **life**, Jesus announced that the King had arrived (Himself). He said, "Repent: for the kingdom of heaven is at hand" (Matthew 4:17). He also gave signs showing what His rule as King would look like. Every healing miracle Jesus performed was a foretaste of what the world will be like when Jesus rules it. In that world, there will be no more blindness, no more leprosy, no more death.

2. In His **death**, Jesus took dominion over sin—the problem that has damaged human rule over this planet ever since the Fall. No king can rule well if he does not submit to the King of Kings! Sin holds everyone in a bad relationship with that King, so you cannot rule your little part of God's world well until Jesus takes care of your sin problem.

3. In His **resurrection**, Jesus took dominion over death, hell, and the Devil. "Through death he . . . destroy[ed] him that had the power of death, that is, the devil" (Hebrews 2:14). And Jesus rose from the dead to sit on His throne and rule (Ephesians 1:20–22). Even centuries before Jesus was born, Isaiah the prophet predicted that Christ would sit "upon the throne of David," and that the Lord would firmly establish that kingdom "with judgment and with justice from henceforth even for ever" (Isaiah 9:7).

THE CHURCH AND THE KING

Herod killed all the babies in Bethlehem out of fear of this new King, Jesus. And he was right to be afraid, because one day Jesus will get rid of all wicked powers (1 Corinthians 15:24). He did, in fact, get rid of Herod.

But Jesus has not yet fully established His rule on the earth. He reigns on His throne from heaven, but He hasn't yet conquered all the territory that will one day be His. He's like a man who buys a plot of land, intending to build a house there, but hasn't yet cleared away all the brush. Or you could compare it to a girl going on a family vacation, who runs into the family's rented cabin and claims a bedroom but hasn't yet brought all her stuff in and set it up.

Jesus has been allowing the thorns in that brush to grow, waiting to set up complete ownership for almost 2,000 years. The New Testament teaches that Jesus "must reign, till he hath put all enemies under his feet" (1 Corinthians 15:25). Clearly, there are still plenty of His enemies around, who haven't submitted to Him yet.

CONQUERING THE CITIZENS

This is where the church comes in. Jesus as Christ the King will come one day and conquer all His enemies in judgment, but the church is full of those He has "conquered" in mercy. The **church** is all the people He has rescued from the kingdom of darkness and brought into His kingdom of light.

When you repent from your sins and trust Christ as Savior, you stop being Christ's enemy. You become a member of Christ's current (and future) kingdom. The church is all the citizens of that kingdom—all the people who, rather than waiting till they are forcibly put under Christ's feet, have willingly submitted to His rule.

When Jesus commands the launch of His church, He does so precisely because He is King. He said to His disciples,

> All power is given unto me in heaven and in earth. Go ye therefore, and teach all nations, baptizing them in the name of the Father, and of the Son, and of the Holy Ghost: teaching them to observe all things whatsoever I have commanded you. (Matthew 28:18–20)

The church is a massively important part of God's plan to restore the world. As the church obeys the Lord's commission to teach all nations, His kingdom is increased with more citizens. It's the first beachhead in a global battle that Christ will one day win. In that day, people from "every kindred, and tongue, and people, and nation" will praise Jesus for redeeming them (Revelation 5:9).

WHAT WE DO AT CHURCH

The earliest Christians "continued stedfastly in the apostles' doctrine and fellowship, and in breaking of bread, and in prayers" (Acts 2:42). Christians ought to do the same today.

Our only access to the teaching ("doctrine") of the apostles is in the Bible. So the church is supposed to teach the Word to the people in Christ's kingdom.

Each church is meant to be a community of love ("fellowship") in which people serve one another's needs and encourage one another toward love and good works.

"Breaking of bread" is communion, sometimes called the Lord's Supper. It is a commemoration of the Last Supper, where Jesus launched the New Covenant.

The church is also supposed to pray together.

Jesus also told the church to "make disciples," so evangelism is part of the church's mission too.

CONQUERING THE HEARTS

In the church, Christ is conquering the most difficult territory there is: the human heart. Through the preaching of the Word and the other things we do inside and outside the church building, Christ is forming us into righteous citizens, increasing His kingdom with better citizens. We'll talk *a lot* more about this in Unit 4.

Meanwhile, the church is surrounded by the enemies that Christ hasn't yet put under His feet. How are we supposed to treat them?

The Bible gives Christians plenty instructions for how to live while waiting for the final restoration. We are *not* told to fight them with swords or guns. Jesus Himself didn't. We are told to love them as our neighbors, to do good for them, to preach the gospel to them—so that they, too, might come into Christ's kingdom.

We are told to suffer persecution with dignity and not with whining, because this isn't *our* world, yet. The Bible is full of word pictures describing this time of waiting. We are ambassadors to a country that our King hasn't yet taken over. We are pilgrims living in temporary housing until we reach the end of our journey. And at the end, we will find a "new earth," a planet restored to the full rule of Christ (Revelation 21:1–5). When Christ comes to earth the second time, He will put the world back the way it was supposed to be.

THE KING WHO REDEEMS

Careful Bible teacher Al Wolters gives a great illustration that helps us understand what it will be like when Christ restores creation.

He compares God's original creation to a newborn baby. Everyone is right to praise a baby's delicate features and healthy appetite. Just as the creation was "very good," a healthy baby is good. It is not good, however, if it stays a baby. A baby must grow and develop.

Wolters asks the reader to imagine that an incurable disease attacks the body of this healthy, growing baby. This represents how the Fall bent creation in an evil direction. The baby continues to grow, but as it does, the disease also bends the body out of its proper shape. While the natural "force" of growth is working on the child, the bad "force" of disease is also twisting and stunting the growth.

Now, what if a cure is found for the disease when the child is twelve? The fully healed child does not revert to a baby state but is a matured person.

Think about how our world has developed since Adam and Eve's time, much like that growing child. If Adam and Eve wanted to go somewhere, they walked. Maybe they could ride an animal. We can get on an airplane and cross a continent in a matter of hours. If Adam and Eve's grandchildren moved to another location, it might have taken days or weeks to send a message to them and receive one back. We can video chat with people across the world instantly.

But all these advances are twisted by the Fall, just like the disease in the child. Our transportation creates pollution. Often, our instant communication is used to harm people—sometimes whole nations. Businesses can pull people out of poverty, but they can also take advantage of poor workers. Restoration is needed for sure, but what will it look like? Is a return to the state of the Garden of Eden what we need?

According to Revelation 21, the world will be made new. Christ will restore it—not back to its "baby" state, the state of the Garden of Eden—but into a perfect, fully filled and subdued planet under His rule. God and His people will live together in harmony in the new Jerusalem, which will be a city, not just a garden.

This day is not yet here, but it is coming. We cannot make it come any faster, but we can live as kingdom citizens to show what that kingdom will be like, just as Jesus did with His life.

THE KING WHO RULES

The King has come to redeem us to Himself and is coming back to claim all. Repent of your sins and follow Christ the King in faith and obedience. Then represent your King to the world by your life of service to others. Win others to the true King by your witness.

Jesus reigns, and He will continue to do so until He has put all His enemies under His feet.

Thinking It Through 2.6

1. How did Jesus finish the job that Adam and all mankind failed to do?

2. How did people know that Jesus was the promised King during His life?

3. How did Jesus' death and resurrection show that He was the promised King?

4. What is the church's place in God's plan of redemption?

5. When will God's work of redemption be complete?

6. How will the restored earth compare with the created one?

What is my
place in
God's story

Where are you in that big story, the big story of the Bible?

You are in the part of the story between Jesus' first coming and second coming. You are in the part called the "church age."

At His first coming, Jesus lived a perfect life and died a reconciling death for your sins. He began the New Covenant and then ascended to heaven. He had really only begun His work of putting the planet under His feet. And His next act was to send His Spirit to begin the church. You are now—or could be, if you repent and believe the gospel—a part of that church.

When Jesus first came, He came in salvation, not in judgment. But after the church age, He will come again—in judgment. He will "put down all rule and all authority and power" (1 Corinthians 15:24). And the powers won't go down easy. They'll fight.

STRUCTURE AND DIRECTION

That fight is not new. It has been going on since the Garden of Eden. The seed of the woman and the seed of the serpent have always been at war. It's going on right now. C. S. Lewis said,

> There is no neutral ground in the universe: every square inch, every split second, is claimed by God and counterclaimed by Satan.

Think back to the child with the disease whom we talked about in the last section. After getting the medicine the child needs, there are three forces at work: the natural force of growth, the twisting force of the disease, and the restorative force of healing. The natural force will always be present. The two other forces—the good and the bad—are fighting over whether that natural force will be successful.

We discussed the natural force already when we looked at creational structure. The other forces, the sickness and the medicine, represent the concept of "direction." (These concepts come from the same writer who gave the sick child illustration, Al Wolters.)

Structure is a word we use to describe the way God created things to be. Structure in a child is the natural force of growth. For the Violins of Hope, structure was their original craftsmanship and good purpose.

Direction is a word we use to describe the two directions in which anything with structure can be tugged. It can be pulled, yanked, bent out of shape by Satan (you've already learned this as "fallen direction"). On the flip side, it can be pushed *back into its structure* by the rule of Christ. This is called **redemptive direction**. In the child, the sickness was bending the body in a fallen direction. The medicine was working to bend the body back in a redemptive direction until it was fully healed. Likewise, the violins were bent in a fallen direction to the cruel purposes of the Nazis in the death

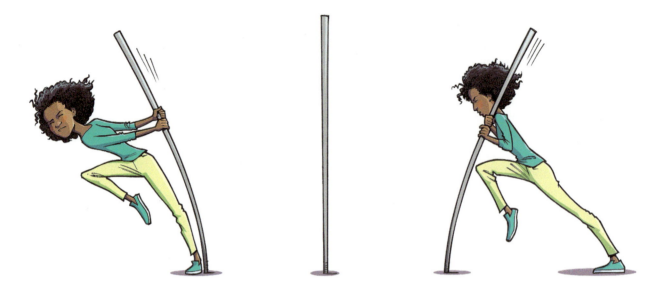

camps. Then the violins were bent back in a redemptive direction toward their structure as the violin maker restored them to their original beauty and purpose.

Think of a car: the structure of the car is what its designers made it to be. When the car gets struck in the passenger door, that door goes in a bad direction—it's out of shape, out of its intended structure. But when the body shop mechanics pound out the big dent and do their magic, making the door look new again, they are sending the car door in a good direction.

Now think of something even more complicated than a car; think of a friendship among three people. The structure of friendship is the way that God designed friends to care for each other. When one friend, tugged by sin, whispers gossip to another about the third friend in the group, that friendship is pulled in a fallen direction. It's out of shape, out of its intended structure. But when the first friend confesses her sin and the one she gossiped about forgives her, the friendship is going in a redemptive direction. It is being put back under the rule of Christ, at least in a small way.

Think of one more example, a popular movie. Go ahead. Think of one. The art of storytelling has structure since it's a good thing God put into creation. But in that particular movie, ask yourself, *is the storytelling going in a redemptive direction?*

Maybe it is. Maybe it is telling the story of how isolating yourself because of a loss doesn't lessen your grief—like in the movie *UP*. In that story, Carl is grieving the death of his wife and hides from everybody behind a grumpy attitude. When he's forced to deal with little Russell, Carl realizes that he still can, and should, love others. This main plotline shows a good direction for storytelling to go.

But maybe the movie you're thinking of is going in a fallen direction. Maybe it's just a setup for a bunch of dirty jokes (Ephesians 5:4). Maybe it's trying to say, like so many other movies, that people should be free to do whatever they want. Now, movies can show sin and still be going in a good direction: *UP* did. It showed Carl's sin. The Bible itself displays plenty of sin, but it obviously pushes people in a redemptive direction.

Everything around you contains something at its core that is "very good," because everything around you was created by God. Satan can't create; he can only bend what God has already created. So, everything has a structure: music, filmmaking, storytelling, education, agriculture, journalism, even politics. But Satan and sinners are always trying to bend structure. And Christ is always working to put it right (hopefully you'll join Him).

You know what's structure and what's direction mostly by reading the Bible—and growing. It will take time for you to learn how to discern the difference between the two. But they're always there.

LIVING A REDEMPTIVE LIFE

Part of your role in this world, at this point in God's story, is to participate with Christ's work of redemption by pushing things back in a redemptive direction. The Lord has given you dominion over certain things in your life. That's the Creation Mandate, remember?

The Lord has given you rule over your free time, over your room, over your friendships, over your piano practicing. And all those things can be bent in a fallen direction. Your free time can be wasted, or worse. Your room can look like a garbage dump after two tornadoes and a small tsunami. Your friendships can become full of sin. Your piano practice can be a tool you use to frustrate your mother.

What if this is you—all these things? And what if you "come to yourself" like the prodigal son and repent from your sin? What will happen? Your room will get cleaner, your friendships will get purer, your piano practice will be productive, and your free time will start to serve the true King.

What is happening every time you push parts of your life back in the right direction? Christ is putting that thing under His feet. Christ is putting things under His feet all the time during this part of the big story, the church age. He is giving you and many others the grace necessary to do **good works**.

Good works will never save you—your sin is too great. But the Bible still tells us to do them. They are part of our calling as image-bearers of God, people told to take dominion over the world.

> We are his workmanship, created in Christ Jesus unto good works. (Ephesians 2:10)

We're told that those who have believed in God must be "careful to maintain good works" (Titus 3:8). This is where believers fit in God's big story right now: they are called to show that they are God's children by living lives of good works. From evangelism and other obviously spiritual things, to mothering, to fathering, to engineering, and to the many other things a student might do one day—you are meant to find the creational structure in some aspect of this world and push it in a redemptive direction.

WORLDVIEW QUEST: TOO FALLEN?

In the late 1700s through early 1800s, William Wilberforce was a member of the British Parliament and was seeking to abolish slavery in the British Empire. As a Christian, he also saw much fallen direction in the world of politics around him, and he considered quitting his work to become a minister.

John Newton, the converted slave trader who wrote "Amazing Grace," wrote a letter that encouraged Wilberforce in the work God had given him. This letter may have changed the course of history, as Wilberforce eventually did succeed in stopping the slave trade. He saw the abolishment of slavery in the British Empire just before his death.

Introduction

Imagine you are a friend of Wilberforce as he faces this crisis. He has written to you about his desire to retire from politics before accomplishing his main goal, the end of slavery.

Task

Write a three-paragraph letter to Wilberforce that (1) acknowledges the fallen direction of politics, (2) points out the creational structure within politics, and (3) encourages Wilberforce in his fight against slavery as a way of living redemptively and pushing politics toward structure.

Procedure

1. Research William Wilberforce for some short articles about his life.
2. Use the internet to find and read John Newton's letter to Wilberforce as an example.
3. Write a three-paragraph letter as described above.
4. Read your letter to your class or family.

THE BIBLICAL STORY AND YOUR DESIRES

At the end of the story, God will accomplish His major goal: He will bring Himself glory. When Christ puts all things under His feet, He will submit Himself to the Father. This is so "that God may be all in all" (1 Corinthians 15:28). That's where the story is headed. God will display His glory through the salvation of sinners and the restoration of creation.

And here's the truly awesome thing about the Bible's big story. Your best desires and God's plan are not in conflict. The best way for you to find the joy you naturally seek is to participate with God in His plan. Be a part of His bringing glory to Himself through the redemption of all creation!

A biblical worldview, then, does not tell you to ignore or deny all your desires. Some of your desires are good—structural, in fact. Good desires include getting married, doing significant work, exploring creation, and getting an A on your math test. But unless you see where you are in God's story—between Fall and full redemption—you won't be able to live rightly in God's world.

And first things first. If you are not yet reconciled to the Creator God, your life is broken and needs to be redeemed from sin. God offers His gift of redemption to you through Christ's death, burial, and resurrection. Will you repent of your sins and by faith be redeemed back to your Creator?

Thinking It Through 2.7

1. Where are we now in the big story of the Bible?

2. Define *structure*.

3. Define *direction*.

4. How can we discern structure and direction?

5. Name two things you have dominion over. What is their structure? What direction are they going in? How can you push them in a redemptive direction?

6. What is God's ultimate goal for salvation and restoration of creation?

Scripture Memory

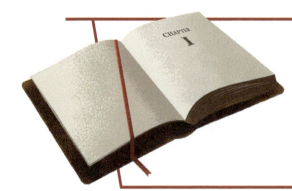

Psalm 19:7–8
Isaiah 46:9–10
Genesis 1:31
Romans 5:12
Genesis 3:15
Revelation 5:9–10
Ephesians 2:10

Recall

1. What are two word pictures the Bible uses to describe how Scripture came to us?

2. What are the three major points of the story of the Bible?

3. Which chapter in Scripture describes the Fall?

4. What were the three major promises of God to Abraham (summarized in one word each)?

5. What are the covenants that are stages for God's redemption?

6. Define *structure*.

7. Define *direction*.

Understand

8. Were there any faults in God's original creation? How do we know?

9. Why did Adam's sin affect the rest of creation rather than just affecting the human race?

10. What blessing-command of the Creation Mandate became more difficult when God cursed the woman in Genesis 3?

11. What blessing-command of the Creation Mandate became more difficult when God cursed the man in Genesis 3?

12. Why do Christians call Jesus the "Second Adam"?

13. What is Christ doing in the world during the church age?

14. How do Creation and the Fall show structure and direction?

Think Critically

15. Would it be better to say God "knew" the future of the world or God "planned" the future of the world? Explain.

16. How does being made in the image of God affect your purpose and value?

17. Why is the New Covenant the most important of the covenants?

18. As illustrated by the growth and healing of the sick child, what will the world be like when Christ fully restores it?

Internalize

19. What do you want to be when you grow up? Now, try to fit that thing into the big story God tells about the world. How does it fit?

20. Give an example of when the effects of the Fall in someone else's life affected your life.

21. When was the last time you saw the effects of the Fall in your own heart?

22. Have you repented of your sins and trusted Christ to redeem you from your fallen direction away from your Creator? Explain.

WHO IS GOD, AND WHY SHOULD I CARE?

What is my greatest need

Do you really need a bright purple puffer stress ball teddy bear toy?

What do you need? What do you *really* need?

Do you think it would be cool if you could have free stuff basically whenever you wanted it?

Some people can actually have pretty much whatever Amazon .com® sells—which is just about everything. These "Viners" get free stuff in exchange for online reviews. They get the stuff in the mail, they give it some stars (1–5), and the stuff is theirs to keep. Seems pretty cool, right?

But when Amazon started cutting back the program, ending the stream of free stuff, a number of Viners were actually *relieved and happy*. They gave different reasons for this. Some felt like the stuff had turned into a burden. Others were unable to enjoy gifts from their family and friends because they already had so much stuff. The very thing most people look to for satisfaction—more stuff—became like a weight to these people.

Ask ex-Viners: more stuff won't make you happy.

ALL THESE THINGS

Jesus said that God knows we need food, drink, and clothing. He said that people who don't know God busy themselves seeking these things. Like a bunch of Viners.

Jesus had different advice:

Seek ye first the kingdom of God, and his righteousness; and all these things shall be added unto you. (Matthew 6:33)

God gave you life. He sustains your life by His provision. He is your greatest need. His kingdom. His righteousness. His love. His justice. His comfort. A bright purple puffer stress ball teddy bear toy is fun, no doubt. But when actual stress comes, the only ultimate relief available comes from God.

IF YOU HAVE EVERYTHING EXCEPT GOD, YOU HAVE NOTHING.

IF YOU HAVE GOD AND NOTHING ELSE, YOU HAVE EVERYTHING YOU NEED.

Can you say this with the psalmist Asaph: "Whom have I in heaven but thee? And there is none upon earth that I desire beside thee" (Psalm 73:25)?

YOUR GREATEST NEED AND THE BIBLE

Because God is your greatest need, you should have a desire to know Him better. Many middle-schoolers in Christian homes and schools *do* have hearts to seek God and know Him. Many of them read the Bible, looking for Him. And what they actually find is a lot of stories and genealogies and poems and rules that may not seem as though they have anything to do with us today. The Bible's world is so far away from our world. Search for *internet* in Scripture, and you won't find it.

You yourself might have read parts of the Bible and wondered, *What does this have to do with me? What possible connection could there be between that world and mine?*

J. I. Packer, in his classic book *Knowing God*, raises this question. And he has a definite answer: God. God is the connection between the stories of the Bible and us today. The same God that was Lord of Abraham, Isaac, and Jacob is Lord of all today. Just like He was their greatest need in their time and place, He is your greatest need in this time and place. And He is the same yesterday, today, and forever.

CASE STUDY: GOD, OUR GREATEST NEED

Many people seek relationships and money to give their lives stability and happiness. It's true that these are real human needs, but even people who have these needs met will eventually find that they're still missing deep, enduring happiness.

Before meeting his future wife, Jeff Bezos would say he was the guy the girls just weren't interested in. However, MacKenzie asked him out on their first date, and six months later they married. A year later, in 1994, Jeff began Amazon. MacKenzie was the company's first employee. They started out very small selling books online, and Amazon grew to be worth over $800 billion in twenty-five years.

A net worth of over $100 billion establishes Jeff Bezos as the richest man in the world.

The Bezoses have four children, whom they've tried to raise normally in a billionaire world. It's an amazing success story. In the view of many, their dreams were complete—until news surfaced of their plan to divorce, after Bezos was unfaithful to his wife.

1. How might a wealthy person like Jeff Bezos come to believe that money will bring happiness?

2. Why is the hope that money will bring happiness a false hope?

3. Will a loving, close-knit family bring happiness?

4. How is it that God alone can meet our longing for deep, enduring happiness?

WHAT GOD IS LIKE

And what is God like in the Bible? If God is your greatest need, you need to know the answer! You won't be able to live successfully in this world without knowing its designer.

Packer asks the reader to imagine dropping off a tribesman from the Amazon jungle into the middle of a city. He doesn't know the language and has never seen cars or buildings. He would be bewildered and terrified. It would be cruel to do this to him. In the same way, Packer says,

> We are cruel to ourselves if we try to live in this world without knowing about the God whose world it is and who runs it.
> The world becomes a strange, mad, painful place . . . for those who do not know about God.

So let's jump in: what is God like? We need to talk about (1) the attributes of God and (2) the Trinity.

THE ATTRIBUTES OF GOD

What is an attribute? It's just something that is true about someone all the time. Red hair is an attribute of some people. Some people are quick to anger; that is a bad attribute. Some people make friends easily; that's a good attribute. But a blue shirt is not an attribute of a person—because they may have a different color on tomorrow.

What are God's attributes? What is God like all the time?

Ask people on the street, and they'll give you plenty of ideas. The most common view of God today in America is that He is a nice uncle who watches out for you from upstairs. This uncle is a little kooky, but in a cute way. And the one thing about him that you can always rely on is that he is quick to forgive and quick to overlook people's faults, if he even notices them to begin with. He's rather distant. He's not just upstairs—he's in the attic. He exists mostly to assure you that you're right and that things will turn out all right.

This view, of course, is completely wrong. Kookiness is not an attribute of God. Nor is cuteness.

The problem with these ideas is that they are creations of our own fallen minds. Should we expect sinful people to have true ideas about God? No, the only way we can know what God is really like is if He tells us.

And as you know, He has. In the Bible.

Careful readers of the Bible have tried to list the attributes of God taught in Scripture. Here are some of them.

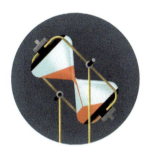

ETERNAL

God exists above and outside time. "A thousand years in thy sight are but as yesterday when it is past" (Psalm 90:4).

PRESENT EVERYWHERE

"Neither is there any creature that is not manifest [visible] in his sight" (Hebrews 4:13).

UNCHANGING

God's attributes do not change. He is reliable, "the same yesterday, and to day, and for ever" (Hebrews 13:8).

OUR GOD IS . . .

ALL-KNOWING

God knows everything. Jesus told his disciples that even "the very hairs of your head are all numbered" by God (Matthew 10:30).

ALL-POWERFUL

"Whatsoever the LORD pleased, that did he in heaven, and in earth" (Psalm 135:6).

SELF-EXISTENT

God relies on no one else for His existence. He told Moses, "I AM THAT I AM" (Exodus 3:14). He has no cause or source. Instead, He is the source for everything else (Romans 11:36).

There are many more attributes: God is good; the Bible invites us to taste and see that goodness (Psalm 34:8). God is love; He reaches out in love to all creation (John 3:16). He is a gracious God who shows mercy to sinners (Exodus 33:19). He is a jealous God: He is angry at anything and anyone who deceives or harms those He loves. He is a God of holiness, of righteousness, of truth, of wisdom.

He is a God of glory. His brilliant beauty shines through the combination of all His attributes. "The whole earth is full of his glory," say the angels in Isaiah 6:3.

As someone once said, ever since God created us in His own image, we have been trying to return the favor. In other words, people create their version of God as someone like them. One of your great goals in life should be to make your ideas about God fit His revelation of Himself, rather than the other way around.

God is your greatest need. Because God is **omnipotent**—all-powerful—you can view things that are hard for you as completely doable with His help. Because God is **omniscient**—all-knowing—you can be sure He understands even if no one else does. Because God is **omnipresent**—present everywhere—you can pray to Him anytime, anywhere; and you know He will hear.

THE TRINITY

Do you completely understand God now? Don't feel bad if you don't. We can't expect creatures like ourselves to have our Creator totally figured out.

If your mind isn't already blown by God's attributes, there's one more thing we have to discuss about God from Scripture: the teaching of the **Trinity**. This is the Christian effort to put together two different truths in the Bible:

1. The Bible insists over and over that there is **only one God**. "I am God, and there is none else," He says (Isaiah 46:9). Belief in one God is called "monotheism" (*mono* means "one" or "alone"; *theism* means "belief in God").

2. And yet the Bible also speaks of **the Son and Spirit as God**. This is less clear in the Old Testament, although the truth is present (see Isaiah 9:6). But it is surely clear in the New Testament. The very first words of the Gospel of John speak of Jesus as divine. John calls Jesus "the Word," and he says, "In the beginning was the Word, and the Word was with God, and the Word was God" (1:1). The Spirit also is divine. Jesus told His followers to baptize people in the name of the Father, Son, and Spirit (Matthew 28:19). The Spirit hears prayers, He fills believers, He is grieved when we sin, and He makes us holy. Only a divine being could do these things.

How can you believe in one God *and* that Jesus and the Spirit are God? The answer is the concept of "Trinity." The word itself is the combination of two ideas: *tri*, meaning "three," and *unity*, meaning "one." In the Trinity, there is threeness and there is oneness. For many centuries, Christians have put it this way: there are three persons in one God. God is a "tri-unity," a Trinity.

This may sound hypothetical or remote. But it is essential to Christianity. Christians can worship only one God. And Christians must worship the Father, the Son, and the Spirit.

Why does the doctrine of the Trinity matter? Here's one reason why: if God is your greatest need, you need a God who doesn't need *you*. You don't need a needy God. And the doctrine of the Trinity shows that God didn't create the world out of His own neediness. God wasn't lonely. Father, Son, and Spirit share a love for one another that is entirely enough. God created us because that love spilled out, like a fountain.

FATHER — IS NOT — IS — IS NOT — GOD — SON — IS — IS — HOLY SPIRIT — IS NOT

HOW YOU SHOULD RESPOND

Christians are people who accept God's love and return it, people who repent from loving stuff more than loving God. When you realize that God is your greatest need, you won't stop needing stuff—we all need food, clothing, and shelter. But you will see God *through* your stuff. *This stuff is so nice; God is so good to me to show His love this way!*

And if you know God is your greatest need, you won't want things He forbids. Your life will evidence more of God's character, His image in you. Goodness, love, wisdom, truth. Not stuff, stuff, stuff.

Thinking It Through 3.1

1. What is your greatest need?

2. What is the most important link between the Bible's ancient stories and your story today?

3. Choose one of the attributes of God from the list in this section and find a verse (one not mentioned in the text) that teaches about that attribute.

4. Which attribute of God would be most comforting to a Christian your age who has just been diagnosed with leukemia? Explain your choice.

5. Which attribute of God would cause the most gratitude for a Christian teen who has just qualified for the Olympic gymnastics team? Explain your choice.

6. How should the fact that God is omnipresent change the way you live?

What is
truth ?

One of the attributes of God is truth. And you're more than old enough to know that different people have different ideas about what counts as truth.

If you've ever seen American TV news, then you know: what counts as truth on Fox News® doesn't necessarily count as truth on MSNBC® or CNN®, and vice versa. The president is either the shrewdest leader in history or a brainless jerk. The president is either 75 percent better than Abraham Lincoln or Hitler's long-lost evil twin.

The same action from the president—signing a bill, dropping a handkerchief—has either saved the world or finally doomed us all, depending on which spin zone you fall into.

And no reasoning, no discussion can happen between the two sides. Just try it. Talking with the other side is like yelling under-water. During a hurricane. While starfish are trying to eat your toes. It's just utterly impossible.

If you do try—just *try*—to take someone else's point of view on any issue, you'll find out how hard it is. It feels like stepping out of reality and into a weird world where people shut their eyes to the obvious. "Truth" is something you can't take for granted.

TRUTH—FOR REAL

Christians should never step out of reality—the reality created by God, that is. Christ's disciples are accountable to God's view of reality twenty-four hours a day, seven days a week. So even when we sit down to define a concept like "truth," we must do our best to submit our mental work to God.

What does the Bible say that truth is?

The Bible talks about truth as what matches reality. Moses said in Deuteronomy that if the Israelites ever saw their brothers wor-shiping and serving other gods, they were supposed to do some de-tective work. They were supposed to find out what really happened. And if "it be true, and the thing certain, that such abomination is wrought [done] in Israel" (17:4), the people who did it were sup-posed to die. You wouldn't just go around accusing others of idol worship and killing them without working hard to find out what really happened. It had to be *true* and *certain* that they committed the crime.

We talk this way too. We say, "I saw the president at a ceremony, and I shook his hand!" And someone else says, "Is that *true*?"

It is confusing to see how many people claim to have the truth, even though their "truths" all differ. In the Western world today, there is a lot of pressure not to claim that your truth is better than anyone else's.

But *true* truth matches reality as it is interpreted by God. God said when He created this world that it was very good. God made a true statement about how the world really is. He interpreted reality *for us*. But why is this so important?

Humans need God to tell them what is really true because fallen people *suppress* the truth (Romans 1:18). Truth presses up into their minds from where God has written on their hearts (Romans 2:14–15), but they shove it back down. God has made some truths completely obvious, such as this one: boys are boys and girls are girls. But many people in the Western world are suppressing even this truth. They are trying to deny it, to pretend it doesn't exist. The more that fallen people try to reinterpret reality, the more we are in need of God's interpretation of reality.

There is another reason people need God's interpretation of reality: we are finite. We are limited. We can't possibly take in all the facts available in order to determine reality ourselves—just think of the vastness of God's world. It is the reality God created, and God created it to tell us truth about reality. But we struggle to understand the created world. We can know only so much—even when we all get together and share what we know.

GOD AND TRUTH

We are fallen. We are finite. How can we know truth?

We must find its ultimate source, like going upstream in a river till we finally find the spring in the ground from which the river comes. That source is, obviously, God Himself. God is truth. God never lies; He "cannot lie," the Bible says (Titus 1:2). All truth comes from Him.

Whatever God knows—*that* is the standard of truth. God's knowledge of your motives for mowing the lawn—that's *true*. God's knowledge of the boiling point of water at one thousand feet above sea level—that's *true*. God's knowledge of the past, His knowledge of the present, His knowledge of the future—true, true, true.

Truth is something God has before anyone else has it. And truth is a gift that He can give by His grace to fallen and finite people like us. We're fallen, so sometimes we refuse to receive God's gift of truth. But this is not God's fault; it's ours. And we're finite, so sometimes we don't receive it very well. We struggle to understand.

A

In Adam's fall,
We sinned all.
B
Thy life to mend,
This Book attend.

The rhyme used to teach the letter *B* in *The New England Primer* says,

Thy life to mend,
This Book attend.

In other words: if you want to fix your life, listen to the person who gave it to you. Listen to God's Word.

Some people think that they can sit out in nature and learn everything they need to know about life. Though creation does speak truth every day everywhere, it doesn't use words; so in the end, it's not the ultimate method to learn truth. (Kind of like how information doesn't really travel to your brain when you sleep with a textbook under your pillow.)

The Bible is God's most important way of giving us truth because it uses God's most powerful tool for truth-telling: language. Words, sentences, ideas. *Communication from God to man.* Without language, we can't know what Jesus' dying on the cross and rising from the dead mean. We can't know that He died "for our sins" (1 John 2:2), or that He rose again as the first in a long line of people that God will raise (1 Corinthians 15:20).

But because we have the Bible, we can know truth. If God "breathed out" the Bible (see Section 2.1) and if God cannot lie, then the Bible's words are true. This was certainly what Jesus thought. "The scripture cannot be broken," Jesus told the Jews. And He said to the Father, "Thy word is truth" (John 10:35; 17:17).

LIVING OUT THE TRUTH

Let's revisit the political divisions of America. How do you know which "side" to be on? God's truth can guide you to know what the reality is for each issue. For example, the legal system in America is a good representation of reality only when it measures up to God's truth. You must follow God's truth in finding your way through complicated issues. And at the end of the day, if God says something is wrong, it doesn't matter how many politicians say it's right—it's still wrong.

Because God is the authority on truth and His Word is truth, you need to love the truth. It comes from God. And you should hate lies: lies come from the Devil. To do anything else goes against God and His nature of truthfulness. Even "little white lies" are serious because they are against the very nature of God. You cannot be right with God while living according to a lie.

Going along with someone else's lie is just as bad. Romans 1:32 explains that you are worthy of the same punishment as the liar if you stand around approving of the situation, even though the lie didn't come out of *your* mouth.

The Bible is clear about the emotions you ought to be having about truth and falsehood:

> [Love] rejoiceth not in iniquity, but rejoiceth in the truth. (1 Corinthians 13:6)

Go ahead—rate your rejoicing-in-truth. One thing is certain, if you are a Christian, God aims for you to rejoice in the truth around you and within you *as much as He does.*

Love the truth. Hate lies.

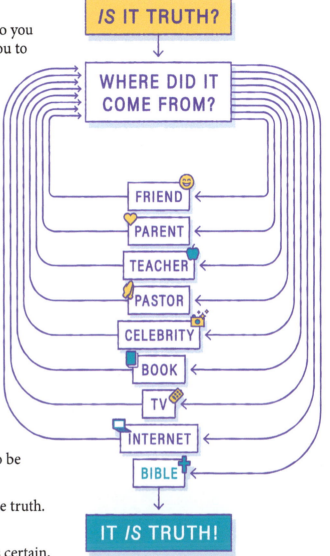

Thinking It Through 3.2

1. How does the Bible describe truth?

2. Why are people confused about the truth?

3. What's wrong with people determining their own truth?

4. Which attribute of God causes Him to be a God of truth?

5. How should the fact that God is the standard for truth change the way you live?

3.3 GOODNESS

What is the difference between good and evil ?

Frederick Douglass was about eight years old when he looked around at his world and condemned it like a little judge. He had to guess his age because, as a slave, he had no way of knowing. But he knew slavery was wrong. Years later he wrote in his second autobiography,

I could not reconcile the relation of slavery with my crude notions of goodness.

There are two ways we learn goodness: from above and from below. Douglass was talking about goodness from below—he learned goodness from the moral **conscience** God had placed in his heart.

Paul said in his world-famous letter to the Romans that when non-Christians "do by nature the things contained in [God's] law," even when they don't know the Bible, they show something. They show that "the law [is] written in their hearts." They show that God gave them a "conscience . . . bearing witness" to the truth of God's law, the truth about right and wrong (Romans 2:14–15).

Without a day of school in his life, without proper clothing, without enough food to eat, without any knowledge whatsoever of his father, without really knowing his mother, this little boy *knew*. He *knew* that the slavery around him was wrong. Evil.

Douglass's writings showed that he was able to discern good and evil because God had written an understanding of these things on the human heart. Douglass knew slavery was evil. Some people, like the slaveholders, suppressed this truth. But the truth was still there.

GOOD—FOR REAL

You know what good is. You know what evil is. And you know them both the same way Douglass did:

GOD HAS WRITTEN THE DEFINITIONS OF GOOD AND EVIL ON YOUR HEART.

But you, like Southern slaveholders of two centuries ago (and everyone else who has ever lived), have been twisted and bent by your sin, so that sometimes you "call evil good, and good evil" (Isaiah 5:20). So you need something more than your own heart and conscience to tell you what is good. Not all your desires are good, and not all your understanding of good is good either!

We need to get an understanding of goodness *from above*: we need to listen to God's descriptions of good and evil given in Scripture. There are many ways to do this.

OBSERVING STORIES

One way is to read the stories of the Bible and learn from its writers, who recorded good and evil throughout history.

The shepherd boy David was clearly good. He sang psalms to the Lord with wholehearted love. He fought Goliath out of jealousy for the name of God. He comforted himself in the Lord when he lost his family. And he refused to kill King Saul, who was trying to kill him. The narrator makes it clear: goodness includes loving and relying on God.

And *king* David, later in his life, was good too—until he committed adultery and murder. The Bible says directly that this was evil: "The thing that David had done displeased the LORD" (2 Samuel 11:27). But you can see that it is evil through the story itself. David repeatedly attempted to cover up his adultery and ended up murdering one of his faithful soldiers.

OBSERVING JESUS

We also learn good and evil by looking at God Himself in Scripture, and especially at the greatest picture of God ever drawn: Jesus.

Jesus was the greater David. He loved the Father with all His heart. His blood boiled when God was mocked—but He also never sinned or even desired to. Far from murdering someone else as David did, Jesus permitted Himself to be murdered. He laid down His life for His friends. One of those friends, someone who watched Him intensely for three years, recognized the truth that Jesus committed "no sin" whatsoever (1 Peter 2:22). Jesus was God in flesh; He was perfectly good.

GOD AND GOODNESS

One of the first things many little kids learn about God is "God is good." Goodness is not an abstract thing in the Bible. No, the Bible presents it as a *personal* thing. *God* is good. This statement means that (1) goodness is not outside God as a ruler over Him and (2) God does not declare something "good" in such a way that He could say something *evil* is good. Just the opposite: He is the definition of good (Luke 18:19).

If someone says, "God can declare cheating good!" then the Bible's answer is simply to point readers, over and over again, to the works of God, which reveal His pure goodness. God loves us (John 3:16), God saves us (Matthew 1:21), God has mercy on us (2 Samuel 24:14), God remembers us (Exodus 6:5), and God notices our needs (Matthew 6:8). God even counts the hairs on our heads (Matthew 10:30). You're at 152,413 right now. (Okay, that's a guess—but God knows.)

In fact, we can't be good outside of God: our lives must match who God is in order to be truly good. And, since He has revealed Himself through the laws, commands, and principles in the Bible, you need to understand that they aren't arbitrary rules but a demonstration of God's pure, perfect character. For your life to be good, it must match God's goodness as revealed in His Word. For those things around you to be called good, they must match God's Word as well.

But we are fallen people. We cannot be good on our own—we cannot even perfectly assess what is good and evil around us. This is the problem Jesus came to solve. Remember how Jesus is the perfect demonstration of God because He *is* God? His righteousness, the righteousness of God, becomes ours when we repent of our sin and trust Him as the Savior (2 Corinthians 5:21).

HOW YOUR WORLDVIEW HANDLES EVIL

We are created by God, and we get our sense of good and evil (our consciences) from Him. It would take a strong act of rebellion to look at God in Scripture and say, "God is *not* good."

But, of course, this is precisely what people do. American writer Mark Twain, author of *The Adventures of Tom Sawyer*, actually said he was morally superior to the God of the Bible.

> The [god] that *I* want to keep out of the reach of is the caricature of him which one finds in the Bible. We (that one and I) could never respect each other. . . . I have met his superior a hundred times—in fact I amount to that myself.

What drove Twain to say this was the existence of evil in the world. The God of the Bible, in Twain's worldview, was a mixture of good and bad—like us. Twain felt he himself had more goodness and less evil than God. But the truth—the reality from God's point of view—is that God is good, and anything that is contrary to God is evil. We have evil within us, not because God made us that way but because we turned from God and disobeyed Him.

A biblical worldview does acknowledge a "problem of evil." It is hard—even impossible—for us to explain how God could be all-powerful and all-good and yet still allow three-year-olds to get painful, deadly cancers. Or to let parents cruelly abuse and neglect their children. Abuse is a moral evil, a sin; cancer is not a moral evil (it's not a sin to get cancer), but it is still a result of living in a fallen world broken by the curse. Thus, diseases and disasters are also often labeled "evil" along with those things that are contrary to God's moral goodness.

GOD'S WISDOM

Yes, there is a problem of evil. But the wisdom and goodness of God deal with it in ways that our finite minds can't. Remember the perspective of Joseph from Section 2.2? He told his brothers,

> Ye thought evil against me; but God meant it unto good, to bring to pass, as it is this day, to save much people alive. (Genesis 50:20)

In the middle of Joseph's darkest moments in prison, it would have been easy for him to conclude that there was no way God could ever turn his circumstances into anything good.

And that's sometimes where we are too. The Bible simply expects us to continue believing that God is good and that He makes "all things work together for good" for us, even when we can't imagine how (Romans 8:28). Since we may never see with our own eyes the end of the story—the justice or the good result—that's where our trust in an infinitely wise God has to come in.

GOD'S MORAL STANDARD

People who reject the existence of the God of the Bible may think they "solved" the problem of evil. Sure, now they don't have to explain how a good God could permit evil. But they create an even bigger problem. Now they have a problem of good-and-evil. How do we even know for sure what good and evil are if there is no God?

If the atheistic worldview is right, then good and evil are just illusions meant to help our species survive. They aren't real. There is no standard by which to judge the goodness or evil of something.

But look in your heart at the laws of good and evil that God wrote there: you know atheists' claims can't be right. The biblical worldview recognizes God as the standard for good, which contrasts with evil. He is the only reason we can say, "That's evil!"

CASE STUDY: EXPLAINING EVIL

How does the big story of evolution explain the existence of good and evil? To the evolutionist, people have adopted certain behaviors to help "the herd" survive and also preserve one's place in it. This "good" behavior morphed into something we call morality. "Bad" behavior—going against the approved morality—limits contact and help from the herd.

In the end, good and evil are all about whatever helps or hurts you. "There is . . . no design, no purpose, no evil and no good, nothing but blind, pitiless indifference," says evolutionist Richard Dawkins. According to Dawkins, not only are humans pointless, they are hopeless.

According to God, however, morality isn't biological, a series of survival instincts; morality is spiritual. Romans 2:14–15 states that God's moral law is written in the heart of every person. Humans flourish when they obey God's good law.

1. How do some evolutionists explain the existence of good and evil?

2. Does the "morality" of evolutionists provide a never-changing standard? Explain.

3. What demonstrates that humans have consciences, not just survival instincts?

4. How does the "morality" of evolutionists change the meaning of love?

GOD'S SOLUTION TO EVIL

People who reject God because of the problem of evil also don't have a Jesus, a "God with us," who came and took our pain on His shoulders. "By whose stripes ye were healed," the Bible says (1 Peter 2:24). Through Jesus' sacrifice, Christians can begin to find redemption for the evils they face within and without. They also cling to the hope of full redemption at the end of the big story of the world.

LIVING OUT GOODNESS

Frederick Douglass came to the same answer that the Bible does about who bears the blame for evil:

> It was not *color*, but *crime*, not *God*, but *man*, that afforded the true explanation of the existence of slavery.

Mankind is to blame for the evil in the world. God is responsible for the good. One day God's good will overrule mankind's evil.

In the meantime, God's goodness can become yours in Christ. You can be good, just as God is good (Galatians 2:20). His law can work in your heart to grow in His righteousness.

Love goodness. Hate evil.

Thinking It Through 3.3

1. What are the two ways to learn goodness? Explain.

2. Is good "good" because God says it is or because it just is? Explain.

3. What answers does the biblical worldview give for the problem of evil?

4. How should a person live in response to God's goodness?

What makes something beautiful ❓☐

The last two sections were about truth and goodness. In a way, they're twins.

- Truth is something a lot of people doubt that we can identify with certainty.
- Goodness is also something a lot of people doubt that we can identify with certainty. They think goodness is defined differently by different cultures.

- Truth is something that, Christians believe, is ultimately defined by God. What He knows is truth by definition.
- Goodness is also something that, Christians believe, is ultimately defined by God. What He is, is good by definition.

But truth and goodness are not twins. They're triplets. There's another sibling in the family: beauty.

Truth, goodness, and beauty go together. When philosophers discuss one, they often discuss the others. And we can say the same things about beauty that we said about truth and goodness.

- Beauty is something a lot of people doubt that we can identify with certainty. They think it is completely in the eye of the beholder. Beauty is anything that *you* see as beautiful. That's all that matters.
- And yet beauty is something that, Christians must believe, is ultimately defined by God. What He sees as beautiful is beautiful by definition.

BEAUTY—FOR REAL

Wait, stop. Think about what this means. At least two things:

1. It's possible for something to be beautiful even if you think it's not. If God regards it as beautiful and you don't, your opinion is wrong.

People don't like to be told this. They believe beauty is completely in the eye of the beholder—and they are the beholders. To them, saying that beauty is something that you can be wrong about is like saying that your favorite color is better than someone else's. It's meaningless.

But adults in your life have probably tried to introduce you to things they saw as beautiful and you didn't. You are old enough now to see the beauty they see in some of those things.

A classic example is classical music. Many generations of Western people have found beauty in classical music, but that beauty is something it takes effort to appreciate. Little kids don't always get it. You must have some compositions explained to you before you can really appreciate them: the creativity, the invention, the artistry. Or you have to work very hard at piano lessons for years before you start to really enjoy the music you're being told to play.

Another example is literary devices—ways of making writing more beautiful, from alliteration to zeugma. Good writers use them all the time, but they don't make a show out of them, so you might not notice. It takes experience and training to see and appreciate literary devices. The beauty is there, but not every reader will see it.

Now, God doesn't list in Scripture which pieces of music or art or writing are beautiful. This is the key point here: beauty is not necessarily "in the eye of the beholder." Often people miss beauty or deny it when it's right under their noses. *We all need to be open to the possibility that there is beauty out there that God sees and we don't.*

2. With God defining beauty, it's also possible for something to be ugly even though many people call it beautiful.

People don't like to be told this. They think that they, as the beholders, can't be wrong.

The most popular video-sharing websites in existence are almost all music videos. Some have not just millions but *billions* of views. And they wouldn't be popular if they didn't contain any beauty whatsoever. But the top videos also generally mix in a lot of sin. Even the videos that are more tame tend to assume a world in which marriage is optional, God's name means nothing, you don't get mad—you get even, and what really matters in life is pleasure. Right. NOW.

All of this is *ugly*. Sin is ugly. But people still flock to these videos by the billions. They love ugly sin. They call the music videos beautiful, but they're wrong. Any beauty the videos have is overwhelmed by sin.

BEAUTIFUL LITERARY DEVICES

Literary devices can make written language beautiful. These two were mentioned:

- Alliteration is starting multiple words with the same sound or letter: "from rags to riches," "dead as a doornail." Sometimes alliteration is just fun, but in the hands of a great writer it can be truly beautiful. Thomas Hardy calls a winter garden a "gaunt gray gallery."

- Zeugma is a clever literary device that uses the same verb one time in two senses: "He took my advice—and my wallet." Wit in a writer can also be truly beautiful. Mark Twain writes of two fighting boys having "covered themselves with dust and glory."

Readers come away from such writing not only knowing information but delighting in it. They enjoy the writing that much more because of the skill it took to make it beautiful.

DEFINING BEAUTY

This section has assumed that you know what beauty is—because you do. You can't be made in the image of God without having, somewhere inside of you, an appreciation for beauty. Even the wickedest man in prison would enjoy a sunset on the beach and a swelling musical chord.

But still, it's worth defining beauty with words to cement and increase our understanding of it. And here's an attempt. It will be hard to understand at first, but we'll get there. These are the words of poet Dana Gioia:

> Beauty is the pleasure we get in recognizing the particular manifestation of a broader, universal order.

Let's start with this definition to get to what beauty is.

1. The poet says beauty is *pleasure*. This is only partially right since something can be beautiful even if a person doesn't recognize it as beautiful. But true beauty should give us pleasure. It should stir up delight and joy. If you have a memory of visiting an amazing, breathtaking place, you know what it means for beauty to stir up pleasure.
2. Beauty is what brings pleasure, delight, and joy at a definite time, at a time when we *recognize* something beautiful. Sort of like spotting a face in a big crowd and thinking, *I know that person!*
3. So what is the something we must recognize (with pleasure and joy) in order for us to truly experience beauty? Gioia says it's *a particular manifestation of something broader*. It's one instance, or one example, of something far bigger than itself.

A JV basketball game is just one particular manifestation of the game of basketball. Basketball is huge: it's a sport played by millions.

4. What is the far bigger thing, then, that sums up beauty? The bigger thing, Gioia says, is a *universal order*. Things in the universe are ordered. There are laws that govern everything God created, including the things we call "the arts." Music, art, theater, dance, poetry, storytelling—all these things are governed by laws that were given by God at creation. They are part of the creational order (think *structure*).

Our job is to discover that order and live our lives according to it. When we do that, we create particular manifestations of beauty that are in harmony with God's beautiful order.

There can be no music, for example, without that creational order. God made it so that certain vibrations, when put together, please the human ear (when the ear is rightly ordered). One chord of just three notes can bring tears of joy or sorrow to someone's eyes. When a composer chooses those three notes and puts them together in a series of other chords and people experience the beauty, that composer is not *creating* beauty itself so much as *discovering* beauty that God already put in His creation.

There can be no art without that creational order either. Color is a divine creation and a human discovery. Symmetry, perspective, balance—all of these are gifts from the Creator.

Every story, every poem, every dance, every sculpture, every nicely sanded and stained piece of wood furniture—every beautiful thing mankind has made is the discovery of something in God's creational beauty.

113

GOD AND BEAUTY

The greatest beauty God sees is Himself. God is the ultimate standard of beauty. It might feel odd to say this, because we don't see God. But God does make His own beauty visible in all sorts of ways, particularly in His creation.

David knew the ultimate source of beauty and sought it:

> One thing have I desired of the LORD, that will I seek after; that I may dwell in the house of the LORD all the days of my life, to behold the beauty of the LORD. (Psalm 27:4)

The goal and final destination of the believer is to behold the beauty of the Lord. There is no greater pleasure. The glory of the Lord—the beautiful, bright light shining from all His perfections—will light up the whole earth. Believers will finally know true beauty. Unbelievers will reject it forever and never see it again.

GOD'S TRUTH, GOODNESS, AND BEAUTY

Listen, these concepts aren't easy. Beauty is a complex topic. But let's again tie beauty to truth and goodness to get some help.

- What is true is what God thinks. Whatever God thinks: that's what counts as truth. There is nothing as true as God.
- What is good is what God is. Whatever God is: that's what counts as good. There is nothing as good as God.

So what about beauty?

- What is beautiful is what God has built into the order of creation. Whatever God created: that's what counts as beautiful. And there is nothing so beautiful as the Creator God.

Only a believer, who is given (by God) a heart to love God and eyes to see Him as beautiful, will ultimately be able to reject what is actually ugly because of its rejection of God or His creational order and take pleasure in what is truly beautiful.

Love beauty. Hate ugliness.

Thinking It Through 3.4

1. Is beauty in the eye of the beholder? Explain.

2. How does the biblical worldview define *beauty*?

3. Why is God the standard for beauty?

4. According to this section, in what ways is beauty like its "siblings," truth and goodness?

Love is what sets Christianity apart. In Greek mythology, Zeus didn't love his believers. He mostly just messed with them as though they were his little toys. Nowhere does the Qur'an say that Allah is love. And in Buddhism there is no personal god to show love. But Christianity, when practiced according to the Bible, is a religion of love. God is love.

The one verse most searched for in online Bibles is John 3:16. "For God so loved the world, that he gave his only begotten Son, that whosoever believeth in him should not perish, but have everlasting life." Love motivated God the Father to give His Son to die for the sins of the world.

Jesus, the Son, was motivated by love too. The Gospel of John says, "He loved [his disciples] unto the end" (13:1). And it was the *very* end. Jesus laid down His life on a Roman cross for His friends. "Greater love hath no man than this" (15:13).

And remember that when Jesus boiled down all the commands in the Bible to their essence, He pointed to love.

> Thou shalt love the Lord thy God with all thy heart, and with all thy soul, and with all thy mind. This is the first and great commandment. And the second is like unto it, Thou shalt love thy neighbour as thyself. On these two commandments hang all the law and the prophets. (Matthew 22:37–40)

Love your God. Love your neighbor. All the complicated laws in the Old Testament "hang" from just those two commands.

Is love real?

DEFINING LOVE THE WRONG WAY

If love is the most important commandment in the Bible, we'd better know what it is.

FUZZY FEELINGS?

Many people think they know what love is: love is the special feeling you get when you're with that special person. It can't be argued with. No one can tell you that what you feel isn't real. You feel it! So follow your heart.

The problem here is that the heart is deceitful (Jeremiah 17:9). Following your heart will often lead to a world of hurt. A lot of Christians recognize the pitfall of this popular definition, so they have put their own spin on the definition of love.

SELF-SACRIFICE?

It's not emotional, some Christians say: love is a choice! They say that love is sacrificing yourself, no matter how you feel.

But the Bible specifically denies this definition of love. In Paul's famous "love chapter," 1 Corinthians 13, he opened by saying that you can perform the ultimate acts of self-sacrifice *without love*.

> Though I bestow all my goods to feed the poor, and though I give my body to be burned, and have not charity [love], it profiteth me nothing. (13:3)

The human heart is so twisted that you can give all your stuff away to poor people *without loving them*. You can give up your body to be burned *without love for God*. You can do otherwise good things out of complete selfishness. It's not that you lack love; it's that you love yourself. Your love isn't pointed toward the people Christians are told to love—God and others. 1 Corinthians 13 describes what happens when you love whom you're supposed to love.

True story: Young Christa gathered a bunch of cleaning supplies into a bucket and informed her mother that she was headed over to someone else's home to clean their basement. She expected her mother to fall down and worship her daughter's superhuman act of self-sacrifice.

That's not what happened. Her mother pursed her lips a bit and said, "Christa, you have cleaning work you've been asked to do in our home, work you have not done. *Our* basement needs to be cleaned. You may not go serve others until you do what you've been asked to do here."

Christa, to her credit, realized what had just happened. She wasn't offering to clean a basement out of love for others, or else she would have cleaned her own basement. She had decided to become a one-day basement cleaner out of love for herself: she wanted to be praised for her self-sacrifice. She was prepared to give up her entire day doing hard labor—but without love it profited her nothing.

Christian love will *lead* to self-sacrifice. If you won't sacrifice your needs for someone else, it is right to question whether you love that person. But you cannot say that love *equals* self-sacrifice.

LOVE—FOR REAL

So what is love? Let's watch how the Bible uses the concept and draw some conclusions.

Notice, for example, that Jesus once spoke of good and bad loves in the same breath.

> Woe unto you, Pharisees! for ye . . . pass over judgment and the love of God. . . . Woe unto you, Pharisees! for ye love the uppermost seats in the synagogues, and greetings in the markets. (Luke 11:42–43)

So here's what love is: it's your heart going out to something. It's liking that thing. It's a feeling of affection for something. If you love it a lot, you feel deep affection. If you love it a little, you might not feel much at all—but your heart still bends toward it rather than away from it. The same is true for loving people.

You're supposed to love God *a lot*—with all your heart, all your soul, all your mind, every bit of you. No part of you is exempt from the requirement to love God.

You're supposed to love your neighbor a lot too—as much as you love yourself. And if you've checked lately, your heart "goes out to" yourself a great deal. You care about your own needs, your own desires, to a very high degree.

So if you think about it, the two **Great Commandments** are very high bars. Love God *with all of me*? Love my neighbor *like I love myself*? You might feel like a pole vaulter with the bar set higher than you can see. But you need to know a few more things about God's love for you before you attempt to jump.

GOD AND LOVE

God doesn't just love. He *is* love. John in his first letter says it in the simplest way: "God is love." He also says that love is from God and that "we love him, because he first loved us" (4:8; 4:7; 4:19). Love is not an invention made by creatures. In fact, it predates creatures by an infinite amount of time. Love has been around for all eternity. Love has always existed—inside the Trinity.

Earlier in this unit, we talked about the Trinity, the Christian belief that there are three persons in our one God. We saw that God didn't create the world out of loneliness. He didn't have any needs. Father, Son, and Spirit shared a love for one another that was entirely enough.

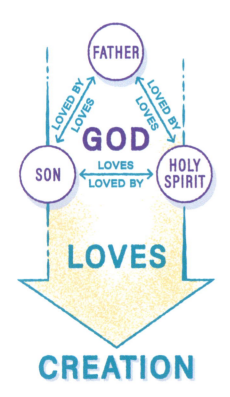

Listen to the way Jesus talked about this love. He prayed,

Father, I will that they also, whom thou hast given me, be with me where I am; that they may behold my glory, which thou hast given me: for thou lovedst me before the foundation of the world. (John 17:24)

Before Creation, love existed among the persons of the Trinity. The Father loved the Son and Spirit; the Son loved the Father and Spirit; the Spirit loved the Father and Son. God is the original lover and the original beloved.

The great American theologian and preacher Jonathan Edwards wrote a famous sermon called "Heaven Is a World of Love." In it he said that God "is a full and overflowing and an inexhaustible fountain of love." Edwards believed that God created the world because that fountain of love spilled out. That's what fountains do: they bubble up and up and up. They spread.

C. S. Lewis said the same thing this way, in his book *The Four Loves*:

God, who needs nothing, loves into existence wholly superfluous creatures in order that He may love and perfect them.

Superfluous means God didn't need us. Our lives are a gift that God gave us so that He could give us more gifts. Truly, God is love. And the Bible insists that nothing—not death, not life, not angels, not things that are now, not things that are coming—can separate us from God's love for us in Christ (Romans 8:38–39).

A PEOPLE FOR HIS NAME

But there's one more thing you need to know from Scripture about the love of God: you are not at the top of the list of God's loves. When the Bible reveals why God redeems sinful people, it isn't ultimately for their sakes—it's for His. God doesn't break His own greatest commandment.

When God had mercy on Israel, He did it for the sake of His name, His glory. He says this over and over.

For my name's sake will I defer mine anger, and for my praise will I refrain for thee, that I cut thee not off. . . . For mine own sake, even for mine own sake, will I do it: for how should my name be polluted? and I will not give my glory unto another. (Isaiah 48:9, 11)

And when He had mercy on the Gentiles, His purpose was "to take out of them a people for his name" (Acts 15:14). For *His* name He acts. "For of him, and through him, and to him, are all things: to whom be glory for ever" (Romans 11:36).

We tend naturally to think that we deserve God's love because we're so lovely. Of course God loves us! Who wouldn't? So it's humbling to see that you aren't at the top of God's list of loves. You were saved, if you are a Christian, as a way to bring glory to God. You are a gift given from the Father to the Son (John 17:6). God's love cleans you up and makes you a gift.

WHEN GOD'S LOVE GOES DEEP

You are not born loving what you ought to love. You are not born loving God. The Bible says that without Christ you have a heart of stone. Your heart doesn't respond to God—it doesn't go out to, or bend toward, Him the way it should.

Remember the parts of your worldview? Your loves drive your basic beliefs, which drive your actions. And the promise of the Bible's big story is that God, through Christ, will reach into your heart and change your loves. It's the New Covenant we talked about in Section 2.5.

> A new heart also will I give you, and a new spirit will I put within you: and I will take away the stony heart out of your flesh, and I will give you an heart of flesh. (Ezekiel 36:26)

When God changes your heart through redemption, the way you think about life and the way you treat the people in your life will naturally change. God will be your greatest love, and His love for you will cause you to love others as well.

Thinking It Through 3.5

1. Define *love*.

2. When did love start existing?

3. List ten things you love. Now put them in order with the thing you love most at the top. What's at the top? What's at the bottom?

Why did God create everything

Why did God create the universe?

As the Trinity, God did not need other loves. As spirit (John 4:24), God did not need the physical universe. So why did He create the universe? In the last section, we dove about six feet down into this question. The love within the Trinity spilled out, we saw, and God created the world. In this section, we'll try to touch the bottom of the pool.

How do you get to know someone? Take your dad, for example. You watch him. You start to clue in to what he likes (maybe basketball?) and what he doesn't like (maybe brussels sprouts?). But somehow what you see goes deeper than the surface of what he likes. You start to notice what drives your dad. You see evidence every day of his loves. Is he motivated by love for God, for Mom, and for the kids—or is it love for alone time, for TV, for six-packs of beer, or for many worse things?

Just as we discussed in Section 1.5, Jonathan Edwards observed that all people are driven by what they love. If there were no love, no one would ever do anything. We'd never get off the couch to go play outside because we wouldn't love play. We'd never even have a couch to get off of because we wouldn't love physical comfort and therefore wouldn't make soft chairs. Without love, we would be inert blobs. But we wouldn't care.

Edwards knew that God was not like this.

GOD IS LOVE, DRIVEN BY LOVE.

HE IS NOT INERT; HE IS ACTIVE.

And Edwards began to watch God like you watch your dad. By carefully studying God's Word, Edwards started to see what it was that God loved. He wrote a whole book about it, called *The End for Which God Created the World*. The word *end* there means "goal" or "purpose." What was God aiming at when He created the universe? What was He loving?

Edwards made a simple, biblical argument: the thing that motivates God throughout His acts in the Bible is very likely the same thing that motivated Him to create the world. He wrote,

> Whatever appears to be God's "ultimate end" in . . . his works of providence in general, that must be the ultimate end of the work of creation itself.

So what is God's "ultimate end" as seen through Scripture? What is His top goal or motivation?

A BIBLE STUDY ON GOD'S ULTIMATE END

See whether you can figure out the answer from the kinds of Bible statements Edwards brought together in his book. Let's join the great theologian in what he did so well: a Bible study.

FOR HIMSELF

Edwards noticed that God calls Himself "first and last," and Christ "Alpha and Omega" (the Greek way of saying "A to Z").

> I am the first, and I am the last; and beside me there is no God. (Isaiah 44:6)

> I am Alpha and Omega, the beginning and the end, the first and the last. (Revelation 22:13)

Edwards also saw that Scripture makes statements like these about the relationship of "all things" to God:

> Of him, and through him, and to him, are all things: to whom be glory for ever. (Romans 11:36)

> By him were all things created, that are in heaven, and that are in earth, visible and invisible, whether they be thrones, or dominions, or principalities, or powers: all things were created by him, and for him. (Colossians 1:16)

SUBORDINATE ENDS AND ULTIMATE ENDS

In *The End for Which God Created the World*, Jonathan Edwards spoke very carefully about the different motivations that drive us all. He noticed that there are "subordinate ends" and "ultimate ends." When you go on a trip to see your grandparents, stopping to pick up snacks for the journey is a subordinate end. The trip to the store is a genuine goal you have, but it feeds into the bigger goal of seeing your grandparents. Seeing them is your ultimate end. It's the main thing you're trying to do; it's something you enjoy for its own sake and not for some greater goal.

The Bible teaches that God created everything *for Himself*. He is the first and the last—the one who came before Creation and the one who will receive all the glory at the end of time.

That God created everything for Himself is not what most people think, and certainly not what they like to hear. They like to hear things like these actual lines from a movie:

"YOU ARE YOUR OWN STAR. . . . FOLLOW YOUR HEART."

This is the general idea out there. Your life is your own, to make of it what you will. You determine the path you'll take. You make your life as fantastic as you want it to be. If you want to stand out, don't let anyone but your own heart tell you what you should do.

But if God comes before everything and if all things are *to Him* and *for Him*, then none of those self-focused goals are true. You don't give meaning to your own life: God does. Your desires are good only if they point, ultimately, to God.

FOR HIS GLORY

Edwards spent some time looking into Isaiah 43, which speaks of God's plan to redeem and rescue Israel. It contains precious promises of God's care for His chosen people.

> O Israel, Fear not: for I have redeemed thee, I have called thee by thy name; thou art mine. When thou passest through the waters, I will be with thee; and through the rivers, they shall not overflow thee: when thou walkest through the fire, thou shalt not be burned; neither shall the flame kindle upon thee. For I am the LORD thy God. . . . Thou wast precious in my sight . . . , and I have loved thee. (43:1–4)

Why did God do all these things? Notice that God answers this question just a few verses later:

> I will say to the north, Give up [my people]; and to the south, Keep not back: bring my sons from far, and my daughters from the ends of the earth; even every one that is called by my name: for I have created him for my glory. (43:6–7)

It is for His glory, "for His name's sake," that God created and redeems His people. That is His ultimate end.

Once you know to look for it, you'll see this everywhere in the Bible. Here are two more examples:

> The LORD will not forsake his people for his great name's sake. (1 Samuel 12:22)

> Our fathers understood not thy wonders in Egypt; they remembered not the multitude of thy mercies; but provoked him at the sea, even at the Red sea. Nevertheless he saved them for his name's sake, that he might make his mighty power to be known. (Psalm 106:7–8)

God will not give His glory to another.

Edwards concluded from his Bible study what we, too, should conclude: "God made himself his end in all his works." Uniquely, "the same Being, who is the first cause of all things," is also "the supreme and last end of all things."

In other words, God loves His own glory. And this must be why He created the world.

GOD AS ALL IN ALL

What is glory? It's God's amazing reputation and fame. It's the glowing magnificence that surrounds Him. It's the splendor and beauty that radiate from all His perfections.

You've seen glory: you've seen it on the faces of athletes who've won an international championship. You've seen it in amazing human achievements, like the time Alex Honnold climbed up El Capitan in four hours—without ropes!

When power or skill or wisdom or strength or cleverness—or beauty or truth or love or goodness—make you say, *Wow*, that's glory. And everything God does brings Him glory. He created His people, and He created the world, for that glory.

And He will get it. The Bible tells me so.

One of the most important statements in the Bible comes just after one of the *other* most important statements in the Bible—they're both in Paul's first letter to the Corinthians. At the beginning of chapter 15, Paul described the gospel, the good news of what God has done for us in Christ. But he didn't stop the story after Jesus died, after He was buried, after He rose again, or after He ascended to heaven. He kept the story of the world going into the future.

And this is what Paul said will happen at the end of time:

> Then cometh the end, when [Christ] shall have delivered up the kingdom to God, even the Father; when he shall have put down all rule and all authority and power. For he must reign, till he hath put all enemies under his feet . . . that God may be all in all. (15:24–25, 28)

One day, when His enemies are defeated and judged,

GOD WILL BE ALL IN ALL:
ALL GLORY WILL BE HIS.
THAT IS THE PURPOSE OF HISTORY.

Everything in the world comes from and points to God. So the next question to ask is, how do *you* bring glory to God?

WHY GOD CREATED YOU

You were created by God. Yes, your parents had something to do with it—but without God's breath of life, there would be no you.

Why are you here? For God. The best thing He can give you is Himself in Christ when you are saved by faith. His glory, shining in your eyes, is the joy you were created to have.

And He shines in all that's fair. The heavens are declaring God's glory all the time (Psalm 19:1). You've seen God's glory in every cool thing in creation that has ever fascinated you, from the tiniest intricate bug to the biggest faraway star. God was giving you tastes of His glory in those things. And when you see God even more directly, such as in the words and the love of Jesus in the Bible, you are getting even more tastes of that glory.

If you live your life as if you were the A to Z of your story, as if you were the first cause and the last end, you will miss the purpose for which you were made, God's glory. God didn't make you because He was lonely (He wasn't) and so you could then give Him attention. God made you so that Christ could reveal to you the glory of God and allow you to join in glorifying Him.

Remember what Jesus prayed for His disciples, just before He died for their sins:

> Father, I will that they also . . . may behold my glory, which thou hast given me: for thou lovedst me before the foundation of the world. (John 17:24)

The love in the Trinity spilled out into the glorious creation you see around you. And all that love is still flowing toward this ultimate end: the glory of the God who will be all in all. Acknowledge this as the ultimate purpose of all you do so that your life will bring glory to God.

Thinking It Through 3.6

1. How do we know God didn't create the world because He was needy, lonely, or bored?

2. How did Jonathan Edwards figure out God's ultimate end in Creation?

3. Define *God's glory*.

4. What is the ultimate end of all history?

5. What is the ultimate end of your life?

God is out there somewhere, but he's definitely not around to help you with your life.

There is no God, just the stuff you can observe and test through science.

What does God have to do with me

?

Everything is part of god, including you, so you need to be at peace with the universe.

God is spiritual. If you could escape this material, wicked world, all would be well.

How does
God relate to
His creation

People in American society love celebrities. They put them high up on pedestals—which is what you do with idols. Americans pay constant attention to what famous actors and musicians are saying, wearing, and doing. In fact, shows and magazines constantly report on what celebrities are doing, even making things up just to sell their story. Apparently celebrities' real lives aren't exciting enough; Americans want more.

There is nothing that so demonstrates the power of celebrity as the fact that actors and actresses get asked important questions about real-life stuff they have no idea about. For example—a very young woman who graduated from high school and then went to acting school for two years got asked on national television to give her opinion about how women can build lasting relationships!

The skill of acting in front of a camera does not make someone an expert on anything except acting in front of a camera. But Americans love their pedestals. Someone standing atop one of those must be able to see farther and better—right? They must know something we don't know about success and happiness.

The truth is, however, celebrities don't live on pedestals. They are somewhere between five and six feet tall, on average, so what they see is basically what the rest of us see.

What we need is someone who can stand far above us and see all the way around the world while, at the same time, living among us so he understands what human life on the ground is really like.

Huh. Where can we find such a person?

SEEING FROM THE HIGHEST PEDESTAL

God, naturally, is the only person who can see around the world. He sits atop the highest pedestal there is. He's also the one true universal celebrity. Sort of. Not everybody's excited about Him; He doesn't get any space on magazine covers; but at least everybody on this planet knows He exists, which is not something you can say about celebrities and their latest relationships. (Remember: people suppress the truth that God exists, but at some level they still know He does.)

In the last section we looked up the full height of that pedestal, and it reached far above the clouds. A God whose major goal in all He does, from Creation through Redemption, is glorifying Himself—that is a God who is very, very high. He's not like us; He's in a different category altogether.

This concept is called "transcendence." It means God is above our level—superior in every way.

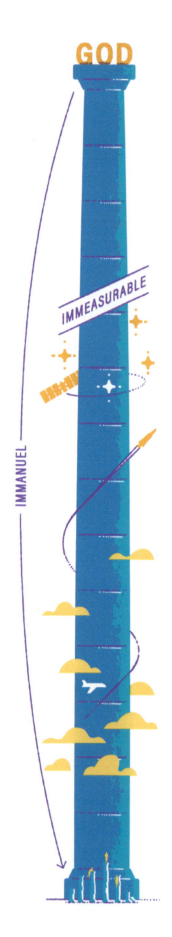

GOD

IMMEASURABLE

IMMANUEL

God explains His transcendence to Isaiah with a comparison:

> For my thoughts are not your thoughts, neither are your ways my ways, saith the LORD. For as the heavens are higher than the earth, so are my ways higher than your ways, and my thoughts than your thoughts. (Isaiah 55:8–9)

God isn't just higher than we are, to an infinite degree; He is bigger. Solomon declares,

> Who is able to build him an house, seeing the heaven and heaven of heavens cannot contain him? (2 Chronicles 2:6)

Nobody can grab God's hand and make Him stop doing something He wants to do (Daniel 4:35). Nobody can step outside time like He does—a thousand years are like a day for Him, and a day like a thousand years (2 Peter 3:8). Nobody can even think of something as big as God. The prophet Isaiah wrote a beautiful poem saying that the Lord can hold the oceans in the palm of His hand, that there's no point in giving God advice because He invented justice and wisdom, and that all the nations in the world and all their people are like a drop in a bucket to Him (Isaiah 40:12, 14–15).

God transcends us in every way. The distance between you and the worst sinner on the earth may seem great, but it's finite. The distance between you and God can't be measured. It's *in*finite. He isn't just you times a hundred; He's not even on a human scale. He transcends all human measurements.

GOD, THE BRIDGE BUILDER

Here's the marvelous thing about the Christian God, the God of the Bible: the distance between us and Him cannot be measured, *but it can be traveled*. And God has done this very thing. In Jesus—God the Son.

Hundreds of years before Jesus was born, God sent Isaiah to tell His people, Israel, that a Messiah was coming. And He gave the Messiah a number of names: "Everlasting Father," "Prince of Peace," "Mighty God"—and one more, "Immanuel." *Immanuel* is a name put together with these Hebrew words: *God + with + us*.

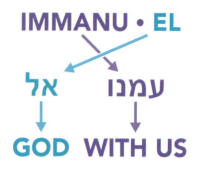

Wait, what? Are we talking about the God on the pedestal, the one who said that all nations—all eight billion people on the planet—are like a bit of the dust from which we were made? How could someone so high and so huge, so transcendent, possibly be *with us*?

Well, you already know the answer to that question if you've read any of the stories of Jesus. Jesus was God, and He was man. He was God in flesh, with us. He bridged the gap; He traveled the distance. He came down from the pedestal and remained on it at the same time; it's mind-blowing. John says that "the Word [Jesus] was with God, and the Word was God. . . . And the Word was made flesh, and dwelt among us" (1:1, 14). We call this the **incarnation**.

AN INVOLVED GOD

You need to know, though, that the incarnation wasn't the first time God had acted in the world since Creation. A biblical worldview includes many other details about God's relationship to the world. We'll start with what it's *not*.

Over time many different worldviews have tried to describe the relationship between the natural world and the supernatural (above nature) world, between creation and the gods.

IN • CARN • ATION
IN • FLESH • NESS

Incarnation means that Jesus took on flesh. A carnivore eats flesh; in Spanish *carne* means "meat"—*incarnation* means that Jesus had literal, physical meat on literal, physical bones.

1. One view says that there is nothing more than matter and energy—the natural world—with no God and no supernatural. Your thoughts are just electrical impulses obeying the laws of cause and effect. That's all they are.

3. A third view believes that all reality adds up to what could be called "god." Every rock, tree, and cancer cell is part of god. The natural world is the same as the supernatural world. There's no distinction.

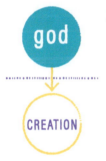

2. Another view says that god is a watchmaker who made the universe, "wound it up," then left it alone to go its own course. The creator left his creation to fend for itself.

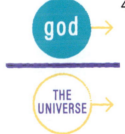

4. A final view distinguishes between natural and super-natural. The natural is bad and completely separated from the good supernatural. Our goal should be to escape the natural and move to the supernatural.

All these views of the relationship of God to creation are contradicted on the first page of the Bible.

In **biblical theism** (*theism* just means belief in God), the natural world is good because the supernatural God made it directly Himself. And in biblical theism, this God still communicates with us in the natural world despite His being above nature. God uses **general revelation** in nature and **special revelation** through His Word to speak to us.

Because of revelation and the incarnation, we have hope. None of the other views gives people much hope in the midst of the pain in this world.

1. If there is only matter and energy, you will one day go *piff*. And then, some day, everything will go *piff*.

3. If creation *is* god, you are part of god—but so is your pain.

2. If god left creation to itself, he doesn't care enough about you to stick around. He's an absentee father.

4. If the evil natural world is battling the good supernatural, we don't know who—if anyone—is going to win.

The incarnation of Christ is massively, unbelievably important. It shows that you won't go *piff*: Jesus didn't. It shows that God is not an absentee Father. He gave us His Son—how will He not with Him also freely give us all things? The incarnation shows, too, that although we are not part of God, God has become one of us (Hebrews 2:14). And by taking on our pain, He has started to remove it. When Jesus rose from the dead, He became a physical human being permanently—and He dealt a death blow to death and evil. There is no doubt who will win in the end.

The incarnation of Jesus is at the heart of biblical theism. This teaching of the Bible shows us what God is like. And it shows us that God is for us and with us. Theologians call God not just **transcendent**—completely separate from and superior to us—but **immanent**, meaning that He has an active relationship to the world He created, including the supreme offer of redemption.

CELEBRITIES

Celebrities may seem immanent. They're here. They're like us. Today's online celebrities—people who make videos and spread them everywhere—seem even more immanent. The internet has made it possible to be a big star from your living room.

But, really, these people are not immanent. You have no real access to them. And even if you did, what you'd find when you got it would be empty compared to what the transcendent God can do for you.

It's a waste of a life to be running from cool celebrity to cool celebrity. Their truth, goodness, and beauty simply pale in comparison to those of God's.

IMMANENCE AND TRANSCENDENCE

You don't have to know the big words *immanence* and *transcendence* in order to understand the concepts they name. But when you have names for things, you tend to be able to see them better. (Just think *nouns* and *verbs*.)

Immanence means that God is intimately involved with His creation: He sustains all creation from day to day (Colossians 1:17). Humans are dependent on God for every breath (Job 34:14–15). He is a present-everywhere God (Jeremiah 23:23–24).

Transcendence is also true of God, however. He is infinitely high and lifted up in His glory (Isaiah 57:15). He is totally distinct from His creation and His creatures. We cannot comprehend Him.

The Bible teaches a number of paradoxes—truths that don't immediately seem to work well together. This is one of the most important: God is both immanent and transcendent. Deny or diminish either truth and you are no longer following the Bible's teaching.

Thinking It Through 3.7

1. How did God bridge the gap between the supernatural (Him) and the natural (us)?

2. How is biblical theism different from the view that matter and energy are the only realities?

3. How is biblical theism different from the view that god left his creation after its start?

4. How is biblical theism different from the view that creation is god?

5. How is biblical theism different from the view of the evil natural world battling the good supernatural?

6. Define *immanence* and *transcendence* as descriptions of God.

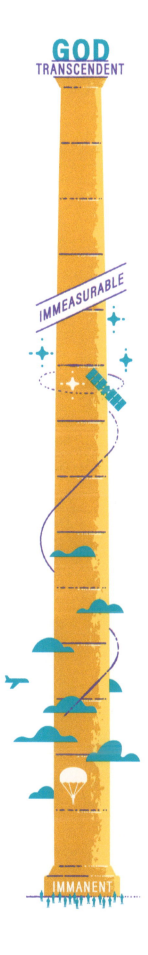

GOD
TRANSCENDENT

IMMEASURABLE

IMMANENT

Scripture Memory

Psalm 73:25
John 14:6
2 Corinthians 5:21
Psalm 27:4
1 John 4:7–8
Colossians 1:16
Galatians 4:4–5

Recall

1. What is the biblical doctrine of the Trinity?

2. Why can't we be the standard for truth?

3. What does it mean to learn goodness from below and from above?

4. Define *truth*, *goodness*, and *beauty*.

5. How does Section 3.5 define *love*?

6. Define *God's glory*.

7. What are God's transcendence and immanence?

Understand

8. Why do people feel disconnected from the God of the Bible? What is the remedy for this?

9. Which of the list of attributes of God from Section 3.1 was Jonathan Edwards speaking of when he said "God made himself his end in all his works"?

10. How can God be both above and with the people He's created and redeemed?

11. What's wrong with saying that beauty is in the eye of the beholder?

12. Is it wrong to love yourself? Explain.

13. How did Jonathan Edwards—and how do we—determine what God's purpose was in creating the universe? And what motivated God to create the world?

Internalize

14. What can you know and enjoy based on the reality of the God of the Bible?

15. What would life be like for you if it were true that God left His creation after its start?

16. What would life be like if it were true that the evil natural world battles the good supernatural as equal forces?

WHO AM I?

4.1 FINDING YOURSELF

How do I find out who I am **?**

The Appalachian Trail is a 2,190-mile-long trail stretching along the Appalachian Mountains from Georgia to Maine. And some people are crazy enough to hike the whole thing! In 2018, 956 people made the entire trek, usually in five to seven months.

Imagine stationing yourself at the beginning of the trail in Georgia, where most people start. You ask people, "Why are you doing this?"

What do you think they would say?

Reporters have asked hikers this question and taken video footage. One common answer that hikers give is that they want to "find themselves."

Really? Hiking two thousand miles up and down mountains helps you find yourself?

People are desperate to find their identity. They will even dedicate five to seven months of their lives to do nothing but look for themselves in the mountains. Identity is what you believe makes you *you*.

American culture is obsessed with identity. Another way of saying "find your identity" is "be yourself." Anyone who watches American culture closely knows that "be yourself" and "follow your heart" are considered wise counsel all over the place. We keep repeating these phrases to ourselves like they're some profound truth.

YOU ARE HERE

MAYBE HERE

OR HERE

ON THIS SPOT

OVER HERE

NO! OVER HERE

AT THIS LOCALE

HITHER BE THY WHEREABOUTS

SOURCES OF IDENTITY

Many Americans find their identity in their favorite parts of popular culture (**pop culture** for short). There are *Star Wars* and *Star Trek* and Marvel fans. There are fans of this or that pop music artist. There are fans of this or that TV show. Americans advertise their pop culture likes (and dislikes) online and gather with other people who share that identity.

Many people find their identity in their work. You've probably had people ask you, "What do you want to be when you grow up?" They're asking, what identity do you want to have? And the answer they expect you to give is the career that you want to have. Work is essential to many people's identity.

Other people find their identity in their wealth. They want to be known as the richest person around. They live in the house they do because it is bigger than the neighbors' houses. They drive the car they drive because it shows that they are wealthier than their friends and family. Or maybe they find their identity in all the fun things that wealth can buy. They want to be known as the person who has the money to give themselves and others a good time.

You may not find your identity in work or in wealth. But maybe you find your identity in sports. You are intent on being known as the best baseball, basketball, soccer, or ultimate Frisbee® player around. Or if sports is not your thing, then perhaps you want to be known as the smartest one in the class. Or the prettiest girl in the room.

People also find their identity in their ethnicity. Maybe your ancestors immigrated to the United States in the past century, and your family carries on the distinctive foods, holidays, and traditions of your ethnic group. Or perhaps your ethnic group has been historically mistreated. You value the way that people of your ethnicity have risen above every obstacle laid in their path. And you intend to overcome as well.

American culture says to them all, including you, "Be yourself."

ETHNICITY

Your "ethnicity" is where you come from. The word comes from the Greek word *ethnos*, which means "people" or "nation."

A BUNCH OF IDENTITIES

But this raises some problems. If everybody goes around being himself or herself, what happens to the connections between people that ought to exist? What happens to the image of God we all share? And, what happens to the biblical worldview's claim that human identity is not found within the human heart?

Mark Lilla, a well-known Democrat, didn't like something about the way his own Democratic Party treated identity. The party's website has separate pages for all sorts of identities, such as Americans with Disabilities, Asian Americans and Pacific Islanders, Latinos, Native Americans, and Rural Americans.

Lilla believed that one of the strengths of the Democratic Party is that it makes sure to look out for the poor and vulnerable in society. And this, in itself, is a good thing. But he also saw that when you divide people into a bunch of separate identities, it's hard for them to come together to win elections. The interests of American Pacific Islanders may have little in common with the interests of Rural Americans. And if their job is to "be themselves," why should they care what other groups need? Lilla saw that everybody was too busy "being themselves" and had no time to "be us."

Many Americans are obsessed with what has come to be known as "identity politics." Without listening to the Bible's explanation that all humans are made in God's image, people find some other basis for their identity. They create countless little groups, each one very vocal about their rights. They are fighting for their identities. And they are *very* offended when they think those identities are threatened or insulted.

There have been big protests at American colleges over identity politics. Colleges are now supposed to be places where your identity, whatever it is, will not be questioned. But, as Lilla saw, giving labels to each little group tends to divide and weaken a society rather than unify and strengthen it.

Tell a whole nation of people, "Be yourself," and herding them in one direction becomes as impossible as herding cats.

GENDER CONFUSION

One problem with finding your identity inside your own heart is the condition of your heart. What if your heart's desires and your self-identity are sinful and wrong?

Let's get specific. (After all, if a biblical worldview can't help you in real life, it's not worth having.) Right now in the West, there is a huge identity-politics fight over a small group: **transgender** people. These are people who were born male or female but who reject this God-given gender and opt to talk, act, and dress like the opposite **gender**.

Whatever drives people to deny the obvious truth about their bodies—it ought to bring out our compassion and not our mockery. But true love for transgender people does not mean going along with the fake world they're trying to create. God "made them male and female" (Matthew 19:4), and what God creates is always good. Love cannot mean telling girls that they are really boys, or vice versa—denying an undeniable reality is not healthy. Christians should be concerned about the health of these people and should work to help them see God's goodness in creating them to be male or female. Christians should help others see how the gospel can free them from sinful desires and self-identities.

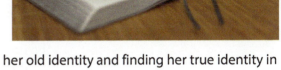

CASE STUDY: SELF-IDENTITY

Rosaria Champagne was an English professor at Syracuse University in New York. As a **feminist**, she believed that social structures like marriage, family, and work are oppressing women and need to be changed or abolished in order to make women free and equal to men. She was also living in something like a "marriage" to a woman. She began researching the Bible in order to argue against it because she thought Christianity to be so strange and even hateful toward aspects of her chosen identity.

And then, Rosaria found Jesus. Through the power of God's Word and the love, gentleness, and patience of a Christian pastor and his wife, this feisty and brilliant woman came to Christ. She repented of her sin. She embraced a biblical identity.

Rosaria Champagne Butterfield—now married to a pastor—wrote a book about losing her old identity and finding her true identity in Christ. She said,

> When we defend our right to a particular sin, when we claim it as an "I am," or a defining character trait, we are cherishing it, and separating ourselves from the God who promises rest for our soul through repentance and forgiveness.

1. How did Rosaria identify herself before she received Christ?

2. What caused her to research the Bible?

3. What did Christ use to bring Rosaria to Himself?

4. In your own words, explain what Rosaria believes now about identity.

Transgenderism is not legitimate. But it is consistent. It's consistent with what people have been telling themselves for decades in the West: "Be yourself." In this fallen world, people will believe all sorts of twisted things about their true identities.

THE BIBLE AND YOUR IDENTITY

Through the Bible, God tells you a different yet also consistent message, *Be your true self.* Look at yourself through the lenses of Creation, Fall, Redemption. You are . . .

1. **created** in the image of God,
2. **fallen** in Adam, and
3. **redeemable** in Christ.

Just as Rosaria discovered, the ultimate foundation for the identity of every person is that each is (1) created in the image of God. Africans and Europeans, rich and poor, athletes and scholars, married and single, saints and sinners are all made in God's image. There is no more stable foundation on which to build human identity than the image of God.

Without the God-given value of this identity, you can have no lasting human rights because some humans will *always* think they're worth more than certain other humans. Right now, our world has millions of people who believe their lives are worth more than the lives of unborn babies. The biblical teaching that mankind is created in the image of God gives incredible value to every soul. We'll talk more about this in the next section.

But we aren't just created in God's image. We are also (2) fallen in Adam. Just as being created in the image of an infinite, glorious God exalts us all, so the sin of Adam is a blot on each of us. There isn't a human on this planet whom sin has not touched (Romans 3:23).

C. S. Lewis packed these two truths into one punch. Aslan says to Prince Caspian in Narnia,

> You come of the Lord Adam and the Lady Eve . . . .
> And that is both honour enough to erect the head
> of the poorest beggar, and shame enough to bow the
> shoulders of the greatest emperor on earth.

WE HAVE NO REASON FOR PRIDE AND EVERY REASON FOR REPENTANCE.

But we also have no reason for despair because we are (3) redeemable in Christ. Many students reading these words *are* redeemed in Christ.

Paul expressed that his redeemed identity was his deepest desire, controlling the rest of his life.

> I have suffered the loss of all things . . . that I may win Christ, and be found in him, not having mine own righteousness, which is of the law, but that which is through the faith of Christ, the righteousness which is of God by faith. (Philippians 3:8–9)

In contrast, all the works in which he used to find his identity he now considered "dung."

God, in Scripture, provides you the only solid basis for identity. Yes, be yourself—the self that God says you are. If you haven't already, receive a redeemed identity, which not only counts you forgiven and restored but also forms you continually into the perfect image of Christ.

Everything else that makes you *you* ought to submit to *that* identity.

Thinking It Through 4.1

1. List a few ways people find their identity aside from listening to their Creator.

2. How do the desires of people's hearts affect how people view themselves?

3. What is wrong with the advice to "be yourself"?

4. Why can't a boy be a girl or a girl be a boy?

5. What are the three parts of a biblical foundation for identity?

4.2 YOUR WORTH

What am I worth ?

After World War II, people were stunned. They had just seen bloody battles raging in Europe, Africa, Asia, and the Pacific. They had seen a bomb more powerful than they could have imagined. And they had seen something else: the bodies of naked, starved Jews piled in heaps. This was on the same soil where Martin Luther had launched the Reformation, where J. S. Bach had composed his cantatas, where some of the greatest minds in history had built an astounding civilization. Yet civilized people showed themselves to be capable of terrible cruelty to their fellow humans.

Democracy wouldn't save the world from more Holocausts. Adolf Hitler had come to power within a democratic system of government. Wealth couldn't save the world either. Germany and Japan had not lacked money and resources.

What would stop the world from seeing more gas chambers, more murder of ethnic groups, or even nuclear war? What could establish a universal standard of human worth?

The world's answer was the United Nations (UN). The UN was formed immediately after World War II to gather countries together to prevent a World War III. As part of that effort, the UN also created a document called the Universal Declaration of Human Rights. The first point it makes is this:

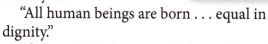

> All human beings are born free and equal in dignity and rights. They are endowed with reason and conscience and should act towards one another in a spirit of brotherhood.

"All human beings are born free."

They are? That's not at all clear. Some are born into debt slavery in India. They don't look free. How do we know they are?

"All human beings are born . . . equal in dignity."

They are? That's not at all clear either. It's hard to call the dignity of the latest British royal baby "equal" to that of a Rohingya Muslim baby whose refugee parents just stumbled out of Myanmar.

The Universal Declaration of Human Rights was not stating how things are. It was stating what its authors thought should be.

After World War II, people believed they needed to pronounce the worth of all human beings so that the gas chambers and concentration camps would not happen again. The UN's declaration, however, did not provide the *basis* for its pronouncements.

GOD AND HUMAN WORTH

The Universal Declaration of Human Rights never mentions God. It has no real authority to proclaim everyone equal or free or dignified. In all outward appearances, people simply are not these things.

But attempting to establish human worth while ignoring God is a major problem. The UN's declaration is a house without a foundation. Its first words hint at this.

> Recognition of the inherent dignity and of the equal and inalienable rights of all members of the human family is the foundation of freedom, justice and peace in the world.

Even if dignity, equality, and human rights are the foundation that holds up freedom, justice, and peace, *what, then, is the foundation for dignity, equality, and human rights?* In other words, what is the foundation for human worth? It can't be floating on nothing.

The Bible shows that God is the foundation for true dignity, equality, and human rights because He is the one who created humans in the first place.

> God said, Let us make man in our image, after our likeness: and let them have dominion . . . . So God created man in his own image, in the image of God created he him; male and female created he them. (Genesis 1:26–27)

An image is a representation of something or someone, like a photograph, or a face in a mirror. What does it mean to be made in God's image? Theologian Cornelius Van Til has put this complex idea very simply: "Man is created *in God's image*. He is therefore like God in everything in which a creature can be like God."

Some say that the image of God consists of those things that make us different from animals. Reason, conscience, emotion, language, and the capacity for relationships are some of those things.

But unborn babies and people in a coma *may not have* those things. Do they lack the image of God? No.

FREEDOM
JUSTICE
PEACE

DIGNITY
EQUALITY
HUMAN RIGHTS

IMAGE OF GOD
IN MANKIND

And dogs *have* all those things, just to a lesser degree than humans (because all creation reflects something of its Creator). But the Bible never speaks of animals having the Creator's image, or even some of His image.

So the image of God must be something that all humans have, and it must be something that sets humans apart from all other creatures. It is best to say that the image of God is found in the whole person.

Reason, conscience, emotion, language, and the capacity for relationships are all characteristics of humans. But they are put together in a unique way to make humans what they are. So it will not do to take one or some of the characteristics that humans have and say that characteristic or those characteristics are *the* image of God. The *whole person* is made in God's image.

IMAGE-BEAR

Why does Genesis say we are made in the "image" and in the "likeness" of God? An image shows the likeness of a person to anyone looking at it. Every person is created to image God, or to represent Him, in the world. Each one shows God's image to others by exercising dominion over God's world.

Even the Fall of mankind did not remove God's image. We mentioned this briefly in Section 2.3. The Bible teaches in at least two passages that His image is still present in everyone:

Whoso[ever] sheddeth man's blood, by man shall his blood be shed: for in the image of God made he man. (Genesis 9:6)

[With our tongues] bless we God, even the Father; and [with our tongues] curse we men, which are made after the similitude [likeness] of God. Out of the same mouth proceedeth blessing and cursing. My brethren, these things ought not so to be. (James 3:9–10)

If you murder someone—anyone—you must die. That's because that person bore the image of God.

ERS OF GOD

And if you curse someone—anyone—you have sinned. That's because that person was made in the likeness of God.

Because we sin, we mess up the image we ought to be showing to each other. We are often very bad mirrors of a holy God. No matter what we do, though, we cannot lose His image.

HUMAN WORTH AND IDOLS

Although the Fall couldn't destroy the image of God, it does something terrible to human worth: it makes people want to build their personal worth on some foundation other than God. It makes them look to created things, to idols. Romans 1 says that sinful people have exchanged "the glory of the uncorruptible God" for "an image made like to corruptible man, and to birds, and fourfooted beasts, and creeping things" (1:23).

People take created things (things made to serve the Creator) and try to yank God off His throne and put those created things there instead. The UN attempted this by pronouncing human rights on their own authority instead of on the authority of the Creator. We do this, too, by making aspects of our lives more important than our relationship with our Creator. As a result (back to our example of a building) we make *those* idols the foundation on which our worth is built.

We will always find ways to serve our idols. And we will make whatever sacrifices they demand.

YOUR VALUE

You are valuable because God made you in His image. If there is no God to guarantee the value of His image, then Hitler will go unpunished for taking the lives of the Jews, which he saw no value in. If there is no image of God in every person, how do you argue against someone powerful who decides that you're better dead? Without a clear idea of what God's image means, you yourself may treat others with disrespect. Or you might conclude that your own life is not worth living.

But if you know that you are made in the image of the glorious God of Scripture, you will have a firm foundation for your own dignity. You will have a firm foundation for the dignity of everyone else. And you will pursue your created purpose to mirror the almighty Creator God.

Thinking It Through 4.2

1. What is the ultimate foundation of the worth of every human?

2. What does "image of God" mean?

3. Why is abortion an attack on the image of God?

4. How should your creation in the image of God affect the way you view yourself?

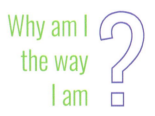

Why am I
the way
I am

If you live in a stable home with loving parents, the most painful effects of human sin may seem far away. You might really have no idea how agonizing some people's lives are.

If you don't have loving parents—if your dad left or your mom drinks or your parents are always screaming—you know the fear and pain caused by sin.

Sin shows up pretty much everywhere, in big ways and little ways. Sometimes the little ways actually hurt the most.

In *Roll of Thunder, Hear My Cry*, the main character, Cassie Logan, is an African American girl living in Mississippi in 1933. The story is set during the time in history when the black population in the American South began to leave in large numbers for Northern cities. Why did they leave? There were many big sins being committed against them: cheating and killing. But in a way, the "little" sins may have been the worst. Every day they were humiliated.

One day, Cassie accidentally runs into a white girl on the sidewalk—Lillian Jean Simms. Lillian Jean orders Cassie to apologize—and to walk in the road, not on the sidewalk.

"[If] you can't watch where you going, [then] get in the road. Maybe that way you won't be bumping into decent white folks with your little nasty self."

Lillian Jean tries to grab Cassie's arm to push her off the sidewalk, but Cassie throws her arm back, out of the white girl's reach.

And someone catches it. Suddenly, Cassie is thrown to the ground by a powerful grip. She looks up into the angry red face of Mr. Simms.

"When my gal Lillian Jean says for you to get yo'self off the sidewalk, you get, you hear?"

He, too, insists that Cassie apologize—right there in the middle of the street in front of a watching crowd.

She stutters out the words they demanded and runs from the scene in tears. It is the cruelest day she has ever known in her life.

LAYERS OF SIN

There are layers and layers of sin in this story.

There are the personal sins of the nasty Lillian Jean. She knows she can torture her black neighbor for what she also knows is a simple accident.

There are the personal sins of Mr. Simms. The same man who, most likely, shows up in church on Sunday grinning and shaking (white) hands is cruel to a girl a third of his size. He humiliates her in front of a crowd. He does not love his neighbor as himself.

There are the sins of that white crowd. They don't step in to protect a weak person from a strong one. They don't see all people as image-bearers of God and value them enough to defend them.

There is also the massive blanket of sin resting on the "system," the culture, which is racist. The fact that there are white people who treat Cassie kindly (as the book shows) doesn't make up for that blanket. Mr. Simms can act the way he does because he knows, he just knows, that other white people will take his side. Cassie *knows* this is unfair, and at home she tells her mother the story. But her mother sighs and says, "That's the way of things."

The way of things was wrong, wrong, *wrong*.

The most difficult thing to say, but we must face it, is that Cassie sins too. Cassie is a victim: this is absolutely and abundantly true. But later Cassie invents a terrible revenge on Lillian Jean. Over time she wins her trust, learns her secrets, lures her into the woods, and then beats her. Cassie threatens that if Lillian Jean tells anyone, Cassie will reveal those secrets.

Maybe the author meant for readers of the book to cheer for Cassie's clever revenge, but from a Christian point of view, what Cassie does is sin. God says very specifically *not* to take revenge. To do so is to try to steal His job and His authority.

The point is not to say that the sins of the two girls are equally bad. The point is that they are both victims—and both sinners. They are victims of the image of God being twisted in them when they are not valued as His image-bearers. They are sinners twisting the image of God in themselves with their own sin.

The image of God is twisted in every character of the story, just as it truly is in each of us.

Internal Twisting:
Racism, pride

CHARLIE SIMMS

CASSIE LOGAN

Internal Twisting:
Revenge, unkindness
External Twisting:
Racism, injustice

LILLIAN JEAN SIMMS

Internal Twisting:
Racism, injustice
External Twisting:
Revenge, unkindness

THE FALL AND YOUR IDENTITY

Sin is like an acid that eats a hole in every container it's put into. Sin has dripped down into every crevice of the human heart and into every aspect of human society. When God looked down at the people of Noah's time, He saw that "every imagination of the thoughts of [their] heart[s] was only evil continually" (Genesis 6:5). Not much has changed a few thousand years later.

By this point in the book, you *know* these facts, but how do they affect how you perceive your own identity? When you sin for the millionth time, after promising yourself and your parents and God not to, do you willingly admit that the Fall has affected you too, down to your very core? "The heart is deceitful above all things, and desperately wicked: who can know it?" (Jeremiah 17:9). And Jesus said,

> From within, out of the heart of men, proceed evil thoughts, adulteries, fornications, murders, thefts, covetousness, wickedness, deceit, lasciviousness [lust], an evil eye, blasphemy, pride, foolishness: all these evil things come from within, and defile the man. (Mark 7:21–23)

The Fall is inside you.

And not just inside you. *All* have sinned and fall short of the glory of God. When you step out into a culture in which "follow your heart" is the supreme law, or in which racism reigns, or in which God is simply ignored—you are seeing the Fall. The Fall is outside you too, eager to take every chance at tempting your heart into more sin.

In fact, here's a sign that all cultures are fallen: they tend to say that your problems come from outside and the solutions come from inside. The Bible, by contrast, says that

YOUR PROBLEMS COME FROM INSIDE YOU, AND THE SOLUTION COMES FROM OUTSIDE.

The seed of every sin lies in the human heart, and only Jesus can root it out.

The Fall twists the image of God in mankind. It makes every person an imperfect mirror of God's glory. And some people are so wicked that God's goodness can barely be glimpsed in them.

THE FALL AND YOUR DESIRES

Someone once asked scientist Stephen Jay Gould, "What is the meaning of life?"

He replied,

> We are here because one odd group of fishes had a peculiar fin anatomy that could transform into legs . . . . We may yearn for a "higher" answer—but none exists.

All this might upset some people, he explained, but actually it's freeing. He said that when we come to the big questions of the meaning of life, "we must construct these answers ourselves."

Does that sound good to you? If he's right, then you are free to follow whatever purpose you decide for your life. You get to choose whatever identity you want. None of your desires could be bad.

But a moment's reflection will tell you that he's wrong. You can look back right now at things you were absolutely sure you wanted as a little kid, things you wanted more than anything else in the whole wide world. You made a deal: "Please, Mommy, please. I promise I will be good for a whole year." And now those things are lying at the bottom of a pile of junk in a treacherous portion of your closet. Or they're disintegrating at the dump. Or you've forgotten about them completely. Or they made you throw up. Or worse. You *know* that not all your desires bring you happiness and that some of them are downright wicked.

And you weren't good for a whole year. You never have been. Remember when your heart absolutely boiled with a desire for revenge for a whole week? Mr. or Miss Revenge was your identity during that whole time. And what do you think about that desire now? Hopefully you see it for the ugly sin that it is.

You aren't very old. No offense, but it's true. Yet even you have hidden regrets, things you hope no one ever finds out about. The Bible tells us why people "loved darkness rather than light" even though they could see the beautiful light of Jesus right in front of them. It's "because their deeds were evil" (John 3:19). Beware of the shadows that darkness will cast over other areas of your life.

When you move toward high school, you are on a journey of discovering who you are, what you believe, what you want to do with your life. But if you don't account for the effects of the Fall in yourself on this journey, you will go far wrong.

> There is a way which seemeth right unto a man, but the end thereof are the ways of death. (Proverbs 14:12)

You must see that sin has gotten its way into you.

STRUCTURE AND FALLEN DIRECTION IN YOU

Who are you? You are someone created good by God, someone made in God's image. But you are also someone who is twisted by the Fall.

Have you ever tried to drive a twisted nail into wood? The solid strength and ingenious design of a simple nail is still obvious, even when it's twisted. The head is still good for striking. The sharp end is still shaped just right for biting into wood. When you bend a nail, it doesn't lose all its good properties.

But a bent nail sure is frustrating when you're trying to use it to tack two pieces of wood together.

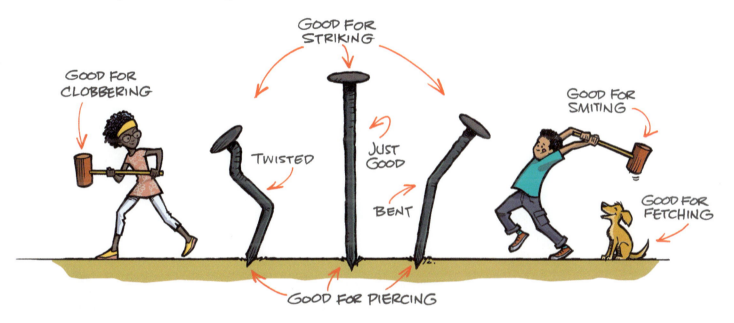

GOOD FOR CLOBBERING

GOOD FOR STRIKING

TWISTED

JUST GOOD

BENT

GOOD FOR SMITING

GOOD FOR FETCHING

GOOD FOR PIERCING

You are made in God's image, so you still have plenty of good, structural "properties." But when the Fall bends and twists that goodness in you in wrong directions, you're no longer quite so good at doing what you were designed to do—to be like God and to represent Him.

The same goes for your school, no matter how good it is. Sin has twisted it in many places. The same goes for your sports teams, no matter how awesome they are. The same goes for your family, for your state, for your country.

And all this sin is bad news because "the face of the LORD is against them that do evil" (Psalm 34:16). In fact, "the wages of sin is death" (Romans 6:23). The Fall is serious business.

In spite of your sin, God loves you (Romans 5:8). We'll talk more in the next section about how He provided Jesus as the Savior to restore His image in you.

Thinking It Through 4.3

1. How might your fallen nature be evident as you read the description of Cassie's revenge from *Roll of Thunder, Hear My Cry*?

2. Is the Fall inside you, outside you, or both? Explain.

3. How should being aware of your fallen nature affect your pride about who you are?

4. What does the Fall do to your created purpose to be like God and represent Him?

How am I
restored ?

The sufferings caused by the Fall are terrible. Right now they fill our lives. But they are nothing compared to the glory that God will, one day, reveal through us.

The whole creation is waiting for this day, the day when God will reveal Christians to be what they are: His sons.

The creation longs for this coming day for one huge reason: it was deeply affected by Adam's fall. God actually put the creation into a kind of slavery, a slavery to death and decay. It is moaning in deep pain even now.

But one day, the creation will be set free from those things—along with all of God's children. Yes: we, too, will be set free. No more death, no more pain, no more suffering. Even our bodies will be perfected. They'll be redeemed from slavery and decay. We'll be fully adopted into the family of God.

What you just read is called a "paraphrase." It's a rewording of something Paul wrote in his famous letter to the Romans. It tells us not only about the effects of Adam's fall but about God's solution, what the Bible calls "redemption." We've talked about redemption—both spiritual and physical—in earlier units. It's the third part in the three-part story of the Bible: Creation, Fall, Redemption.

153

TWO FAMILIES

Now we need to talk about how redemption applies to *you*. There will come a day when you are fully revealed to be God's child—or someone else's.

Jesus talked about these two families when He was confronting hypocritical Jews. "If God were your father," He told them, "ye would love me: for I . . . came from God" (John 8:42).

That's one possible family: God's family.

But there's another. Jesus then spoke terrifying words to His hearers. He told them that they were from their father the Devil. This was clear because they wanted to do what the Devil desired (John 8:44).

That's the other possible family: the Devil's.

Because of Adam's sin, we are not born sons of God. The Bible calls us "children of disobedience" (Ephesians 2:2). But it is the goal of God to bring countless people into His family. For that to happen, you must be born *again*. You must be adopted out of the Devil's family and into God's.

REDEMPTION THROUGH ADOPTION

There once was a little girl from a very troubled family (this is a true story, though the names have been changed). We'll call her Britnee. Drugs and alcohol made her parents nothing short of terrible to live with. They hit and neglected their children.

But Britnee did get to go to a neighborhood Bible club. (Her parents were happy to have the free babysitting.) And there she met a young college student named Ruth, who befriended her.

During all four years of college, Ruth kept up a friendship with young but growing Britnee. Meanwhile, Britnee's family situation grew worse. As Ruth neared graduation, she was engaged to be married. An idea came into Ruth's big heart: maybe she could adopt Britnee.

That is precisely what happened. Ruth got married, and she and her husband suddenly became the parents of a young teenager. Soon, Britnee's little brother Cody was adopted into their family as well. Ruth became a faithful mother to Britnee and Cody. Ruth's husband became their loving father.

Life had to change for the two kids: the television and video games they were used to were replaced by better things. For example, Cody was usually left to himself to play video games in his old family. But he could barely read, even though he was in seventh grade. Ruth dedicated herself to teaching Cody, who made huge improvements.

We saw the word **adoption** in the paraphrase from Romans at the beginning of this section. In Paul's day, adoption meant what it means today: moving from one family into another one. It gives a new name to the adopted child: the father's name.

The problem is that we clearly don't belong in the family of God. Our sin has messed up His image and has placed us all in the Devil's family. Even if God wanted more people in His family, how in the world could He make it happen?

GOD SENT HIS SON TO DIE IN ORDER TO BRING MORE SONS INTO HIS FAMILY.

When the fulness of the time was come, God sent forth his Son, made of a woman, made under the law, to redeem them that were under the law, that we might receive . . . adoption [as] sons." (Galatians 4:4–5)

Jesus came to redeem sinners, to pay the price for their release. He bought them through His blood. And He did it so that they could be adopted as brothers with Him in the family of God.

This was the great plan of God: that sinners might be "predestinated . . . unto the adoption of children by Jesus Christ to himself, according to the good pleasure of his will" (Ephesians 1:5).

Let's try that in easier English: God's goal before the beginning of time was to adopt as His sons those who believe, through the work of His capital-*S* Son, Jesus. And just like we saw in Section 3.6, God makes Himself the ultimate end of all things—even adoption. He adopted believers *to Himself*.

The Bible's big story goes from Creation to Fall to Redemption. And redemption produces adoption.

YOU CAN BE A SON OF GOD— BECAUSE OF THE SON OF GOD.

155

SANCTIFICATION

What if someone were to challenge Britnee and Cody to prove they're really and truly the daughter and son of Ruth and her husband? DNA testing, after all, would show conclusively that they have no blood relationship to their adoptive family. And legal papers can be forged. Maybe it's all a hoax?

Here's the proof: look. Look at their biological parents, look at their adoptive parents, and look at them. Ask them questions. Listen to them talk. Find out what they value. Learn about their faith in Christ. Watch how they now are raising their own children. Yes, Britnee and Cody look physically like their biological parents. But in every other way they look more like their adoptive parents. The most important family resemblance, *the one that has to do with Christian character*, proves beyond doubt who their "real" parents are.

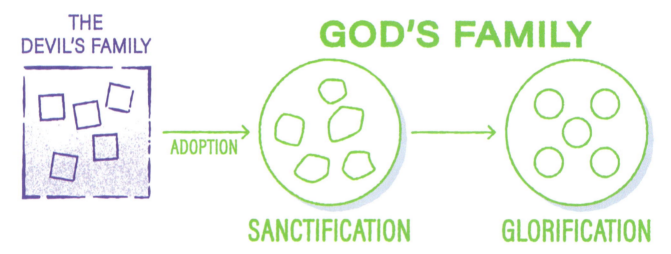

Britnee and Cody's adoption experience can help you understand why the Bible talks about adoption in two ways: (1) as something that has already happened, and (2) as something that will be fully accomplished and proved in the future. Within a couple of paragraphs, you can see Paul talking both ways about adoption.

First he talked about it like it's something that has happened. We get to call God "Father" *now*.

> Ye have not received the spirit of bondage again to fear; but ye have received the Spirit of adoption, whereby we cry, Abba, Father. (Romans 8:15)

And yet just a few verses later, he talked about it like something that hasn't happened yet.

> We ourselves groan within ourselves, waiting for the adoption, [that is], the redemption of our body. (8:23)

Paul was not contradicting himself. He talked this way because something happens in between adoption as salvation (8:15) and adoption as full redemption (8:23), something to demonstrate that someone has truly been brought into God's family. That something is called **sanctification**. When we are brought out of the Devil's family and into God's, Christ cleans us up from our sin. But because the Fall still affects us, we get dirty again. We have to keep going to Him for cleansing. And, sure enough, His blood keeps cleansing us (1 John 1:7).

Those who have been adopted will begin to look more and more like their new family. Although there will be times of stumbling, Christians always—*always*—grow and change to look like their new Father and like their new older brother, Jesus (2 Corinthians 3:18).

In the end, when full redemption comes to this planet, the family resemblance will be made complete. Our bodies will be glorified, fully redeemed from the sin nature. We will be transformed into Christ's image (1 John 3:2). No one will ever mistake us for children of the Devil. We will again be what we were created to be: people who are like God and who represent Him perfectly.

REDEEMED IDENTITY

The only true foundation for human value comes from God through the Bible. God is the only source of true worth among humans. Recognizing one's true identity requires seeing identity through the lenses of Creation, Fall, Redemption.

Creation
People do not need to be on a perpetual search to discover "who they are." God has already told us: we are, fundamentally, bearers of His own image.

Fall
If bearing God's image gives us all equal honor, the Fall gives us equal shame. But instead of being ashamed, many people embrace their fallen, twisted desires. They say, "That's the real me! That's my identity!"

Redemption
The damaged image of God can be restored in you. Your sins—and the Devil's family—won't define your identity any more. The redeemed are made sons of the heavenly Father.

THE GOSPEL

You can't redeem yourself. You need the grace of God through the gospel.

When Jesus hung naked on a Roman cross, all of God's anger against all human sin came rushing onto His shoulders. Wave upon giant wave. It pleased the Father to crush His Son, the Bible says. It pleased Him because He was laying on Jesus the sin of the world—precisely so that He could forgive people and bring them into His family. Jesus was buried, and along with Him was buried all of God's wrath against human sin.

Three days later, of course, Jesus rose from the dead. He carries with Him the power of an indestructible life, Scripture says. Hundreds of people saw Jesus walking around—the same Jesus who days earlier had given up His spirit and died. And though people back then were not very good with computers, they were smart enough to know that the resurrection of dead people was uncommon.

The Bible says you must turn from your sins and believe that Jesus paid for them with His blood. You must believe that He rose again. Then you will be saved. You will be redeemed. You will be adopted into God's family—like a Britnee and a Cody. And like them, you will begin to take on the family resemblance.

That is who you really are, once you're a Christian. You are created, fallen, and redeemed.

Thinking It Through 4.4

1. What is the word the Bible uses to describe how people become part of the family of God?

2. Is there such a thing as a Christian who doesn't grow to share God's family resemblance? Explain.

3. Do a person's previous sins have to determine his identity for the rest of his life? Explain.

4. If you are a Christian, how do sonship (adoption) and sanctification relate to your identity?

5. How do Creation, Fall, and Redemption relate to your identity?

Just hope nobody finds out.

Try to work harder to not fail again.

I've really messed up—what should I do now

?

Ask for forgiveness.

Ask God for victory.

Avoid admitting you've done anything wrong.

4.5 YOUR VICTORY IN CHRIST

How do I
overcome
my sin **?**

The Bible uses several word pictures to describe what happens when Christ saves someone from sin. We looked at adoption in the last section.

Two other important ways of describing salvation appear in the same sentence. Romans 3:24 says that Christians are

> justified freely by [God's] grace through the redemption that is in Christ Jesus.

That first description—justified—is taken from the courtroom. **Justification** pictures Christ as a judge presiding over a criminal trial. *Your* criminal trial. You are the defendant. And because Christ Himself steps down from the bench and takes your place, He is declared guilty instead of you. You are "justified," declared *not* guilty. At the same time, you receive Christ's perfection on your record. Justification is something that happens at the same time as adoption—as part of salvation.

The second word picture—redemption—is taken from a place you've never been to and probably will never see: the slave market. The Bible pictures Christ coming to a slave market where, because of your sin, you are standing on the auction block. In redemption, Christ buys you out of slavery to sin by the price of His blood.

God helps us understand these realities of salvation by pointing to earthly realities we already know about—families, courtrooms, slave markets.

UNION WITH CHRIST

But there's one word picture for salvation that you can't know quite so well from experience: **union with Christ**. When you are saved, you are "united" with Him. Nothing in your experience is exactly like it.

VINE AND BRANCHES

But one illustration Christ gave for this union probably *does* overlap with your experience. In John 15, He compared Himself to a vine. His Father is the farmer. Christ's followers are branches on the vine. Branches cannot produce fruit unless they remain connected to a vine. The same is true for Christ's followers: they cannot bear fruit unless they remain in Christ and He remains in them (15:1, 4–5).

What is the point of this illustration? As long as we are separated from Christ, everything that He did for us—living a perfect life, dying on the cross, rising from the dead—will not help us one bit. In order to receive all the benefits of salvation, we need to be united to Christ. Salvation is not just about getting blessings from God; it's about getting Christ, getting connected to the Vine. When you get Him, all the life-giving benefits come along with Him. But Christ is who you want.

Other verses also clearly teach that this union is very important.

- Paul said that "our old man is crucified with him, that the body of sin might be destroyed" (Romans 6:6). *In other words: Christians, because they have a union with Christ, were crucified with Him.*
- Paul also spoke of Christ's death this way: "If one died for all, then were all dead" (2 Corinthians 5:14). *In other words: Christians, because they have a union with Christ, died with Him.*
- Paul said that God has "raised us up together, and made us sit together in heavenly places in Christ Jesus" (Ephesians 2:6). *In other words: Christians, because they have a union with Christ, were raised with Christ from the dead to have new life, and they are given authority with Christ in heaven.*

HEAD AND BODY

Union with Christ is not an easy concept to understand. But Paul repeatedly insisted that true Christians are "in Christ." And, like Jesus, he did give an illustration that makes this idea easier to grasp. Paul described Christians as "the body of Christ." They are all "members," or parts, of that body (1 Corinthians 12:27). Christ is "the head of the body" (Colossians 1:18).

Your feet and hands are part of you; they are united with you. But they are, in a sense, separate too. It's not fun to think about, but you can live without them. Many people do. A well-functioning body, however, maintains "union" between the parts and the whole, between the parts and the head.

This unit has been asking the question "Who am I?" Or "What is my true identity?" Hollywood has one fairly consistent answer to that question: you are who you really want to be. But we have looked at answers drawn from the biblical teachings of Creation, Fall, Redemption.

1. **Creation:** I am made to be like God and to represent God.
2. **Fall:** I am twisted from the inside by Adam's fall, along with the rest of mankind.
3. **Redemption:** I can be restored to Christ's image and be brought into the family of God through Christ's death and resurrection for my sin.

Union with Christ takes us a step further into what it means to be redeemed. It means you are placed *into* Christ. If you are a Christian—if you have repented and believed the gospel—then your identity is wrapped up in Christ. Your various sub-identities (as a member of your family, a player of a certain sport, a lover of a certain book series, and so on) must all be submitted to your main identity. You are *in Christ*.

A great artist's hands look the same as anyone else's, yet the head controlling them makes them skillful. A great soccer player's feet look the same as anyone else's, yet the head controlling the muscles give those feet an agility others don't have. The value of the parts in a body comes from the value of the head.

Christians are *in Christ*. Don't follow your heart. Follow your Head!

Sydney's parents took her to church every week. She grew up learning Sunday school songs and Bible verses, but she never really cared about any of it. By middle school, all she cared about was clothes, makeup, and her popular friends. Her parents didn't like her friends, so she often lied about whom she was hanging out with. And since her mom wouldn't give her money to buy makeup, Sydney started shoplifting. "It was kind of exciting, and it impressed the other girls. I felt important!" Sydney says.

After the second time Sydney was caught stealing, her parents laid down the law. "They took away my phone and told me I was going to summer Bible camp. I didn't have a choice," says Sydney. "I was so angry! I didn't want to leave my friends."

But at camp, Sydney finally started listening to God. She realized she had been seeking worth in the wrong place. "I learned that because God created me and loves me, I don't need to try to impress Him—or anyone else!" Sydney explains. Ever since she repented of her sin and trusted Christ, she has reached out to her unsaved friends. "It's taken a while, but one just agreed to go to camp with me next summer!"

1. Where did Sydney find her identity before Christ?

2. What did Sydney learn from camp about her value?

3. How would her new understanding of her value help with her struggle with sin?

4. How did Sydney's new understanding change her relationship with her friends?

OVERCOMING SIN

If you are in Christ, if you are working to follow your Head, you will find obstacles in your way: the world, the flesh (your fallen sin nature), and the Devil. If you've ever screamed at your sister—and then felt guilty about it but powerless to stop, you need to understand union with Christ.

Paul explained that union with Christ is the answer to your sin problem. He raised this question: if people's sin led to God's grace (and it has), then why not sin more—in order to get even more grace? Paul's answer to this question: "No way!"

This is what he said to people who ask whether they should sin so that they could get more divine grace:

> How shall we, that are dead to sin, live any longer therein? Know ye not, that so many of us as were baptized into Jesus Christ were baptized into his death? . . . Our old man is crucified with him, that the body of sin might be destroyed, that henceforth we should not serve sin. For he that is dead is freed from sin. (Romans 6:2–3, 6–7)

Christians have been "baptized into Jesus Christ." They have therefore been "baptized into his death." Their union with Him applies all the benefits of His death to them, including this one: "he that is dead is freed from sin."

Paul knew that it wouldn't necessarily *feel* this way for you, or for any Christian. Sin doesn't feel dead. It's not only alive, but it's kicking you every day. Christians don't feel all the time like they are united with Christ. But Paul insisted that it's true:

> Reckon [consider] ye also yourselves to be dead indeed unto sin, but alive unto God through Jesus Christ our Lord. (Romans 6:11)

If you are a Christian, you must reckon that these things are true: *In Christ*, you are freed from sin. *In Christ*, you are justified, declared not guilty of sin and righteous instead. *In Christ*, you are already seated in heavenly places. *In Christ*, you can and will overcome sin because, in Him, you're dead to it.

To receive all the benefits of salvation, you need Christ to be yours and you to be His.

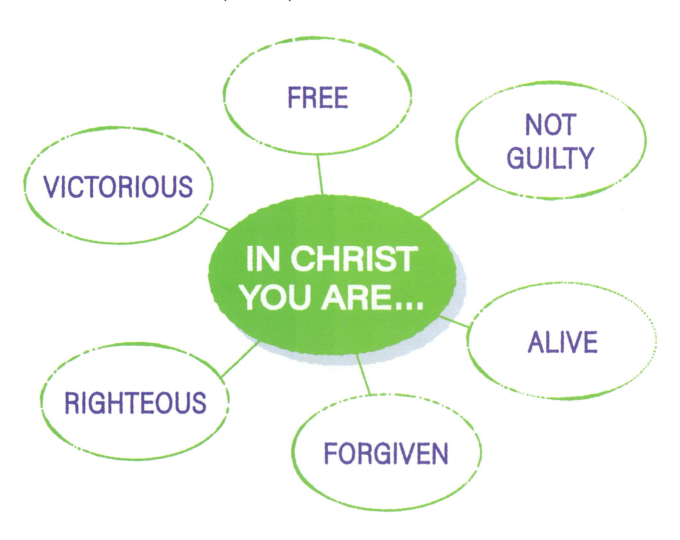

FREE

NOT GUILTY

VICTORIOUS

IN CHRIST YOU ARE...

ALIVE

RIGHTEOUS

FORGIVEN

IF YOU LOVE ME

Chris was a fifteen-year-old boy with an eleven-year-old brother, Justin, and a two-year-old sister, Leti. Little Leti had a terrible, deadly disease in her blood, and she needed a bone marrow transplant. Doctors hoped one of her brothers would be a match, so they tested their marrow.

The boys' parents sat them down and told them the results: Chris was a match! But Justin started crying.

His parents asked him why. He was happy that Chris could help Leti, he said, but he was very sad to have to lose his brother. Justin thought that giving up bone marrow meant giving up your life.

Justin's parents suddenly realized that *when that boy walked into the doctor's office to be tested, he did so believing that if he was a match, he would have to die to save his little sister.*

Think of the love in that boy. Think of what love made him willing to do. Love is the most powerful of all motivators. Ultimately, it's the only motivator.

Think of that fact as you hear Christ's words:

If ye love me, [ye will] keep my commandments. (John 14:15)

Adoption, justification, redemption, union with Christ—all of these things are evidences of Christ's love for you. And all true Christians can say, after looking at these evidences, "We love him because He first loved us."

If you wish to overcome sin, look to the love Christ has shown you. It will stir your love for Him. You *will* struggle; a Christian's love for Christ is not perfect in this life (see Section 4.6). But your love will motivate you to overcome sin, to live like you're dead to it. The body *will* serve the Head.

Thinking It Through 4.5

1. List all the Bible phrases you can find in this section (at least four) that indicate that Christians are put into a union with Christ.

2. Why was "Head" capitalized in "Don't follow your heart. Follow your Head"?

3. How does union with Christ give value to people?

4. How did Christ conquer sin in Christians, according to the explanation of Romans 6?

5. How can a Christian be motivated to overcome sin?

How do I
defeat my
fallen nature **?**

Aldrich Ames was one of the worst traitors in US history. His father worked for the CIA, and when Aldrich grew up, he also joined the CIA. Aldrich Ames was not an especially good spy. He wasn't an especially good man either. He wasn't faithful to his wife.

He found out that divorcing her was expensive, and his new wife had expensive tastes. Ames needed a way to get rich fast. And he knew just the way: he became a spy for the Soviet Union in 1985.

At that time the United States had some very important spies working against the Soviet Union. The spies gave the US government information about what Soviet leaders were thinking, information that would protect our military in a war with the Soviet Union. Some of this information helped bring the Cold War to a peaceful end.

But Ames betrayed all these people for money. Many spies were captured and killed by the Soviets. Aldrich Ames was a traitor. He was a traitor to his wife. He was a traitor to his country.

Now look into the mirror, into your eyes. If you know yourself as the Bible shows you to be, you will see a traitor too. Inside you there is an enemy against you. It is you. And it's not you.

THE FLESH

The Bible—and especially the apostle Paul—calls this enemy "the flesh." Look how Paul referred to the flesh as both him and not him:

> I know that in me (that is, in my flesh,) dwelleth no good thing. (Romans 7:18)

The flesh is the fallen nature of a person, whether Christian or non-Christian. But you can't blame your flesh when you sin, as if you had nothing to do with it. Your flesh is you. You are guilty of your betrayals.

If you're a Christian, you were redeemed to fight on God's side—against your flesh—but you've probably given yourself over to this enemy on a daily basis.

Why has God allowed this traitor, this enemy within, to remain inside you? Well, why did He allow Satan to enter the Garden of Eden? He has His own good purposes, and He doesn't have to tell us all of them. We simply need to know that the flesh is evil:

> They that are in the flesh cannot please God. (Romans 8:8)

The opposite of living in the flesh is living in the Holy Spirit. The first, Paul taught the Romans, leads to death. The second leads to life and peace (see Romans 8:1–17).

If you're still fuzzy on what the flesh is, Paul got specific in Galatians 5. Every kid that went to Sunday school knows the fruit of the Spirit: love, joy, peace, patience, kindness, goodness,

FRUIT OF THE SPIRIT

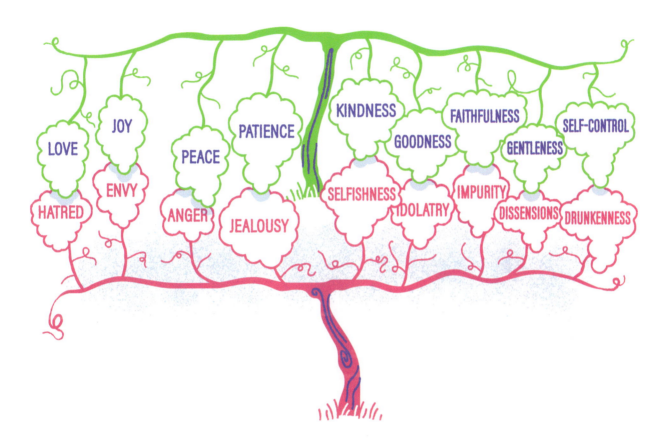

WORKS OF THE FLESH

faithfulness, gentleness, self-control (5:22–23). But few people memorize the list Paul gave right before this one, the list of the works of the flesh (5:19–21). Here are most of them: impurity, idolatry, hatred, jealousy, outbursts of anger, selfish ambitions, dissensions (causing division), envy, drunkenness.

Paul ended his list by saying "and such like"—in other words, "things like these." The list he gave isn't every work of the flesh.

The flesh is like a cancer, eating away at the goodness of *all* human activities. Like Satan, the flesh doesn't create anything. It's not creative; it's destructive. It takes the good gifts of marriage and family and twists them till it breaks your life in pieces. It takes good things in God's creation and turns them into idols. It takes the righteous emotion of anger (even God is angry against sin) and blows it up into a murderous explosion. It takes the plants God has given us and makes them into mind-altering beverages.

Christians are right to want life and peace instead of death. So they are right to set up walls of protection around their lives. After all, the unredeemed world doesn't have the Holy Spirit to help them say no to the works of the flesh. There are threats out there that can harm your soul. It really is best to stay away from some places, some activities, and some people. We'll talk about this more in the next section: it takes the work of a community of Christians to strengthen one another against outside enemies (Hebrews 10:23–25).

But Christians must never think that all the sin is on the outside of their protective walls while all the holiness is on the inside. No, allowing even one Christian "inside the walls" of the church means allowing some sin in the camp. No church is perfect as long as people are part of it. (If you ever find the absolutely perfect church, don't go there. You'll ruin it.)

Truly wise Christians will set up walls not to keep all evil out; that's impossible. They do it to keep the evil "out there" from touching the evil "in here." You don't play around with stirring up sinful desires, or even joke about it (Ephesians 5:4). You don't dabble with idolatry, as if a little is okay. *Because there is a traitor living inside you.* And if you let *outside* enemies through your walls, that traitor *inside* will work together with those enemies. And those walls will come tumbling down faster than you can say "Jericho."

John Bunyan, author of *Pilgrim's Progress*, wrote another famous book called *The Holy War*. He pictured a man as a city with gates: the eye gate, the ear gate, the feel gate. It matters what you let in through those gates because of the traitor that already lives in the city: your flesh.

IDOLS OF THE HEART

Non-Christians who read Scripture or Christian theology (studies about God and the Bible) are sometimes put off by all the Bible's dark warnings about the power of the flesh in every person's heart. It all feels pessimistic to them. The Christian teaching of original sin—the idea that all humanity is born with a bent to evil—feels gloomy and even offensive to them. In the *New York Times*®, America's most prominent newspaper, Molly Worthen dismissed "the grim vision of original sin in traditional Christian theology."

But the evidence points clearly in the direction of the Bible: people never, ever stop sinning against God. John Calvin, an influential teacher during the Protestant Reformation, described the human heart as an idol factory. Your flesh is always worshiping something other than God.

The second of the Ten Commandments forbids idols, of course.

Thou shalt not make unto thee any graven [carved] image, or any likeness of any thing that is in heaven above, or that is in the earth beneath, or that is in the water under the earth: thou shalt not bow down thyself to them, nor serve them. (Exodus 20:4–5)

There are almost certainly many people in your town or city who do worship physical idols. They pray to them; some offer food to them. But to you, this command might seem like the easiest one to follow out of all ten. How many students reading this book are actually tempted to worship statues? Probably not many.

But look at what Colossians 3:5 says: "Covetousness . . . is idolatry." Just because there are no statues of Jesus or Mary (or Buddha or Vishnu) in your house doesn't mean you're not an idol-worshiper. To covet something you shouldn't have—to desire it, to want it, to think about it, to scheme to get it—is idolatry too.

In middle school, you're probably not scheming to get super bad things. You don't covet cocaine or other criminal things. But maybe you worship approval from your peers. And that idol can lead you into all kinds of sin. "All the cool people are doing it" (or just, "Sarah's mom lets her do it") is an idol for many kids.

Another thing a lot of kids covet is entertainment. They act like it is a human right to watch TV or play video games. They begin to look forward to those things in an unhealthy way, to even live for them. And though God gives us some good pleasures in entertainment, a lot of kids give up much *better* pleasures in order to have screen time. Be honest: which kind of day is more fun—one spent watching random stuff or one spent playing outside and having adventures? Which pleasure is more solid and lasting?

The non-Christian writer David Foster Wallace said,

> There is no such thing as not worshipping. Everybody worships. The only choice we get is *what* to worship.

What are some of the idols your heart desires? Things that your conscience, or even the Bible, says you shouldn't have—and shouldn't want?

CONQUERING THE ENEMY WITHIN

One of the terrible truths about worshiping idols is that you tend to become like whatever you worship. If you worship movie stars, you will become like them. And if you take a second to look at the Wikipedia pages of movie stars, you'll discover that their lives have a lot of pain in them. Many, many of them can't seem to stay married—and it's no wonder so much of our star-worshiping culture has the same problem. Worshiping idols always corrupts you.

But one of the wonderful truths about worship is that *you tend to become like whatever you worship, God included.* We talked in Section 4.5 about how to overcome sin. And a lot of the advice there boiled down to this: if you are a Christian, become what you are in Christ. In Christ, you are someone with a love for God. So, you will find that over time your love for God will grow. Your worship will grow. And you will become more like God.

Opposition from your inner traitor, the flesh, will never cease. But in the same letter where Paul said that "covetousness . . . is idolatry," he gave this advice for those who want to conquer the flesh:

1. Put off the old self.
2. Put on the new self.

The whole Christian life is one of repentance—a change of mind, a transformation (Colossians 3:9–10). You keep putting off the works of the flesh, and you keep putting on the image of God. You keep turning away from idols, and you keep turning toward serving the living and true God.

Remember the confusing verse where Paul said that in him dwelt no good thing—but then he said it was actually in his *flesh* that nothing good dwelt? He talked in a similar way about the *good* that was in him. Watch:

> By the grace of God I am what I am: and his grace which was bestowed upon me was not in vain; but I laboured more abundantly than they all: yet not I, but the grace of God which was with me. (1 Corinthians 15:10)

You want to ask, *Which is it Paul? Is the grace of God the reason for your good works, or did you just work harder than everyone else?*

The answer: both. Look at how Paul said it. The hard work he did ("I laboured more abundantly than they all") is sandwiched between two statements about God's grace: "By the grace of God I am what I am . . . yet not I, but the grace of God which was with me."

Whenever you do repent from idols and put off your flesh, you will find that the grace of God was sandwiching you all the way.

Thinking It Through 4.6

1. Why can't you do right all the time?

2. List some idols that you think are common to kids your age.

3. What are Christians to put off and put on?

4. Is it God who works to put off the Christian's flesh, or is it the Christian? Explain.

The latest gadget.

Making the basketball team.

This new online game.

WORLDVIEW DILEMMA #378

What should be most important in my life

?

Getting good grades.

Working as hard as you can at church.

How do I defeat the fallenness in the world **?**

The British redcoats of the 1700s were accustomed to facing other European armies on open fields, with everyone lined up like gentlemen in neat lines. They found it difficult, therefore, to fight American farmers who failed to wear proper uniforms—and who refused to line up to be shot!

The enemy, for both sides, was *still* clear. It was the person holding a gun and pointing it at you.

Fast forward to the "war on terror" that the United States of America (along with other nations) has been fighting, especially since 2001. The enemy darts in and out, frequently failing to show itself clearly. It leaves hidden bombs by roadsides. It impersonates innocent civilians. It fades into the crowd in a marketplace. It hacks computers.

This enemy is much harder to fight.

Some spiritual enemies are redcoats. They line up in formation against Christ and His disciples. They are obvious dangers. Think of an abortion clinic, where they kill babies *and sell their body parts for profit*. There's no subtlety there. What they're doing is openly evil and chilling, even demonic.

But if you expect all your enemies to wear uniforms and blow trumpets, you're going to get hit with attacks you didn't see coming. You need to be prepared for the inside enemy (the flesh—that was the last section) and outside enemies.

OPPOSITION FROM WITHOUT

Christ could have made it so that once you are saved you are instantly raptured to heaven. There would be no church, in this case, because there would be no Christians on the earth. He could use angels as evangelists to preach the gospel and lead people into the kingdom.

But that's not what Christ chose to do. He chose to leave His followers in the world. He prayed right before His crucifixion, as He was about to leave the world,

> Now I am no more in the world, but these [disciples] are in the world. . . . I pray not that thou shouldest take them out of the world, but that thou shouldest keep them from the evil [one]. (John 17:11, 15)

This is the situation Christ's followers are still in. And here in this prayer Christ names our two biggest enemies: the world and the evil one—the Devil. Let's talk about these two enemies so that you can watch out for them.

THE DEVIL

The Devil is a source of opposition for every Christian. Christ's disciple Peter warned us,

> Be sober, be vigilant; because your adversary the devil, as a roaring lion, walketh about, seeking whom he may devour. (1 Peter 5:8)

Satan is crafty, scheming, and hungry. Paul said something similar:

> Put on the whole armour of God, that ye may be able to stand against the wiles [schemes] of the devil. (Ephesians 6:11)

Satan is not a redcoat, or not usually. He doesn't tend to announce his presence or fire a warning shot. He's more like a tricky terrorist. The Bible doesn't get very specific about how Satan acts against us, but the two times in Scripture when he interacted directly with humans give us some warnings. Those two times were in the Garden of Eden and in the wilderness where he tempted Jesus early in His public ministry.

In the garden, Satan was the definition of crafty. His question deceived Eve: *Did God really say what you think He said?* And that strategy is still one of his favorites. He casts doubt on God's words.

Satan has successfully tempted many, many people to deny the teaching of Genesis, for example. Genesis says that this world and life itself were created by a God of eternal power. And after getting people to deny God's creation, Satan makes them even easier prey by getting them to doubt his own existence—which we first learn about in Genesis 3.

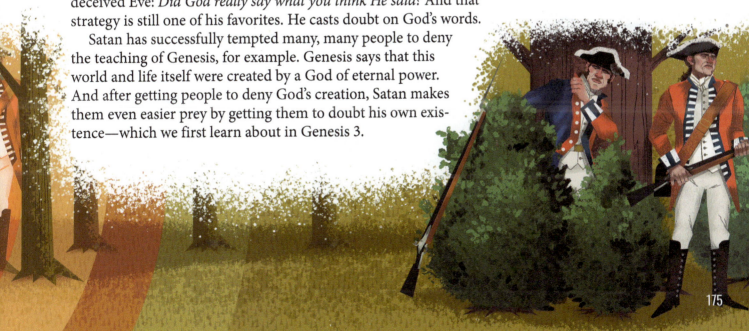

When he tempted Jesus, Satan didn't question what God said; he twisted it. He tried to use God's words to trip God's Son. (It didn't work—read Luke 4.)

You can see this strategy among the many people who work hard to make the Bible say things it doesn't say—or work hard to make it seem as though what it says doesn't apply. Paul says, for example, that **homosexuality** is sinful.

> Know ye not that the unrighteous shall not inherit the kingdom of God? Be not deceived: neither fornicators, nor idolaters, nor adulterers, nor effeminate, nor abusers of themselves with mankind . . . shall inherit the kingdom of God. (1 Corinthians 6:9–10)

"Effeminate" men and "abusers of themselves with mankind" are homosexuals. And if they refuse to repent, they will not enter heaven. But Satan has managed to trick an increasing number of professing Christians into changing the meaning of what God says quite clearly in Scripture.

While we're here, notice that Paul says "idolaters" don't get into the kingdom either. No matter which sins you hold on to, you won't get through the gates into Christ's kingdom. No matter which sins you need to repent of, including homosexuality, you can be washed clean by the blood of Christ. Paul says this clearly too—see verse 11.

Satan is called a "tempter" (1 Thessalonians 3:5). And one of his major temptations, apparently, is to get you to deny or even just misunderstand what God has said. Beware.

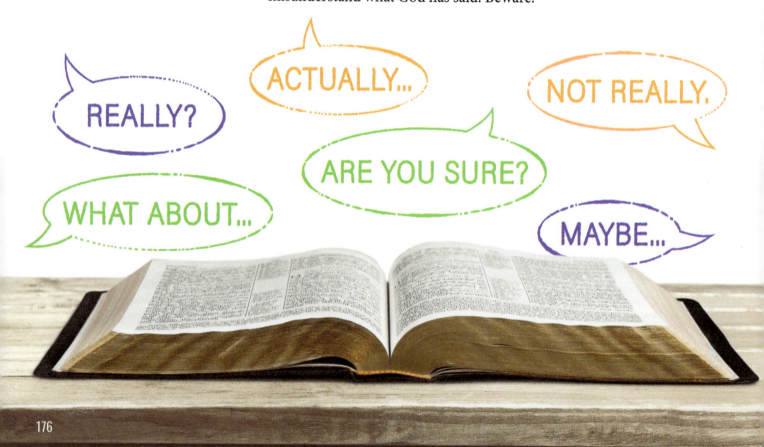

THE WORLD

Satan is also called "the prince of the power of the air" (Ephesians 2:2). He's a ruler. And his kingdom—the territory he rules—is called "the world." The world is the second outside enemy you need to be warned about.

And the Bible does offer warnings, very direct ones:

> Love not the world, neither the things that are in the world. If any man love the world, the love of the Father is not in him. (1 John 2:15)

In other words, you cannot love God and love Satan's kingdom at the same time. The world is your enemy; it is God's enemy.

And Paul has an especially interesting warning about the world:

> Be not conformed to this world. (Romans 12:2)

The world is a special kind of temptation. It's the kind that hems you in on all sides, like when you're walking in a huge crowd of people—which is precisely what you're doing. The world pushes you to think and act and feel a certain way. As theologian Kevin Vanhoozer put it, "Culture and society are in the full-time business of making disciples." *You are going to be either Christ's disciple or the world's.*

Let's test you, to see who has been shaping your thinking. How does this statement, drawn by Alastair Roberts from a recent scientific study, make you feel?

> The average man is stronger than 99.9% of women.

Or how about this?

> Women should wear modest clothing in public.

If you have been shaped by the world, then these statements of truth will be offensive to you. Even if you sense, somehow, that you shouldn't say these things out loud in front of most people, then you have felt the conforming pressure of the world.

It is a God-given truth that men have greater upper- and lower-body strength than women. It was reported in a scientific journal—not in a Christian one, but in *Evolution and Human Behavior*. But right now, the Western world is placing incredible pressure on people to deny that men and women are different. So even scientifically measurable differences are not permitted to be spoken of in public.

It is a God-given truth that women should wear modest clothing in public. (Men should, too, of course.) The Bible is straightforward:

women should "adorn themselves in modest apparel" (1 Timothy 2:9). And yet right now the Western world is placing incredible pressure on people to say that women can wear whatever, whenever; and no one can say a public word against it. If you try, you will not be shouted down—you will be screamed down.

The world has great power to affect your thinking, even when you try to fight against it. It is a powerful, powerful enemy. The world is all those parts of culture that are evil. It is the organized system of opposition to God. And it looks different in North America from how it does in India or in Saudi Arabia or in South Africa. The cultures there are different, so the "world" in each place is different. The pressures you feel to conform to the bad parts of your culture might be the opposite of what they are for another student reading this book in another part of the planet.

The "world" in the West tailors every one of its strategies to appeal to your flesh. The bad part of culture appeals to the bad part of you. Beware.

The world is offering you absolute, non-stop entertainment. It is putting pressure on you to believe that the good life is one full of movies and TV.

The world is offering you absolute, non-stop immoral enticement. You are young, but you must know and understand this if you are to fight against it.

The world is pushing you to value money over people.

The world is pushing you to act as if God and His Word are irrelevant to every bit of your life except maybe a couple of hours on Sunday.

The world mocks authority figures in your life and tells you to disregard them.

RESISTING THE DEVIL AND HIS KINGDOM

Only one kingdom lasts forever. Even mighty Egypt and Rome fell. Satan's kingdom will one day fall. The wicked world, John told us, will pass away (1 John 2:17).

Until then, the Bible gives these commands: *flee* and *fight*.

Some temptations are so strong and so dangerous that you must run away the instant you see them. The temptation of impurity is one of them.

> Flee also youthful lusts. (2 Timothy 2:22)

Sometimes, however, you must stand and fight.

> Put on the whole armour of God, that ye may be able to stand against the wiles of the devil. For we wrestle not against flesh and blood, but against principalities, against powers, against the rulers of the darkness of this world, against spiritual wickedness in high places. Wherefore take unto you the whole armour of God, that ye may be able to withstand in the evil day, and having done all, to stand. (Ephesians 6:11–13)

Your fight against the world is a fight against incredible powers, satanic ones. But you (if you're a Christian) have armor—and weapons—forged in heaven. You are *in Christ*. You have prayer and the instruction of the Bible. You have Christian authorities in your life and a church. You need not be defeated by the enemies out there.

LOVE AND FIGHTING

The redcoats of Britain seemed like an unstoppable force. But the scrappy American colonists of the 1770s had an advantage over their opponents. They were fighting for freedoms and lands they loved.

If you love Christ, you will fight for virtue, for righteousness. *And you will win.*

> Submit yourselves therefore to God. Resist the devil, and he will flee from you. (James 4:7)

Thinking It Through 4.7

1. Who are your two major outside enemies?

2. What are some ways that you personally feel pressure from the sinful world?

3. Name two strategies the Bible gives for fighting these enemies.

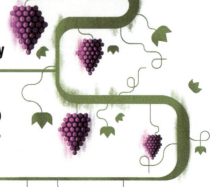

Scripture Memory

Jeremiah 9:23–24
Philippians 3:8–10
Ephesians 4:22–23
1 John 2:15

Recall

1. Name several ways people in American culture find their identity.

2. What is the word the Bible uses to describe how a Christian is brought into the family of God?

3. What is the technical name for the process by which God restores fallen people to His image?

4. What is the major enemy of God inside you? What are the two major enemies of God outside you?

Understand

5. In your own words, describe what it means to be made in the image of God.

6. What way of relating to Christ, which was discussed in this unit, is evident in these words from Paul's letter to the Romans? "We are buried with him by baptism into death: that like as Christ was raised up from the dead by the glory of the Father, even so we also should walk in newness of life" (Romans 6:4).

7. How is it that Jesus' death in the past helps a Christian overcome sin today?

Think Critically

8. What's wrong with a non-Christian saying that it doesn't matter *why* we all believe in human rights as long as we *do* believe in them?

9. When should you "follow your heart"?

10. When should you "be who you are"?

11. What relationship is most important for the identity of the believer? How should the believer maintain that relationship?

12. What do you think the most popular idol is among people your age in your culture?

Internalize

13. When in your life have you needed to be humbled by your fallenness?

14. When have you needed to be encouraged by your being made in the image of God?

15. What temptations from the Devil and pressures from the world affect you most?

16. Name some sins you must put off.

17. Name some good things you must put on in their place.

HOW SHOULD I SPEND MY TIME?

5.1 CREATED TO CREATE

Not everyone is called to be a pastor or foreign missionary (and those who *are* called to these vocations aren't always obedient). Praise God if you are called to one of these, and obey God if you are. It is a privilege to serve the Lord in these ways, because these callings are sharply focused on eternity.

But many of you will have some other calling—an engineer, an insurance adjustor, a salesperson, a nurse, a janitor, a teacher, a scholar, an artist, the greatest basketball player in the history of the universe (statistically unlikely but not impossible), or the greatest and hardest of all jobs: Mom.

Why should I work ?

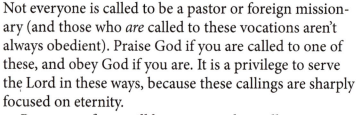

Praise God—and obey Him—if He calls you to be any one of these. And yet it's not always easy once you're in your job to believe that your work matters for next week, let alone for eternity. Wash a dish, and it will get dirty again tomorrow. Sell a lot of widgets, and your boss just might raise the number you'll have to sell next month. Someday you may find that it's hard to do your work because it feels so meaningless. You might feel the same effects of the Fall as the preacher of Ecclesiastes did when he said that life seems empty.

Some of these jobs are truly *hard*. Have you seen any adults who hate Monday mornings? What will motivate *you* when you have to get up in the morning and go face the workweek again?

Well, you have some options.

- You could go to work for the fame, for the praise you get from other people. But not only does that praise usually fall away after a while; it's a rather empty reason to go to work. And there just aren't many jobs where you'll get it. Very few jobs outside professional sports come with cheerleaders.
- You could go to work solely to make money. Making money is not a bad thing. You will find as an adult that eating food and wearing clothes become difficult without money. But working only for money is like marrying only for money: something essential is missing.

As always in the Christian life, that essential thing is *love*. The key to doing the right thing is always loving the right things in the right amounts. Love money, and it will grow wings and fly away (Proverbs 23:4–5). It will also take root and grow into evil (1 Timothy 6:10). Love praise from others, and you will have an empty, fleeting reward (Matthew 6:2). You'll also have a cruel master that always demands more.

Your motivation in work—as in everything—needs to be love for God and love for neighbor.

THE IMAGE OF GOD AND THE CREATION MANDATE

What is the first thing we find out about God in the Bible? He is a creator.

God created you in His image, which means that you, too, will create. In fact, you have a mandate to create: remember the Creation Mandate?

God blessed them, and God said unto them, Be fruitful, and multiply, and replenish the earth, and subdue it: and have dominion over the fish of the sea, and over the fowl of the air, and over every living thing that moveth upon the earth. (Genesis 1:28)

You learned way back in Section 2.3 that a mandate is an official command to do something. And God blessed us with these two commands:

1. His image-bearers are going to be fruitful and **multiply**. We must replenish, or **fill**, the earth God has given us.
2. His image-bearers are going to **subdue**, or tame, the earth. We must have **dominion**, or rule, over it.

In each case we are to create. In the first, we are creating new life. In the second, we are creating

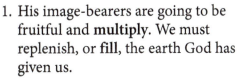

solutions to the problems that stand in our way as we try to subdue and have dominion over the earth.

Your parents created you. They were fruitful, and they multiplied. And their work almost certainly subdues and takes dominion over the earth in some way.

THE "CULTURAL" MANDATE

Think about what would have happened with this Creation Mandate—these creation blessings—if Adam and Eve had never fallen into sin.

In a perfect world, Adam and Eve would still have to farm, or someone would. The Garden of Eden didn't cover the entire earth. As people went out to live all over the earth, they would encounter new territory where they would need to grow food. To subdue a plot of ground far away from Eden would take hard work: removing trees, tilling fields. It would mean—as it did come to mean in our fallen world—taking dominion over some animals such as horses and oxen. Plowing is awfully difficult without them.

Filling the earth, subduing it, and having dominion over it would also mean building roads. People in one area of the world who grew cotton would want the spices that grew in another part of the world. And the people who grew the spices would want the cotton. It's difficult to have trade without roads.

And without carts and wheels and leather straps for horses. And inns and bridges and towns and all kinds of things that quite naturally develop when people fulfill God's original Creation Mandate.

As people noticed the properties of reeds and of wood and of catgut, they would make flutes and harps and guitars. (This is precisely what happened, even in our fallen world. Genesis 4:21 tells us that Jubal was the "father" of people who play the harp and flute.)

We're coming now to an extremely important concept in this book. It's one for which you will need not only a thinking cap but also an extra battery.

Here it is: the Creation Mandate is also a *Cultural* Mandate. Humans tend to make buildings and music and even leather straps in distinctive ways. That is, people tend to make these things the same way as others in their group do—but not the same way as those in other groups. They develop distinct *cultures*.

The Pueblos' adobe buildings look one way; Kamean huts in Papua New Guinea look another. Kazakh folk music sounds one way; Armenian folk music sounds another way. Yoruba art from Nigeria is different from Chinese art. Italian food offers different tastes and textures from those provided by French cuisine. Russian choral music sounds different from New Zealand choral music. Japanese greetings are different from Brazilian ones. Folk dances of the Quechua in Peru differ from those belonging to the Maasai of East Africa.

And this is what God intended. When people live out the Creation Mandate, what results is **culture**. And when humans in different parts of the world live out the Creation Mandate, they produce different human cultures.

The differences are not necessarily good or bad. There are different good ways to live out the Cultural Mandate. The Fall, of course, has affected all cultures; the dances and music and art and even greetings in a culture can be deeply ruined by sin. But the mere existence of multiple human cultures is a good thing.

The Cultural Mandate is a blessing from God on *all* peoples.

CREATED FOR CULTURE

You were created to create—for the glory of your Creator and for the good of your neighbor. You were created to be part of a culture.

Right now in your life, you are learning your culture. You may be learning Western culture's style of music by studying the long tradition of skills of playing the piano or the violin. You may be learning Western art by studying techniques honed by generations of artists going back (at least) to the Greeks. On your way toward creating something yourself, you will be *cultivating* the already-created culture around you. It is your job to cultivate the traditions you are handed, whatever your calling might be.

You are like a farmer who inherits land. That land has already been cleared by your great-great-great-great-grandparents. There are no more huge rocks or tree stumps in the field to stop the plow. Your land has already shown what it can produce. You have been handed seeds that have been domesticated over centuries. You have been handed relationships with other farmers and with customers. Your job is to take the good things you've been given—especially that land—and cultivate them all. If you do, you will eventually be able to *create* something valuable for the glory of God and the good of your neighbor. You will take what you are handed, refine it, and then add to it.

It's just this way in all the good parts of human cultures. You cultivate, and then you create.

Let's get practical by trying to imagine your future.

187

ENGINEERS

Engineers take the raw materials God has provided in creation, discover their properties, and make extremely useful machines and bridges and power plants for the good of their neighbors.

INSURANCE ADJUSTORS

Insurance adjustors create a world in which terrible accidents don't wipe out all the money people have saved. That's a good service to their neighbors.

SALESPEOPLE

Even people who sell things for a living—if they love their neighbors—are helping those neighbors by letting them know about useful products at good prices.

TEACHERS

Teachers take the raw material inside your head and shape it into something capable of skills like advanced math and clear writing, skills which are tools for serving your neighbor.

SCHOLARS

Scholars focus intently on some aspect of God's creation, and they work to cultivate existing knowledge until they make new discoveries and creatively build upon them.

NURSES

Nurses cultivate the skills of their profession, and they create an environment of healing care for their neighbors. They lift people up—sometimes quite literally—in their suffering.

JANITORS

Janitors push back the daily effects of the Fall in the public places we use. They protect us from the effects of awful things that grow in the grime and trash we leave behind.

ARTISTS

Artists cultivate the tradition they've been handed, and then they create beautiful art for the glory of the God who is beauty—and for the enjoyment of their neighbors.

BASKETBALL PLAYERS

Even basketball players cultivate and create. They take the game as it was handed to them and turn it into something new through innovative playing styles. Their shots delight their neighbors and bring glory to the God who designed the human body.

MOTHERS

Working the greatest and hardest of all jobs, moms create and sustain their children. Ideally, they create a home, something that is incredibly precious, something that everybody needs almost more than food (and moms create that too).

Christians believe that everything they do has a basis in the Bible. It only takes reading the first chapter to get the first instructions for glorifying God as an image-bearer. The Cultural Mandate helps us see why jobs like those described in this section are biblical jobs, *good* jobs.

EVERY GOOD, GOD-HONORING, NEIGHBOR-SERVING JOB GROWS FROM THE CREATION MANDATE.

Your job will be to cultivate and create, just like God told Adam and Eve to do.

Thinking It Through 5.1

1. Name from memory the commands in the Creation Mandate.

2. How does knowing that you have been created in God's image help you fulfill the Creation Mandate?

3. Why is the Creation Mandate sometimes also called the "Cultural Mandate"?

4. Is it a good thing to be a software developer or a florist or a construction worker? Pick one and explain why, using the words *cultivate* and *create* in your answer.

5.2 GOOD, BETTER, BEST

How does
wisdom help

Have you ever felt like you wasted a day?

Maybe you were at Grandma's and she let you watch as much TV as you wanted, and she even let you use her phone. So you sat on the couch staring at screens.

At first it all seemed pretty awesome.

But then, at the end of the day, you felt vaguely bad. And at the end of three days of nonstop screen time, you felt that gross, over-sugared feeling, like you'd eaten a whole box of Hostess Twinkie® cakes in an hour. You felt like you had *become* a Twinkie.

Maybe you've reached that special moment of maturity when you realize that, maybe, just maybe, it was more fun to be a kid a long time ago. You know, back when there weren't TVs or phones and kids just had to go outside and do what kids used to do: play.

Admit it—you never feel like a Twinkie after three days of non-stop outside play. You feel tired but also invigorated. Your dinner tastes extra good because you are so hungry. You sleep soundly, and you wake up itching for more play. No time for a shower. (Also your conscience isn't bothered by good play like it sometimes is by the TV.)

It is a *good thing* to watch TV sometimes. There are shows and movies that are amazing examples of creativity. Writers and actors and camera operators and editors are showing that they are creators made in the image of God by producing a good and beautiful and true story. All this is one way to fulfill the Cultural Mandate.

As your mom may already have told you, you can have too much of a good thing—and it becomes a bad thing. And growing up means noticing that there aren't just *good* things in life; there are *better* things and even *best* things.

How can you tell the difference between the good, the better, and the best?

You need wisdom.

READING FOR WISDOM

Wisdom—biblical wisdom—is a skill. It's a *reading* skill. **Biblical wisdom** means fearing the Lord so that you read His Word and His creation in such a way that you end up knowing and loving and doing what is truly *best* in each situation of life.

You see, there is an order out there in creation. Human lives and choices tend to run according to certain rules. Here's one: if a friend has a fight with another of your friends, and they stop being friends . . . then you probably don't want to take sides unless you're really certain you've heard both sides. But if a friend has a fight with an-other friend, and they stop being friends, *and* it has happened three or four other times—all with different friends . . . then probably there's something off about that friend. Beware. You might be the target of the next fight.

Here's another one: when you set up a big project, no matter what it is, something will go wrong that you didn't anticipate. So anticipate that you'll need some extra time or money or help.

Here's another bit of wisdom: some animals can be tamed and others just can't. A dog makes a good pet; a Nile crocodile doesn't.

The Bible doesn't say all these things, exactly. But creation does. God made His world to work a certain way. And wise people observe the ways of God's world—*and they remember*. They watch the humble little ant, and they learn a lesson about preparing for the future during harvest time (Proverbs 6:6–11). They watch the way of fools, and they learn lessons about where not to go (Proverbs 7). It takes time to develop wisdom, because wisdom generally comes through experience. And experience takes time.

But then some people get to wisdom faster than others, and some never get there. Some people are always choosing the best, and some people barely ever even choose the good.

THE FEAR OF THE LORD

Why do some people have wisdom and not others? The key verses in the key Bible book about wisdom—Proverbs—tell us:

> The fear of the LORD is the beginning of knowledge: but fools despise wisdom and instruction. (1:7)

> The fear of the LORD is the beginning of wisdom: and the knowledge of the holy is understanding. (9:10)

True wisdom, and even true knowledge, grow in a heart that is pointed toward God. Fools have their hearts pointed in the wrong direction. They hate the instruction that is meant to help them.

True wisdom begins with the **fear of the Lord**.

But that just raises more questions, doesn't it? Does the Bible really tell us to be *afraid* of God?

Yes and no.

Let's start with the no. There is a kind of fear that we should not have toward God. That's the fear of a prisoner whose jailer is wicked, or of a girl being made fun of in public, or of a teller who has a gun shoved in her face during a bank robbery. That fear is painful emotion caused by impending danger or evil, state of alarm, dread, anxiety for one's safety.

Abused children know at some deep level that they don't deserve punches and bruises from their father. Their dad's actions are unpredictable. He punishes unfairly. He is an impending danger who causes anxiety. The children of a bad dad are afraid. The child of God should not be afraid of God in this way. God does not change; He is always good. And He never punishes unjustly.

But now the yes: the children of a good dad *are* afraid of Dad in a specific way. Because they love their dad, they are afraid to act in a way that would grieve him.

They also know that Dad has power and authority (the right to use his power). They know he sets up guardrails around them for their good. He stands up to their complaints about having to eat their spinach, and he doesn't make compromises. They also know his deep love. When their punishment for sibling-hitting or lying or disrespecting Mom is over and when they have said they are sorry, Dad sweeps them up in a hug.

God is the ultimate good Father who guides His children in the path of life, away from danger and death. His children know His great love for them, but they also respect His great authority and power. God rewards their humility and punishes their pride. They cannot bribe Him to get out of consequences for their sin. But He does forgive them when they confess.

Do you see the difference now between the fear of an *abused* child and the fear of a *loved* child? The fear of the Lord is the emotion of a *loved* child toward a powerful, holy God.

BECOMING WISE IN ONE LIFELONG STEP

If your heart is pointed toward God in this kind of loving fear, you will start to be able to "read" His creation better. You'll start to become wise. You'll start to discern the difference between good, better, and best.

People who don't fear the Lord aren't looking to remember and benefit from the rules He built into creation. They are looking to push back against those rules. And one major way they do it is by ignoring the rules about creation that God decided to have written down in actual words.

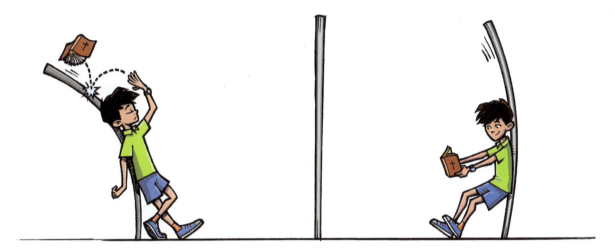

In order to understand how to live well in God's creation, you must understand what God says in the Bible. The psalmist of Psalm 119 did. He wrote,

I have more understanding than all my teachers: for thy testimonies are my meditation. (119:99)

Now, you're never supposed to be wise in your own eyes (Proverbs 3:7). But even very young people can become wiser than certain adults—if they fear the Lord and soak their souls in His words. This could be you. Meditating on God's testimonies is a lifelong step, but it can begin to make you wise very quickly.

Proverbs also encourages you to hang around wise people so that their wisdom rubs off on you (13:20). Two great ways to do that are to get good education and read good books.

Wisdom is available in many places.

LOVING THE BEST THINGS

As you grow, you will face more and more choices about how to spend your time—and you will need more and more wisdom for those choices.

Will I play soccer this year or basketball? Will I read this book or that book this week? Will I take choir or study hall next year? Will I just listen in church or listen and take notes? Will I spend my money on this game or that rafting trip?

Wisdom—*Christian*, biblical wisdom—looks not just at whether any of these choices is good or bad. It looks at which are good, better, and best.

Look at what Paul prayed for the Philippians:

This I pray, that your love may abound yet more and more in knowledge and in all judgment [discernment]; that ye may approve things that are excellent. (Philippians 1:9–10)

Love is supposed to come with knowledge and judgment, or discernment. Loving God and loving others is the starting place for discerning what choices you should make. These loves, or values, will make you approve *excellent* things, not just good ones.

So how can you tell which is the *best* of more than one good option?

There are some tests you should use to help you discern the best—whether you're facing a small decision or a life-changing one.

1 **The first major test is the glory of God.** Which of the possible choices will best bring glory to God (Colossians 3:17)? Which will help you fulfill that God-given purpose for your life?

2 **Another test is how much power the thing you choose has over you.** Paul talked about not being under the power of any action (1 Corinthians 6:12). Will your choice bring you under its control? Some choices, though not prohibited by the Bible, may become all-consuming habits for those who choose them. Know your weaknesses. The best choice for you will be what you can show self-control in.

3 **A third test is how it will help others please and serve God** (Romans 14:13, 19). Will your choice be like throwing a banana peel in the path of fellow Christians to make them slip up? If so, another choice will be the best one—especially the choice that will encourage them to fulfill their role of glorifying God.

4 **The final test is whether the choice is inconsequential** (not having much importance). Which accessory you wear with your outfit or which kind of potatoes you order is probably not a decision guided by any of the tests above. It's simply a matter of personal preference.

Be careful of assuming that most of your actions are in this last category. Many things are available to us, but not all things are the best—according to the first three tests. If you are a believer, you are to glorify God, avoid choices that would control you, and avoid being the reason that another believer stumbles.

Discern what is excellent.

Thinking It Through 5.2

1. What is biblical wisdom?

2. When you stand before a massive elephant, you will tremble a little at his sheer power—even with bars between you and him. Is this the good kind of fear (the kind we're supposed to have for the Lord) or the bad kind of fear? Explain.

3. What are some ways you can get wisdom?

4. When you want to do the best thing and your friends argue to do a wrong thing or even a good thing that you know isn't the best, how would you convince them to choose the best?

5. Name something you did yesterday that was good but not best (in that situation).

Have some screen time for just a little bit to recharge, then start on the highest-priority assignment.

Grades are really important. Ignore fatigue and push on to make the best grade in the class!

WORLDVIEW DILEMMA #68

What should I do after school when I'm really tired but have a lot to do

?

Get a little time outside first to recharge, then start on the highest-priority assignment.

Homework can wait until tomorrow. Binge-watch Netflix®!

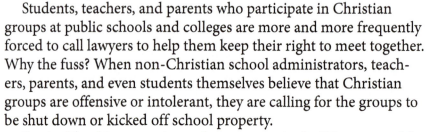

How can my light shine brightest?

Christian lawyers have never been busier.

Students, teachers, and parents who participate in Christian groups at public schools and colleges are more and more frequently forced to call lawyers to help them keep their right to meet together. Why the fuss? When non-Christian school administrators, teachers, parents, and even students themselves believe that Christian groups are offensive or intolerant, they are calling for the groups to be shut down or kicked off school property.

Stories like this are getting to be common in the Western world. A Christian wedding cake baker in Colorado and a Christian florist in Washington State are persecuted by their governments for believing what the Bible says (true stories). A businessman is forced out of the company he started because his employees find out that he believes marriage is what the Bible says it is (also true). A Christian graphic designer is removed from a graphic design conference for the same reason (also true—it happened three days before this was written).

It's maddening. It's so unfair! How should Christians respond?

Christians need to remember what Jesus called the second Great Commandment: we must love our neighbors as ourselves, *even when they persecute us*. We must promote forgiveness and resist bitterness. And instead of just pointing out the sins of our enemies, we must let God search our own hearts for things we need to repent of and seek God's help to change. Our responses must be humble but still boldly truthful.

Persecution should not surprise Christians or shame us into silence. Jesus said, "The servant is not greater than his lord. If they have persecuted me, they will also persecute you" (John 15:20).

LIVING LIVES OF GOOD WORKS

Surprisingly, one of the first things Jesus told His disciples was to rejoice when persecution comes.

> Blessed are ye, when men shall revile you, and persecute you, and shall say all manner of evil against you falsely, for my sake. Rejoice, and be exceeding glad: for great is your reward in heaven. (Matthew 5:11–12)

And immediately after this, He addressed a big temptation you might have during persecution: Retreat. Hole up. Lock yourself in a bunker. Stay away from people who hate you and try to hurt you.

Jesus said just the opposite. He called us to live lives of good works in this wicked world.

> Ye are the salt of the earth: but if the salt have lost his savour, wherewith shall it be salted? it is thenceforth good for nothing, but to be cast out, and to be trodden under foot of men.

Ye are the light of the world. A city that is set on an hill cannot be hid. Neither do men light a candle, and put it under a bushel [basket], but on a candlestick; and it giveth light unto all that are in the house. Let your light so shine before men, that they may see your good works, and glorify your Father which is in heaven. (Matthew 5:13–16)

The temptation faced by Christian groups is to give up their distinctive taste and do what the school administration says. But the whole point of salt is to add a distinct tang to food. If those Christians give up their beliefs and instead accept the beliefs of the school administration, they wouldn't be adding anything to the school that the school didn't already have. It would be like trying to spice up your bland popcorn by adding more popcorn instead of salt. Jesus said "Christians" like that would be good for nothing.

The point of light is to shine. Christians, Jesus said, are an illuminated city on a hill—something that can't be hidden. And who in the world turns on a flashlight but sticks it under a basket so the light can't be seen?

If you're a Christian, at some point you'll find yourself persecuted for what you believe. When the Salt Police comes to tell you to keep your salt to yourself, *add some more*. When the Darkness Commission comes to tell you to cover your light, *shine your good works even brighter*.

You need to know, though, that doing good works doesn't always bring good results on this earth. When you shine a Christian light, people frequently, even usually, cover their eyes. They might even lash out.

LOVING YOUR NEIGHBOR WITH YOUR JOB

The New Testament most definitely teaches that Christians who do good works where non-Christians can see them will be persecuted. But the image of God remains inside people who hate Him, and they don't *always* hate what is good. Sometimes they appreciate it.

Jesus said that people who see your good works might end up "glorify[ing] your Father which is in heaven." And Paul said that church leaders are supposed to maintain a good reputation among those outside the church (1 Timothy 3:7). It is possible that a Christian who is "careful to maintain good works" as Titus 3:8 commands will end up being praised by unbelievers.

There are all kinds of good works you can and must do in this world, out of love for your neighbor—works they might even like. It is now time to make an important connection that will help you do this very thing for the rest of your life.

The main way you will do good works out of love for your neighbor is probably through whatever job you will have. Right now your job is school, and you love your neighbor-parents when you do your work without complaining or needing to be forced, and you love your neighbor-classmates by helping them with their work (where that help doesn't involve cheating!). This job—along with other part-time jobs you might have between now and the time you get your first adult job—is your opportunity to practice for the future. Practice makes perfect.

There is a lot of emphasis today on getting jobs in science, technology, engineering, and math (STEM). Each of these fields is a fantastic way to do good works out of love for your neighbor.

Science is one fantastic way. Take medical science. The good that you could do as a scientist for cancer patients and sufferers of heart disease is enormous.

Technology is a tool for showing love to your neighbor too. Software developers are in very high demand right now. (Take a tip: learn some coding skills!) Some of them are supporting evil in this fallen world. But there are also companies full of developers who are doing awesome good works by making useful software for churches and Bible students.

Engineering is full of good works for neighbors. Every bridge that doesn't fall is a gift from engineers to their neighbors. Every app that connects you with distant friends. Every printer that works exactly like it's supposed to so you can get that last-minute homework done. And all kinds of other cool stuff.

Math is a powerful tool for good works. Mathematicians do all kinds of cool things for their neighbors, even if those neighbors don't understand them. Mathematicians process

massive amounts of weather data, for example, so that you can know whether to ride out a storm or run from it. How cool is that!

Tying your future work to loving your neighbor can help you right now if you are bored learning the skills you'll need later. STEM is full of heavy-duty tools for doing good works.

Of course, there are jobs you might get outside of STEM. There are plenty of neighbors around who need to see truth, goodness, and beauty through music, painting, poetry, fiction, essays, and journalism. Now's the time to develop skills in those areas.

The opportunities are truly endless. They're also so important that we'll keep talking about them for the rest of this unit.

CASE STUDY: LOVING YOUR NEIGHBOR WITH A CHICKEN SANDWICH

"To glorify God by being a faithful steward of all that is entrusted to us and to have a positive influence on all who come in contact with Chick-fil-A®." This is the Corporate Purpose statement of Chick-fil-A. The man who started Chick-fil-A was S. Truett Cathy. Here are some things he said in his autobiography *Eat Mor Chikin: Inspire More People*.

> Unexpected opportunities almost always carry with them the chance to be a faithful steward and to influence others positively.

> We built our business and made friends at the same time, always seeking to meet their needs wherever we could. If we learned that a customer was in the hospital, we sent food to the house. Likewise, if a customer died, we sent food to the family.

The restaurant business gives us a wonderful opportunity to mentor young people and help guide them toward adulthood. Hundreds of thousands of teenagers have worked at a Chick-fil-A restaurant, and I like to think we have been a positive influence for each of them.

Cathy modeled for those around him the second Great Commandment. Even today, many Chick-fil-A employees practice this love for others by doing extraordinary things for those they serve, from fixing their cars to rescuing them from floodwaters.

1. How do these statements and actions relate to the second Great Commandment?

2. How did S. Truett Cathy demonstrate that all people are our neighbors?

3. How did Cathy use a restaurant selling chicken sandwiches to obey the second Great Commandment?

4. How did Cathy influence those around him?

WISDOM AND GOOD WORKS

Someday, when you find your calling, you will begin to learn that there are good, better, and best ways of doing your job (often called a *vocation*, which means "calling"—since every Creation-Mandate-obeying, neighbor-loving job is a calling from God).

There's a good way to do science: running experiments. And there's a better way: running experiments over and over. And there's a best way: running experiments over and over and having your work checked by other scientists.

This is the wisdom we talked about in the last section. If you really love your neighbor, you will learn the order in God's world as carefully as you can with your schoolwork so that you can do your vocation *in the best way possible*. This is precisely why you're in school now. It is your vocation—your calling—right now. And it is preparing you for your vocations of the future. (God may give you more than one work to do in your life, like most people!)

God's call for you is to glorify Him out of love for your neighbor, specifically by doing good works for them, and especially through wise work in your vocation.

And if you get persecuted, keep being salt and light through your good works.

And if you don't, praise God—and keep loving your neighbor.

Thinking It Through 5.3

1. What did Jesus mean when He told us to be salt and light?

2. What is probably the main way you will do good works for your neighbor when you grow up?

3. How can a person show wisdom in the works he or she does?

4. What is the main way you can prepare right now to do good for your neighbor?

WISDOM AND SCHOOL

The beginning of school is so awesome. There's the smell of new pencils, the promise of a fresh notebook, the feel of pristine shoes, the anticipation of delicious peanut butter and jelly. Then there's reconnecting with friends if you go to a school—and recess even if you don't. (Homeschoolers should get recess too!)

But you know that those delicious feelings of back-to-school pleasure usually last only 12.3 minutes, only to be replaced by utter terror.

You mean, I'm going to have to go through that whole book? And that one? And that one? And that kid is going to sit next to me? And my teacher/mom won't actually let me get away with stuff? And I have to practice piano or else no video games? And recess isn't starting until I'm forty-six?

And then you actually pick up one of the books and open up the cover. Even on the first page there are words you don't know, like "antidisestablishmentarianism"—which doesn't sound good. It kind of sounds like a disease.

You think, *This isn't right. This isn't fair!*

And you have a question, a serious question arising out of your deep feeling of dread. Maybe if your mom or teacher hears how pained you are, she will let you feed the antidisterablish . . . (oh, bother) book to your little brother, because he will eat anything. Your question is this: *Why do I have to learn this stuff?*

Now stop.

Think.

If your teacher or mom gave you a Christian answer, would you accept it—because you are (hopefully) a Christian? If you could see that God wants you to learn math or English or history, would that change your attitude toward it?

Why do I have to learn this stuff

"BECAUSE I SAID SO!"

Let's first, however, get past one common answer—not because it's bad but because you're getting too old for it.

All the students who are reading this need to know something: your parents get tired, maybe especially your mom. You can know this when you see your mom vacuuming. What happens when she comes to a tiny Lego®? Does she bend over and pick it up, or does she let the vacuum eat it? If the vacuum eats it, she's tired.

So give your mom a little break if you say, "Why do I have to learn this stuff?" and she says, "Because I said so!"

That answer *is* a Christian answer. And if you get this answer, you have been told by God's holy Word that you must obey. "Children, obey your parents" (Ephesians 6:1). "Obey them that have the rule over you" (Hebrews 13:17). Those are straight Bible. So, students, if your mom says, "Learn these spelling words *because I said so*," you know the will of God for your next twenty minutes. You don't have to pray for guidance: *O Lord, should I learn how to spell* antidisestablishmentarianism, *or should I doodle pictures of small dogs?* No, you know the answer: God says learn to spell the word.

"Because I said so" is not wrong to say. Sometimes God says it, like when He told a somewhat whiny Moses, "I am the LORD: speak thou unto Pharaoh king of Egypt all that I say unto thee" (Exodus 6:29). There's no arguing. He is the Lord.

But God does often give explanations and arguments. And you're at the age now when you can handle these more complex biblical answers. Christian students ought to want biblical *reasons* for learning all this stuff.

Here are three.

1. BECAUSE YOUR YOUTH IS THE TIME TO BECOME WISE

The first reason is that the Bible treats youth as a special opportunity for gaining wisdom in all areas of life. You are probably already more than halfway through the one time in your life when you will get a free education (at least, free to *you*). In as few as six years or so from now, you might have to go to work full time. Your opportunity to get an education may be over—or much, much more difficult.

And God speaks directly to you about education, through the lips of Solomon. In Proverbs 4:1 Solomon says, "Hear, ye children." And what should you hear? His counsel:

> Get wisdom, get understanding: forget it not; neither decline [turn away] from the words of my mouth. Forsake her [wisdom] not, and she shall preserve thee: love her, and she shall keep thee. Wisdom is the principal thing; therefore get wisdom: and with all thy getting get understanding. . . . Take fast hold of instruction; let her not go: keep her; for she is thy life. (4:5–7, 13)

God doesn't say many things directly to children in the Bible. But all these words come pouring from His lips (through Solomon's) just for you. And they all say the same thing: *get wisdom.*

Wisdom takes time to get—we saw that in Section 5.2. But the writer of this book once had a college teacher (a graphic design teacher, actually) give him some wisdom about wisdom. "Experience is the best teacher," he said, *"but education is quicker."*

Spelling and grammar and writing and literature and art classes—they are full of wisdom. Math and science and history and health classes—they are full of wisdom.

Your teachers are trying to give you the wisdom God put into these fields. And now's your best chance to get it. Now's your *quickest* chance to get it.

It may not seem that way; school may seem like it lasts forever. But people who don't learn wisdom as children may never learn it.

Why do I have to learn this stuff? Because now is your best chance. You are young: get wisdom.

2. BECAUSE SCHOOL HELPS YOU DO GOOD WORKS OUT OF LOVE FOR OTHERS

A second reason you have to learn all this stuff is that education hands you tool after tool to help you do good works for others.

Just a few years ago, there were lots of things you couldn't do that you can do now. Maybe you can write a logical paragraph, summarize American history, or conduct a science experiment. Maybe you can throw a football twenty yards to an open receiver. Maybe you can sew a patch on a pair of jeans. Maybe you can do the backstroke or draw a dog or solve a Rubik's® cube.

A REMINDER
ABOUT WISDOM

Biblical wisdom means fearing the Lord so that you read His Word and His creation in such a way that you end up knowing and loving and doing what is truly best in each situation of life.

Just imagine what it would be like for your abilities to grow and grow. You are made in God's image. You are blessed with dominion over His creation. There is a *lot* you can do if you will learn the skills of wisdom.

In particular, there's a lot you can do for *others*. We looked at many of those things when we talked through the good works people do through STEM fields. It's worth repeating: every Creation-Mandate-obeying, neighbor-loving job in this world is full of good works.

You've probably been hearing "What do you want to be when you grow up?" since you were little. It's truly OK if you have no idea. But maybe you *do* have some idea. You should begin right now to connect your love for that work to the well-being of your neighbor.

How can your love of animals help you do good works for your neighbors? How can your love of writing or sports or fishing or biology or money-saving or technology help you do good works out of love for the people around you?

You will never know if you don't listen in school.

You will never develop all the abilities God has given you if your teachers offer you wisdom and you reject it. Remember: it's "fools," Solomon says, who "despise wisdom and instruction" (Proverbs 1:7).

Here's an example: A few years ago, *Newsweek*® magazine came out with a cover story attacking Christians and the Bible with open mockery. The internet went a little crazier than usual, and people were sharing the article all over the place.

The author of the article, Kurt Eichenwald, made many specific arguments about complicated issues. He said, for example,

> No [one] . . . has ever read the Bible. . . . At best, we've all read a bad translation—a translation of translations of translations.

This is completely wrong. But would you know how to answer him? Many Christians didn't. They needed help responding to this attack. It took Christian scholars with years of deep study of Hebrew and Greek (the original languages of the Bible) to answer Eichenwald. They had to work hard and work quickly to write articles combating his false claims.

Every one of them had to go to school for a long time to be able to do these good works for their neighbors.

Why do I have to learn this stuff? Because school is handing you countless tools to help you do good works out of love for your neighbor.

3. BECAUSE SUBMITTING YOUR LIFE TO GOD MAKES YOU FLOURISH

The third reason you have to learn this stuff is simple: God. If you want to be blessed, you must submit your life—including your schooling—to God.

Even some non-Christians have discovered that *without some ultimate end* (remember from Section 3.6 what that means?), education becomes empty. Molly Worthen wrote in the *New York Times* that college education today leaves students with "the inability to ask, and answer, serious questions about life's ultimate purpose." She said that students want "what we all desperately want: to submit to . . . an ideal larger than ourselves, without losing ourselves entirely."

This is what the Christian faith offers. It gives life an ultimate purpose: to love God and glorify Him. And it gives us an ideal larger than ourselves: to love our neighbor as ourselves. And we won't lose ourselves entirely if we join in with God's plan in the world. We will instead find our true calling.

Submit to God in school, and you'll be like a fruitful tree planted by rivers of water—you'll be blessed (Psalm 1). Submit to God in school, and you will suddenly have good reasons to learn all this stuff.

Thinking It Through 5.4

1. What are the three reasons this section offers for why you should learn all the stuff they're trying to teach you in school?

2. Can you think of a way your favorite school subject might help you show love for others?

3. How will your pursuit of wisdom lead you to answers about the purpose of life?

Use it to make cultural contributions to your digital community.

Use it to be aware of your culture.

How should I react to social media as a Christian ?

Don't use it, because people gossip and are unkind on social media.

Use it to make a difference in your digital community for Christ.

206

ATTITUDES TOWARD CULTURE

One kid's mom lets him watch *anything.* He's up on every major show and every movie and every viral video, and he can quote every pop music lyric that came out after 1965.

Another kid's mom lets her watch *nothing.* She's up on every major show—as long as that show is *Andy Griffith.* She's seen only the viral videos and Disney movies that were made *before* 1965, and she can quote every hymn her church sings.

Where are your family's standards in relationship to pop culture?

How should I think about my culture ?

DIFFERENT KINDS OF CULTURE

Pop culture is the set of movies, shows, books, albums, online videos, sports teams, Broadway shows, and other kinds of entertainment that are popular at any given time.

But there are two other major kinds of culture: folk culture and high culture.

Folk culture is something people come up with when they don't have mass media like radio and TV. It's local. It's accessible to people because it doesn't require advanced outside training. Folk culture in the United States is bluegrass music and barbershop harmony and state fairs and rodeos and Cajun food and tales of Paul Bunyan.

High culture is *refined* culture. But don't let that word make you scoff. To refine your powers of singing or piano playing is to take dominion over them like God told us to do in the Cultural Mandate. It is to push human abilities to their top level. If you've ever heard what a world-class violinist can do, you've heard refinement. You've heard high culture. High culture in the West is classical music, art painted by the old masters, skillful literature, and satire (a special kind of humorous writing that uses irony).

Every culture in the world has a folk culture. Many have a high culture. But only in the last century has it been possible for them to have a pop culture—because popular culture requires technologies like radio and TV.

Even though pop culture didn't exist not too long ago, it's really hard to ignore now. In 1850, it was more than possible to live so far from civilization that you just didn't know what was popular. Today, when even babies seem to have phones, it takes an act of will to stay away.

Christians have to look at all kinds of culture—pop, folk, and high—through biblical lenses. And that means seeing them through the lenses of Creation, Fall, Redemption.

1. **Creation:** Because these kinds of culture are natural products of God's Cultural Mandate, they all have some real goodness in them.

2. **Fall:** Because of the Fall, they also have at least some evil in them (sometimes more, sometimes less).
3. **Redemption:** Because of Christ's power of Redemption, Christians can use each form of culture to bring glory to Him. And because of the push of redemptive direction, some kinds of culture have more value to them than others.

All this means that you need to learn *discernment*. You have to be able to tell the difference between the things in culture that are worth your time and those that aren't. It's just like our section on structure and direction from Unit 2: you have to see the creational structure underneath things in your culture, and you also have to see the directions those things are going.

Writer Andy Crouch has suggested four possible attitudes toward culture. This section will introduce those four different attitudes, or reactions, you could have toward something you see in culture. Each one will be appropriate at different times.

CONDEMNING CULTURE

Sometimes the best attitude you can have toward something you see in pop, folk, or high culture is to *condemn* it. Profanity is part of pop culture, and it is absolutely wicked. It is wrong. It is sin. "Thou shalt not take the name of the LORD thy God in vain" (Exodus 20:7).

Some TV shows and movies and music and video games are so full of impurity, violence, and bad language that it is impossible to think of a Christian reason for watching them. Some are so full of wrong thinking about God that they, too, should be condemned.

Some art found in areas of high culture is also terrible. It's purposefully ugly and blasphemous. It's made only to shock people. It actually *attacks* beauty.

The Bible is your guide. If the Bible condemns something, then God does. And you should too.

MARCEL DUCHAMP'S *FOUNTAIN*

In 1917, French artist Marcel Duchamp flipped a urinal over, signed it "R. Mutt 1917," and called it "art." But it was actually an attack on art—an attack on beauty. If everything is art, then nothing is.

But beauty is not just in the eye of the beholder; it is something that ultimately comes from God. So an attack on beauty is an attack on God. Duchamp's work should be condemned—not consumed, copied, or even just critiqued.

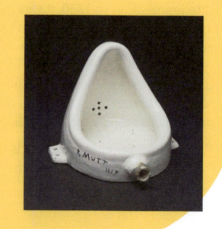

Don't feel embarrassed when kids on your sports team are all giggling about something wicked they just watched, and you have no idea what they're talking about. Whose opinion of you is more important: theirs or God's? God says, "But fornication, and all uncleanness, or covetousness, let it not be once named among you" (Ephesians 5:3). By saying this, God condemns most of American entertainment culture.

CONSUMING CULTURE

But He doesn't condemn all of it.

There are excellent movies, good TV shows, beautiful folk songs, rich pieces of classical music, and life-changing pieces of art. Psalm 24:1 says, "The earth is the LORD's"—God blessed mankind to be creators and provided the raw materials all around us. Christians and non-Christians alike can create things of incredible beauty.

A life without art, or the rest of culture, isn't just a poor life—it's an impossible life. You will be part of some culture or other, whether you like it or not. You need to *consume* the good things that your culture gives you: they are gifts of God. All good things are. And you shouldn't refuse them but take them with thanksgiving to God (1 Timothy 4:4).

The easiest way to understand this is to go home and pull up a chair to your dining room table. Whatever your mom serves you is probably going to come from your culture. Consume it. Enjoy it. Americans, eat your hot dogs, hamburgers, takeout pizza, and casseroles. Canadians, eat your poutine. Brits, eat your bangers and mash. It's good to consume what your mom gives you.

But know that certain things should be consumed less than other things. Hot dogs are great for summer picnics. Pizza is great for family game night. But hot dogs and pizza every day is unhealthy. An occasional movie can be fun. Bingeing on movies every weekend is unhealthy.

Some things are worth consuming on a regular basis. If you want to avoid the bad stuff in your culture (and you should), make sure you replace it with a steady diet of the good stuff. Ask trusted adults for good book recommendations; read Christian movie reviews before watching a film. Try to develop the ability to really enjoy the good things your culture gives you.

Work hard at deepening your enjoyment of all the good stuff until you start noticing a change in yourself. Read *The Hobbit* until you can enjoy the journey-like pacing and rich details without rushing (or worse, skipping) to the action scenes. Practice piano until Bach is a delight and not a chore. Become a cook yourself, and you'll start to enjoy all food more. Some cultural pleasures in God's creation are only available to people who will work to gain them.

CRITIQUING CULTURE

Some things your culture will set in front of you won't be clearly wicked or excellent; they'll land in the categories of good, better, and best. They require *critique*.

Some video games are good. They're artistically interesting. They make for an enjoyable challenge. But they also make for a *pretend* challenge. You get all the exciting feelings from taking risk—but none of the actual risk. It's fake adventure. Are there any *real* adventures out there that might be a better use of your time? Maybe building something or learning to survive in the wilderness or pushing yourself to see how good your jump shot can get?

A discerning person knows how to critique what he or she sees. A wise person knows how to distinguish good, better, and best. And when you're faced with something in culture that you aren't sure how to critique, ask for help from God. He is a generous giver of wisdom (James 1:5).

A wise person reaches for the best, not just the good. For example, the Warriors series of books are super popular. The adventures of the different clans of wild cats are read by boys and girls alike. But you won't find any adults reading them (except at bedtime when they read them to their kids!). You *will*, however, find adults reading The Chronicles of Narnia, even though they seem to be for kids. A wise young person notices this and looks to understand why.

It *isn't* wise to fit everything in your culture into either the condemn or the consume categories. Some things require evaluation and judgment. They require critique.

COPYING CULTURE

Lastly, sometimes the attitude you must have toward a thing you see in your culture is to *copy* it. This is particularly true when you are young and learning how to draw, paint, play music, build with wood, cook, or anything else that requires skill.

When you first learn to cook, you copy exactly what other cooks have done: that's what recipes are for. Of course, after some time passes, you will be able to create your own dishes. But when you're starting out, copying is fine. Wanting to copy is actually the best attitude you could have toward some things in your culture.

Christians in America, however, have done a bit too much copying of their culture. They want to win over non-Christians to the gospel (which is good), and they have often tried copying non-Christian culture as a way to do it (which is not always so good). Although we live in the fallen world, we are not supposed to join in with the sinful world system (John 17:14–16). That's why Section 4.7 taught you how to battle the world's temptations.

One culture critic named Chris Williams, who used to work at a Christian bookstore, describes what they sold there:

> There was music that sounded kind of like what you'd hear on the radio; it might not be as good, but at least it was clean, right? There were horror novels that never got too intense and wrapped things up with a conversion experience or spiritual victory. . . . The idea was that the retailer knew that its shoppers enjoyed things of the world, and they provided items that were copies of that, but were "safe."

Copying the world is a very good way to be conformed to it—which is exactly what Romans 12:2 tells us not to do. It makes Christians look desperate, like we can't create culture ourselves.

NEXT UP

And that is what we will talk about in the next section: how we are supposed to interact with culture. The four *c*'s in this section—condemning, consuming, critiquing, and copying—are not enough. The Bible calls us to two more: cultivating and creating.

But before we get there, you need to practice these four attitudes toward the culture around you. Ask yourself the next time you're at a friend's house and everyone wants to watch a movie: *Is this something I should condemn or consume? Or should I critique it? And if I ever make my own movie for fun, is there anything in this one that I might copy?*

Thinking It Through 5.5

1. List three things in your culture that you think you should condemn.

2. List five good things in your culture that you have consumed in the last week.

3. Name one thing in your culture that you think you should critique.

4. Name one thing in your culture that you should copy.

5.6 INTERACTIONS WITH CULTURE

SCRIPTURE MEMORY 1 Timothy 4:4–5

How should I act within my culture ?

Have you ever noticed that paintings over the centuries became more and more "round"?

Look at the first painting below, which the Italian master Giotto created around 1305. The characters are well-defined, and the colors are rich and vibrant. But everybody in the picture is *flat*. Two-dimensional. It looks kind of like they're all cut out of paper and pasted one on top of each another.

Now look at the second painting, which the American painter John Singer Sargent created around 1885. He painted without photographs to look at, and yet the image looks something like a photo but more alive. It's three-dimensional—it's round. It's full of energy.

(left) *Betrayal of Christ* by Giotto
(center) *Carnation, Lily, Lily, Rose* by John Singer Sargent
(right) *Advent* by Mary Whyte

Now look at the last painting, which the twenty-first-century painter Mary Whyte created recently. Whyte's style would be impossible without the history of Western art. Whyte built on Sargent and other painters. She learned from them. No other culture has produced anything like Western art.

And Sargent and those other painters relied on and learned from earlier painters, who learned from earlier painters, who learned from Giotto. And Giotto learned from even earlier painters. There's a long tradition in Western art. *Tradition* just means "things handed down."

It works the same way in other cultures. Chinese calligraphers and Japanese painters and African mask-makers and Indian sculptors all have their own traditions. Tradition is a fundamentally good thing, because it grows right out of the Cultural Mandate. God blessed us all to subdue the earth and have dominion over it. And when any culture obeys that mandate, one of the things that come out is art—and a tradition of art.

TAKING THE NEXT STEP

Every tradition, from every culture, is affected by the Fall of mankind into sin. So remember the previous section:

- Sometimes you must *condemn* what your culture hands you.
- Sometimes you should *consume* what your culture hands you.
- Sometimes you need to *critique* what your culture hands you.
- Sometimes you may need to *copy* what your culture hands you.

Each one of those *c*'s is an appropriate attitude—sometimes, but not at other times.

But did you notice something? These *c*'s are all about you reacting to things in your culture, not about making them yourself. And yet that's what the Cultural Mandate (Genesis 1:28) calls you to do. You can't have dominion over the earth if you don't get any farther than thinking about the culture others have made.

So Andy Crouch wrote about two last *c*'s that allow you to actively push culture in a redemptive direction: *cultivate* and *create*. Unlike the four from the previous section, these two are always good to do.

CULTIVATING CULTURE

But what does it mean to cultivate?

Think again of art. Maybe you are an artist. If you are, your task will be to learn from Mary Whyte and other contemporary artists, and build on what they have done. While you are learning, maybe you will first want to copy them. Their brushstroke style, their compositions, their backgrounds—all these things and more will instruct you. They are a tradition that is being handed to you. You will *cultivate* the tradition by learning it and preserving it.

This is true if you are being handed a tradition of woodworking, hunting, needlework, graphic design, medicine, or whatever it is you want to do when you grow up! You will learn from the tradition that others hand you. You won't invent your job by yourself.

But as you take hold of that tradition, something will happen: You will notice that there are things in the tradition that you do not want to copy, because that tradition is touched by the Fall. You will notice what are basically "weeds" in the garden of your tradition—things that do not honor God. You may wonder how you can join in that tradition with a clear conscience if God says you are supposed to work with your whole heart for Him (Colossians 3:23). You will have to weed some things out of the tradition you are handed. In other words, you'll need to do some *cultivating*.

OK, now some examples.

(top) J.E.B. Stuart on Monument Avenue by Fred Moynihan (bottom) *Rumors of War* by Kehinde Wiley

As you look at these sculptures, you will notice that one thing artist Kehinde Wiley is doing is confronting people. He takes people off the street and poses them to mimic famous historical pieces of art. He is—partly—mocking and undermining the traditions of Western art.

One of the powers of art is that it can confront people. In a fallen world, sometimes people need to be confronted with the problems of their sin. But so much of Western art today is busy confronting and protesting that often beauty gets left to the side. It is good that Wiley doesn't forget beauty amid his protest. But Christian artists have to ask themselves very hard questions about what art is for and whether their protest is truly serving the common good. They will want to *cultivate* art. They may want to weed out ugliness or unnecessary confrontation. They may wish to dedicate their art not to protest but instead to rich, God-glorifying beauty.

Woodworkers might notice that old ways of furniture-making are dying because of power tools. There's nothing necessarily wrong with this: an electric drill is certainly progress over a hand-powered drill. But some of the old ways were good traditions that ended up producing more beautiful furniture, rather than the throwaway furniture people often buy nowadays. Christian woodworkers will want to *cultivate* woodworking. They will want to weed out of their woodworking the idea that furniture is meant to last only five years. They will want to make the kinds of pieces that can be handed down to their grandchildren.

Nursing provides another example. The tradition of nursing is an honorable one. It is an extremely important and necessary service. And if hospitals dedicate themselves more and more to making a profit rather than serving the community, Christian nurses can push back. A Christian nurse's highest calling is love of neighbor. Profit cannot be neglected, but loving care is essential to the tradition of nursing. A Christian nurse will *cultivate* this profession.

CREATING CULTURE

But at some point you will find that you are tired of just cultivating. You will think of new things to create, things all your own. Your creations will build on what others have given to you, and they will make it possible for others to build on your work.

So imagine that you are an artist, a woodworker, or a nurse. You love your God; you love your neighbor; you love your job. You want to be the best artist or woodworker or nurse—for the glory of God and the good of your neighbor! And yet you see that the tradition that is being handed to you is not entirely good.

What can you do? How can you change the culture around you in the art studio, or in the woodworking shop, or at the hospital?

Andy Crouch says this: "The only way to change culture is to create more of it." You are blessed by God to do this, to make culture, to *create*. So prepare to create.

If you're an artist someday, make art that pushes your tradition back in a redemptive direction. *Create* art that weeds out as much of the Fall as you can. Make art that makes it possible for other people to learn from you and create their own art.

If you're a woodworker, *create* beautiful furniture that shows off the amazing beauty God put into wood. Do it for your neighbor. And see if you can make it possible for other woodworkers—like your own children, maybe—to learn your insights. Make an online video channel teaching your skills. Write a book. Or just let the furniture speak for itself.

If you're a nurse, be a God-honoring nurse. And if the Lord ever gives you any authority or power, work to make nursing at your hospital or clinic the best that nursing can be. If the schedule requires nurses to work long shifts that keep them away

CASE STUDY: CHRISTIAN CREATING

Makoto Fujimura is a Christian who paints abstract art in the traditional Japanese style with colorful crushed minerals. He seeks to glorify God and witness of Jesus Christ through his art. This is how he closed a letter written to guide students viewing his art.

> Art can train us to "see" with our eyes, or even "listen" through our eyes, and that experience can help to tap into the "eyes of your heart." Your faith journey depends on being able to see things through these eyes, to see through the "dangers of the world" to the "mystery of the Gospel" that St. Paul speaks of. [. . .]

> Go into the world, and pay attention to miraculous things. See "heaven in a wildflower" all around us! Share that with each other and begin to "name" these experiences through art, music, drama and poetry . . . actually, through any activity. You can be a nurse or doctor dealing with Ebola [. . .], or an engineer trying

> to solve how to create a better city, or a politician who leads with compassion and empathy rather than usurping power. You can bring beauty into the world through all these means. Ponder why St. Paul called the Good News "the mystery." Your life will then become generative.

1. What does Fujimura mean to "pay attention to miraculous things"?

2. How can people "share" the miraculous through various vocations?

3. Why is it important to bring beauty into the world?

4. Look up the definition of *generative*. Why does Fujimura use this word to describe what your response ought to be to the gospel, "the Good News"?

from their families and make them irritable, *create* a new schedule. Push back (nicely!) against the administration if you can see that they are sacrificing good patient care solely for financial reasons.

NOW DO IT

Right now, you're not a professional artist. You're not an expert woodworker. You're not a nurse. You're still learning.

And all this talk about cultivating and creating may seem four hundred light years away. What can you do *now*?

Now is mainly a time to cultivate. By all means, cultivate your spiritual life: Get to know God. Learn the Bible. But the Bible isn't all you need to know. The Bible itself tells you to get wisdom. Especially while you are young, learn wisdom through the traditions of math, science, history, music, writing, spelling, and athletics (and maybe art and woodworking and health) that your teachers are handing you. Try a lot of different stuff to find out what interests you.

And when you find your interests, throw yourself in. Copy, copy, copy. Watch all the YouTube® videos you can about how to do that thing well. Sing, draw, build, train, cook, design! Find a competition for kids your age and join it. Find a mentor, someone to guide you in that field.

> And God blessed them, and God said unto them, Be fruitful, and multiply, and replenish the earth, and subdue it: and have dominion. (Genesis 1:28)

Take the little part of this earth that the Lord gives you, and cultivate it, subdue it. Rule it with your whole heart directed toward the Lord. Look for things that don't seem right because of the Fall and weed them out. Then work to make something that will glorify Him and serve your neighbor.

Prepare to create like your Creator made you to do.

Thinking It Through 5.6

1. List out all six of the *c*'s you've learned in this section and the last—from memory.

2. What Bible verse says you should perform the two *c*'s that we talked about in this section?

3. Look into the future as best you can. If you are *not* a pastor or missionary, what percentage of your time do you think you will spend in Bible reading, prayer, evangelism, preaching, and other obviously spiritual things? What percentage of your time will you spend either responding to or creating culture?

WORLDVIEW QUEST: THE TWO GREAT COMMANDMENTS

You've already learned the two Great Commandments—love God and love your neighbor as yourself. These commandments provide Christians with the right motivations for pursuing excellence in their fields of study and work. Christians should be pushing against the effects of the Fall in their fields—in other words, they should be living redemptively, pursuing the very best things that align with God's creational structure. Many Christians have become some of the experts in their fields because of their devotion to God, good works, and His structure for the work they do. Where they excel, the others in their fields notice.

Introduction

Fast forward into your future to when your interest has become your career. You have excelled in your field so that what you produce is in demand, and you are considered an expert in your field. Because of your expertise, the national association of _____ (your field) wants you to produce something for their yearly gathering.

Task

Research a Christian expert in your field. Learn from how they have obeyed the two Great Commandments while working in that field. Gather ideas for producing something that pushes the field in a redemptive direction. Your product must be something that could be presented to or performed for a gathering of professionals in your field. (For now, your "gathering of professionals" will be your class or your family. If you are already involved in a group related to your interests, you may present to them as well.) Your presentation or performance should demonstrate the best of your current skill level.

Procedure

1. Research a Christian expert. (Examples: Christopher Parkening for the music field, Nikki Grimes for the writing field, David Robinson for the athletics field, or a member of Christians in the Visual Arts [CIVA]. If you have another field of interest, ask your teacher or parent to help you find a Christian professional to research.)

2. Using your research, write a Christian way of thinking about your field and ideas about how to push it in a redemptive direction toward its creational structure.

3. Produce something in your field that can be performed or shown to an audience.

4. Perform for or show your product to your class or family (and to a local group of professionals in your field, if you wish).

How can
I make a
difference

Someone once said that everybody wants to change the world, but nobody wants to take out the trash.

You could replace "take out the trash" with "make the bed," "clean up after dinner," "break up a fight between your siblings," or a long list of other things that just aren't fun but have to get done.

But the Bible says your life should be full of good works like these, even if nobody else wants to do them. It is by doing those things that you may change your world.

DEVOTED TO GOOD WORKS

Christine is a pastor's wife in a small city in New England. No one gave Christine any tests to see whether she qualified to be a pastor's wife. She just became one when her husband became a pastor. But if there were tests, she would pass them. She has a heart that can include far more people than the average. She loves people.

But she has a body that doesn't always work right. She's frequently tired and cannot get good sleep. She has children to care for—including multiple adopted children. And one of her children has special needs.

One day Christine brought some of her children to the local library and saw another young mom. Christine prayed silently, "Lord, if you want me to talk to that woman, you'll have to have her come up to me, because I simply do not have the energy."

The woman, whose name was Melissa, did just this. And soon she was coming to Christine's church.

Melissa grew up in a very broken home—and her own home wasn't much better. Melissa was a baby Christian who had many questions and many needs. Melissa grew much as a Christian while attending Christine's church, but her needs kept coming in big waves.

Christine stood by her through it all. She babysat Melissa's four kids. She answered many phone calls from Melissa. She created a family culture in her little home that had space for others. Through it, she taught Melissa how to be a Christian wife and mother.

And when the day came that Melissa had the hardest trial of her life—the day the police found out that her husband had committed crimes—Christine was there again. Day after day, she supported Melissa. She prayed for her. She gave her wise advice from the Bible.

Christine lives a life the Bible describes with these words: "careful to maintain good works" (Titus 3:8). She is "zealous of good works" (Titus 2:14), the way God says Christians should be.

She will never win a major award on earth for those good works. Only God knows every good work she's done. But quite a number of lives have been significantly touched by this one woman who just keeps doing whatever good works seem to be next. Her own kids, the kids she and her husband have adopted, women in the church, especially Melissa—many people have been touched by Christine's love.

And some people do notice. People listen to Christine speak about her faith because they see her good works. They know her love. Even when her thirteen-year-old son talks about Christ with kids on his baseball team, those boys listen to him in part because of Christine's love. Her love has shaped her son, and the boys themselves have seen it.

THE GOOD WORKS OF CULTIVATION AND CREATION

Now, all this may seem like a totally different topic from what we've been talking about in the last few sections. We've talked about all the possible attitudes toward culture (condemn, consume, critique, copy), and the two big things you yourself are supposed to do to make culture (cultivate and create). Christine's story may not look, at first, like it has anything to do with cultivating and creating.

But it does. It really does. Cultivating and creating most frequently look like what the New Testament calls "good works." It says about Tabitha that she was "full of good works" and had made coats and clothes for many people (Acts 9:36, 39). Most of the time, those good works aren't earth-shaking. They're simple—like sewing good clothes for people if you're a seamstress.

It is good to be inspired by a big vision of what your life could do. But your calling probably won't be a global one in which you write the greatest novel of the century, or reinvent art for the Western world, or produce a training video that becomes required viewing for every other nurse on the planet. If those opportunities come, take them for the glory of God. Let your light shine so that others will glorify Him! But don't feel like you have to change the entire world. You have a better chance of getting struck by lightning while being bitten by a shark who has won the lottery. The world is a big place.

Your calling to cultivate and create will probably look like being "full of good works" that are seen only by the people around you. At the very least, your calling to cultivate and create will look like that at the beginning. Only later in your life will you have greater influence.

To the future mothers who are reading this book—you will spend decades of your lives serving your children and your church.

CASE STUDY: REMEMBERED FOR CULTIVATING AND CREATING

Amos Fortune was an African slave who purchased his own freedom at the age of sixty in 1770, a few years before the United States achieved theirs. Fortune was a tanner whose good works included making beautiful leather for his neighbors in Massachusetts and later in New Hampshire. As one of the best tanners in the area, he had customers from distant towns.

Fortune spent his own money to purchase the freedom of a dying slave named Lily and then married her. She died within the year. The next year, he purchased the freedom of a woman named Violate, whom he also married.

Along with these good works, Fortune hired apprentices and taught them how to be good tanners. He adopted two daughters during his life. He was a founding member of the library in the town where he lived. He even bound some of their books for them. Before he died, he decided that his money should be given to his church and the local school.

This is what their pastor wrote about Amos and Violate on their tombstones, which you can still see in New Hampshire:

Sacred to the memory of Amos Fortune, who was born free in Africa, a slave in America, he purchased liberty, professed Christianity, lived reputably, and died hopefully, Nov. 17, 1801, [age] 91.

Sacred to the memory of Violate, by sale the slave of Amos Fortune, by marriage his wife, by her fidelity, his friend and solace, she died his widow Sept. 13, 1802, [age] 73.

Fortune could have had no idea that Elizabeth Yates would write an influential children's book about him 150 years after his death. His simple good works glorified his God and made a difference in our world, a world he could never imagine.

1. How did Fortune glorify God with his work?

2. How did Fortune glorify God with his interactions with his neighbors?

3. Why do you think people still talk about, and even write books about, Amos Fortune?

4. What are some good things Christians can do in their community to love their neighbors?

Your job will be to cultivate a home culture like Christine's and to create emails and text messages and devotionals and private prayers that are good works for others like Melissa. Maybe someday your good works will help change the lives of many people. Maybe not. That's in God's hands.

To the future workers of all kinds who are reading this book, future men and future women—you will spend decades of your lives serving your neighbors in every job imaginable (and in some jobs that no one has yet imagined). Your job will be to cultivate a God-honoring culture in your office or construction site or schoolroom or operating room. You will create things that help make these more redemptive places. And people will see your efforts and call them "good works."

INFLUENCING

Jesus said that all Christians are like salt, and all Christians are like light. Salt flavors. Light shines. Each one of these things changes its environment. Popcorn without salt just isn't good. Kind of like reading without light.

If you will look at your calling in life as an opportunity to do good works for your neighbor—cultivating and creating a better world—you simply do not know how many people you will "salt" or how far your light will travel.

So do what the Bible says: humble yourself to do even the simplest good works and let God take care of how broad your influence is (1 Peter 5:5–6). Take out the trash, and you might just change the world in a way that matters.

> Let your light so shine before men, that they may see your good works, and glorify your Father which is in heaven. (Matthew 5:16)

Thinking It Through 5.7

1. How could doing good works give you an opportunity to glorify God or share your faith? Tell a true story or make up a possible one.

2. What good works could *you* do today?

Scripture Memory

Genesis 1:28
1 Corinthians 10:23–24
Romans 12:1–2
Philippians 4:8
1 Timothy 4:4–5
1 Timothy 4:12

Recall

1. What are the parts of the Creation Mandate?

2. What is biblical wisdom?

3. What is the beginning of wisdom?

4. When is the best time in your life to become wise?

5. List the six ways people can react to and interact with culture.

Understand

6. When Paul said to "approve things that are excellent" what principle from this unit was he teaching?

7. How can working in the field of science be good for your neighbor?

8. Based on your answer to number 4, why is that particular time the best time for you to become wise?

9. What is the main difference between the first four *c*'s you learned in this unit and the last two *c*'s?

Think Critically

10. Why is the Creation Mandate also called the "Cultural Mandate"?

11. In twenty years, what do you think will be the main way that you will do good works for your neighbor?

12. If a TV show never mentions God in any of its seasons, what critique could you give of that show? (Think, perhaps, of a specific show.)

13. How does the Cultural Mandate make possible the Great Commission?

Internalize

14. List three things in your culture you think you should condemn.

15. List three things in your culture your parents and teachers think you should consume.

16. List three things in your culture your parents and teachers have had you copy.

17. What is the very next thing you must do (after answering this question!) to prepare to live a life of doing good works for the glory of God and the good of your neighbor?

HOW SHOULD I RELATE TO OTHERS?

What does it mean to be a man?

In *Calvin and Hobbes*, the world's greatest comic strip, six-year-old Calvin is in a constant love-hate battle with his neighbor Susie Derkins. He needs her math skills to cheat on tests (Calvin: "What's 12 + 7?" Susie: "A billion." Calvin: "Thanks!"). But he also lives to "paste Susie's pate" with a well-aimed snowball. He and his stuffed tiger, Hobbes, even form a club called G.R.O.S.S.—**G**et **R**id **O**f **S**limy Girl**S**. Calvin proclaims himself "Dictator-for-Life" and drafts a G.R.O.S.S. resolution "condemning existence of girls"!

Girls are *not* gross, just so you know. And they *should* exist, or else the rest of the human race will all stop existing. The comic strip is having fun with the age-old rivalry between boys and girls. Which one rules and which one drools is the never-settled question, because by the time the two are old enough to figure it out, they settle their differences instead and get married. Men and women may never fully figure each other out, but their differences become fascinating to each other rather than annoying.

We need to talk about being a man (this section) and being a woman (next section).

The differences between the two are some of the first things every child notices about the world. From their earliest days, boys and girls play differently, and they play with different things. Boys generally love competition; girls generally love nurturing. Boys tend to gravitate to trucks and balls and Legos; girls tend to gravitate to dolls and jump ropes and princesses. Boys often love playing with boys; girls often love playing with girls.

But if you have been listening to your culture, the last few sentences probably made you feel a little uncomfortable. At the very least, a little objection arose in your mind as you read. *Well, not all boys love competition and trucks, and not all girls are nurturing and love dolls.*

This is all true. But the general tendencies are still overwhelmingly obvious. Variations don't eliminate them.

It would take a culture that has gone crazy to deny that boys and girls are different—and different in more ways than could ever be fully understood, let alone counted. You can't be human and not notice that from the way they walk and talk to the jobs they gravitate toward, the differences between men and women go very, very deep.

GOD CREATED MAN IN HIS IMAGE

Of course, their similarities go just as deep, as deep as Creation, Fall, Redemption.

Creation
All men and all women are created in the image of God—"Male and female created he them"—and it takes both men and women to "be fruitful, and multiply." God gave the Creation Mandate to both of them. (Read Genesis 1:27–28.)

Fall
All men and all women are bent by the Fall—bent into sin, and then bent into old age and death.

Redemption
The percentage of men who can be redeemed by Jesus Christ is the same as the percentage of women who can be redeemed: 100 percent.

But from the very moment Eve is introduced into the Bible's story, she is different from Adam. She is the helper; he is the helped (Genesis 2:18–25). The man was created first (1 Timothy 2:13); the woman was created from his side (Genesis 2:22).

Men and women are the same in important ways, and they are different in ways that are also important and foundational.

MASCULINE CHARACTER

What does it mean to be a man?

God tells us in two ways: the Bible and the world. Remember special revelation and general revelation from Section 3.7? We need the Bible to help us read the world rightly, but we also need to make the effort to read the world itself.

SPECIAL REVELATION ABOUT MEN

Let's first notice one simple point from Scripture: there is such a thing as "being like a man." There has to be because of this verse:

> Watch ye, stand fast in the faith, quit you like men, be strong. (1 Corinthians 16:13)

"Quit you like men" doesn't mean that men are quitters. It's older English for "act like men," or "be courageous," or "be valiant." And the writer, Paul, seemed to assume that standing fast and being strong are also manly.

This, too, is offensive to Western culture. *Can't women be courageous and valiant and strong?* Yes, of course. But physical strength and courage are qualities the Bible ties here to men in a special way.

Here are some more character qualities the Bible gives to show what it means to be like a man: Old men are supposed to be "sober, grave, temperate, sound in faith, in charity, in patience" (Titus 2:2). Young men are supposed to be "sober minded" and "shewing . . . a pattern of good works: in doctrine shewing uncorruptness, gravity, sincerity" (Titus 2:6–7).

The Bible says in other verses that men are to be the leaders in at least two specific places:

1. Men are to be leaders in the **home**. Scripture says of the family: "The head of the woman is the man" (1 Corinthians 11:3). And Paul told the Ephesians the same principle: "Wives, submit yourselves unto your own husbands, as unto the Lord. For the husband is the head of the wife" (Ephesians 5:22–23).
2. Men are to be leaders in the **church**. This doesn't mean that every man is supposed to be a church leader; only men with certain character qualities can be church leaders (1 Timothy 3:1–13). But, the Bible says, women are not permitted "to teach, nor to usurp [take] authority over the man" (1 Timothy 2:12).

The world right now truly hates these teachings of the Bible—in part because they have seen so many men sinfully abuse their authority. It's very sad: men often do this. But they *don't* do this if they're following the Bible. Right after being told that they are the heads of their homes, husbands are also told to love their wives tenderly and self-sacrificially:

> Husbands, love your wives, even as Christ also loved the church and gave himself for it. (Ephesians 5:25)

And church leaders are told something similar. Peter tells them not to lead in a domineering, cruel, "I'm-the-boss-so-you-have-to-do-what-I-say" kind of way. They are supposed to lead instead by example (1 Peter 5:2–3). Leaders must certainly lead, but that leadership itself is supposed to be a loving service and not a show of power.

The Bible does not teach that all men are the leaders of all women. Husbands lead their own wives; pastors lead their own churches. But even outside home and church, men should generally be the ones to stick their necks out and lead rather than waiting for women to do it. God laments it when men get lazy like that:

> As for my people, children are their oppressors, and women rule over them. (Isaiah 3:12)

If you are a current boy, you are a future man. You should prepare yourself even now to step up and take leadership. When a bully approaches your little sister and her friends, you speak up and step between them. When something heavy needs to be moved, you jump up to help. When everyone is super tired at the end of a long hike and you realize that someone left the car key half a mile back up the trail, you be the one to volunteer to run back and get it. When you are part of a mixed group of boys and girls, and you all do something dumb and get in trouble, you be the one to step up and answer for the group when an adult confronts you.

The Bible never says that women can't be leaders ever. It never says that all men should be leaders at all times. If everyone were a leader, there wouldn't be anyone left to follow. But in the home and in the church, men are leaders. They need to have the character of leaders: courage and servanthood.

GENERAL REVELATION ABOUT MEN

The old rule on sinking ships was "Women and children first into the lifeboat!" It was (and still is) considered dishonorable for men to shove their way into the first lifeboat and make the women and children wait for the next one.

Why?

Because men are physically stronger than women (and children), and that strength comes with responsibilities.

Two scientists named William Lassek and Steven Gaulin wrote a paper not long ago in which they showed that the average man has more upper-body strength than 99.9 percent of women. They showed that men have an average of 50 percent more muscle mass in their legs than women, and are 65 percent stronger in their lower body overall.

The two scientists said that evolution must be the reason for these huge differences. But this is not true. It is God who made the woman "the weaker vessel" (1 Peter 3:7). It is God who made men stronger and faster. And when God gives power, He also gives responsibility.

That's where general revelation comes in: when God gave men and women the bodies He gave them, *God was saying something about the way they ought to act.*

When you see that the vast majority of jobs that require physical interaction with the environment—firefighting, timber cutting, offshore fishing—are filled by men, what do you think?

When you see that the vast majority of jobs that require relational interaction with people—nursing, social work, teaching (especially elementary)—are filled by women, what do you think?

It is possible that our society has gotten the differences between men and women all wrong, saying that it is prejudiced against men or against women to say that they have different interests. It is possible that men and women like different things because God made them different *on purpose.*

Young men ought to work to grow to be mature men. And you need to know that it is good, not bad, for men to be interested in manly things.

The Bible does not define in detail what counts as masculine and what counts as feminine. But God did give you a personality, and He did (and will continue to) give you areas of interest. Some men have personalities that are outgoing, charismatic, bold. Others have personalities that are reserved, thoughtful, inquisitive. Some men are naturally more interested in hunting and carpentry; others in music and art. Many of these differences stem from differences between cultures and between families—what opportunities were introduced to you as a kid and what things your family had interest in. But all these interests and personality traits can be lived out in a

way that is truly masculine. Just like we talked about at the end of Unit 5, throw yourself into developing those interests and personality traits to the glory of God.

Because our world is so confused right now about what manhood is, you may feel confused too. You (boys) may wonder whether your interests fit inside the masculine category. You can and should talk to your parents and your pastor about this if you have questions. What you cannot do is decide that masculinity doesn't matter.

No. Act like a man.

Thinking It Through 6.1

1. What similarities between men and women land in the category of Creation?

2. What character qualities does God expect men to have, and why?

3. What does Ephesians 5:25 suggest is the difference between good male leadership and bad?

6.2 WOMANHOOD

What does it mean to be a woman?

If you haven't noticed already, our culture is very, very confused about the differences between men and women.

In many modern movies, the girls beat up the boys. Disney character Mulan®, for example, disguises herself as a man in order to fight in a war. The most famous song in her movie is "I'll Make a Man out of You." In it, a strapping young captain teaches his army—including Mulan—how to fight.

At first, Mulan isn't so good at all the things soldiers need to do. She can't carry heavy weights on hikes in the mountains; she gets a black eye in hand-to-hand combat training; she's not too great with weapons.

But by the end of the song Mulan knocks down her martial arts trainer, an expert fighter twice her size, with a roundhouse kick to the face. She is the fastest hiker in the army. They've made a man out of her.

The very powerful movement in our society called feminism cheered at this. Many feminists say that men and women are *equal in every way*. Women can be just as strong as men, they say.

And there are some women who have amazing physical strength. So a few Mulans are a healthy reminder that God made some women to be exceptionally physically strong.

But do this in movie after movie, and it actually ends up condemning the women who *aren't* as physically strong as men—and that's almost all women. Remember, the average man has greater upper-body strength than 99.9 percent of women. Men are taller too: go find two thousand random people above six feet tall, and most likely only one of them will be a woman.

Think about this, and think hard, because equality between people can be a good thing. The Bible affirms that in certain very significant areas men and women are equal (we'll review these areas in a minute). Blind people and seeing people are equal in all the most important ways too. But there aren't any people campaigning for driver's licenses for the blind—because blind people and seeing people are *not* equal when it comes to the one thing most relevant to driving: the ability to see. You can't just call people "equal." You have to describe carefully the ways in which they are equal and the ways in which they're not. Differences matter as well as equality.

Your culture is trying very hard to persuade you that men and women are equal in *every* way. It says there are no important or essential differences between men and women. *This is not true.* Men are better at some things because of how God created them, and fighting is one of them. Women are better at other things; God gave them other major strengths beside physical strength.

WARRIOR PRINCESSES

Christian writer Alastair Roberts calls out the irony of "action heroines"—women in movies and TV shows who can beat up men, like Captain Marvel®, Wonder Woman®, Katniss Everdeen®, and Rey® from *Star Wars*.

Roberts says that in shows like these, "women, we are assured, can fight just like men. These characters are highly confident characters who routinely outclass men in combat, despite their typically short, thin, and conventionally attractive frames."

GOD CREATED WOMAN IN HIS IMAGE

It is absolutely true that, in the most important ways, men and women are equal. And only the biblical worldview knows this.

Creation
All men and all women are created in the image of God and given the blessing-commands of the Creation Mandate.

Fall
All men and all women are bent into sin.

Redemption
All men and all women can be redeemed by Jesus Christ.

But from the very moment Eve is introduced into the Bible's story, she is different from Adam. She is the helper; he is the helped (Genesis 2:18–25). The man was created first (1 Timothy 2:13); the woman was created from his side (Genesis 2:22).

Our point is the same as the last section: men and women are the same in important ways, and they are different in ways that are also important and foundational.

The worldview that runs the Western world—called **secularism**—rejects these truths, so it has to create pretend equalities between men and women. Secularism and feminism have to invent things that aren't true because they deny the things that are. And the result? The current trend of powerful women being portrayed as aggressive, action-oriented fighters like men can make women think that they have to act similarly to men in order to be a "real woman." Women should be valued as *women*—and valued as made in the image of God.

FEMININE CHARACTER

What does it mean to be a woman?

Again, God tells us in two ways: special revelation and general revelation.

SPECIAL REVELATION ABOUT WOMEN

In the Bible, the differences between men and women are not portrayed as a competition. It's not like when one wins, the other loses. In a family, a man and a woman are both needed. They will both contribute their strengths to the good of the family. The same goes for the church and for the rest of society.

Whereas our culture pays attention to the very few exceptional (and perhaps fictional) women who are taller and stronger and better fighters than men, the Bible celebrates women for the real talents that set them apart.

The Bible dedicates almost a whole chapter to the strengths—in both character and action—that women have. It's Proverbs 31.

And the introduction to that section is very interesting:

> Who can find a virtuous woman? for her price is far above rubies. (31:10)

These words are interesting because that word *virtuous* can be translated in other ways. It can be translated "capable" or even "strong." She is a "wife of valor." "She girdeth her loins [dresses herself] with strength, and strengtheneth her arms," the writer later says (31:17). *The Bible celebrates strong women.*

But the woman of Proverbs 31 isn't a soldier. She isn't a mixed martial arts fighter. She doesn't beat up guys. Her heroic strengths are not the same as man's.

Her focus is the home. Can you see it in all the things Proverbs 31 says about her?

- Her husband's heart trusts in her; she does him good and not evil for her whole lifetime. She is his helper, like she was created to be.

- She looks for plants she can use to weave clothing.
- She works diligently. She brings in food.
- She plants a crop in a field she bought.
- In her home she creates things of good quality to sell.
- She serves the poor and needy.
- On her lips are kindness and wisdom.
- She looks after her household carefully.
- Her children and her husband praise her.
- She may have charm and beauty, but more importantly she has the fear of the Lord.

Western culture says women are valuable when they are either (1) strikingly attractive or (2) equal in strength to men (and preferably both). As you can see, the Bible focuses on other better feminine virtues.

Now, some women will be single. Their focus will not be the home. They are actually told to dedicate themselves to the Lord, in body and soul (1 Corinthians 7:34). And they can still have "spiritual children" by bringing others to Christ and discipling them, just as the apostle Paul did with many people. Paul himself was single and told single men the same thing. This is an honorable calling. But because God blessed humanity to be fruitful and multiply, most women will be mothers like the wise woman of Proverbs 31.

Other parts of the Bible also talk about virtuous women. Titus 2 says that older women in the church are supposed to teach the younger women "to be sober, to love their husbands, to love their children, to be discreet, chaste, keepers [working] at home, good, obedient to their own husbands" (2:4–5). Again the focus is the home.

The Bible also addresses women's appearance, something Western culture is obsessed with. It tells Christian women *not* to be obsessed. First Timothy 2:9–10 instructs women to dress modestly, in an appropriate and self-controlled manner. They're to focus more on living in a godly way than on outward accessories and hairstyles.

GENERAL REVELATION ABOUT WOMEN

A few years ago, Google software engineer James Damore wrote a letter and made it available to other Google employees. In it he tried to explain why so few women were software engineers. He said, "Men and women biologically differ in many ways." Two of his many arguments were that "women on average show a higher interest in *people* and men [show a higher interest] in *things*" and "women on average look for more work-life balance while men have a higher drive for status on average."

In other words, Damore said, maybe fewer women were software engineers because they didn't *want* to be software engineers, given the way the job requirements were currently constructed.

A lot of the internet got very mad at this. "No!" the internet shouted. "Women are being left out of this important job because of bias and prejudice! This is unfair!"

Damore said he'd love to see more women working in his field. But pretending that unfairness is the reason that software engineers are overwhelmingly male isn't helping bring more women in. What are we going to do, force women to do jobs they don't want? Instead, he argued that Google should make adjustments that accommodated for the differences between men and women.

Google fired Damore. And the National Labor Relations Board found that his "statements regarding biological differences between the [genders] were . . . harmful, discriminatory, and disruptive."

You, whether you're a boy or a girl, will probably be told at some point in your life, "You can be anything you want to be." And it is true that smart women were once kept out of certain jobs just because they were women—jobs they could have done just as well as the men. But our culture is so intent on showing that men and women are not different that it has forgotten to ask what men and women actually want (not to mention what God wants). It has begun to assume that unless every kind of job is filled by 50 percent men and 50 percent women, something is wrong.

Far more surgeons and machinists are men. Far more nurses and occupational therapists are women. What if the jobs in which women have the majority tell us something about what women want, and not about oppression in society? General revelation is telling us that men and women are different, and that's all right.

Even general revelation shows girls that they don't have to be good at all the things boys are good at—or like all the things boys like—in order to be equal with them.

> "FILMS THAT EXPLORED THE HEROISM OF ICU NURSES WOULD BE WONDERFUL. ICU NURSES DON'T NEED TO BE ENGAGED IN COMBAT OR TO HAVE INCREDIBLE MARTIAL ARTS SKILLS IN ORDER TO BE HEROIC."
>
> —ALASTAIR ROBERTS

You may be good at and like things very different from boys, and that's OK because you're not a boy. You may like some things boys like, and that's OK too. Follow the Bible and let God show you His place for you as a godly woman in this world. Girl heroes don't have to be exactly like boy heroes.

Proverbs 31 treats the "virtuous woman" like a hero. And she is. When a woman pushes back against all the forces of sin and builds a loving home for her family, she is a hero. Maybe today would be a good day to go home and hug *your* hero.

Thinking It Through 6.2

1. What similarities between men and women land in the category of Redemption?

2. Read Titus 2:3–5 and summarize the character qualities of the mature Christian woman.

3. How do these qualities from Titus 2 help a woman carry out the Creation Mandate?

4. What is the difference between feminism and biblical womanhood?

How do families work ?

"All happy families are alike, each unhappy family is unhappy in its own way."

These are the famous opening lines from Russian novelist Leo Tolstoy's book *Anna Karenina*. That was in the 1800s. And in the world today there are still many unhappy families.

In fact, marriage is actually dying out in some poor areas of the United States. Poverty does not always lead to family breakdown. But it is doing so now in the United States. People desperately need to know what God says about husbands and fathers and wives and mothers.

HUSBANDS: LOVING LEADERS

As you heard in Section 6.1, God gives to husbands the position of authority in the home. Paul speaks of this authority in several places; here's one for review:

> The head of every man is Christ; and the head of the woman is the man; and the head of Christ is God. (1 Corinthians 11:3)

The final decision about taxes and car purchases and church attendance and which sports the kids are involved in is the responsibility of the husband. He is the head of the family, and his wife is supposed to submit to him as if she is submitting to the Lord (Ephesians 5:22–23).

And when you aren't in charge of anything except your room and your homework, you might be tempted to want this kind of power. You might think that leadership *equals* power.

Actually, leadership looks like this: the King of Kings giving up heaven to sacrifice Himself for human sin. Jesus didn't come to be served but to serve and give (Matthew 20:28). Godly leadership looks like the one who created human feet stooping down to wash the particular feet owned by His disciples.

> Ye call me Master and Lord: and ye say well; for so I am. If I then, your Lord and Master, have washed your feet; ye also ought to wash one another's feet. (John 13:13–14)

Leadership equals service. The character Spider-Man® might not reference Jesus, but his mantra is biblical: *with great power comes great responsibility.*

It is especially important today, when many people think that a husband's authority and power are bad, to remember what else Paul said to husbands:

> Husbands, love your wives, even as Christ also loved the church, and gave himself for it. (Ephesians 5:25)

Husbands are supposed to have such deep affection for their wives that they are willing to sacrifice their time, their energy, their bodies. And, since husbands and wives are "one flesh," husbands who do this are doing good for themselves at the same time:

> He that loveth his wife loveth himself. For no man ever yet hated his own flesh; but nourisheth and cherisheth it, even as the Lord the church. (Ephesians 5:28–29)

God gave wives as partners to help their husbands. Part of a husband's leadership is to listen to his wife, understand her, and look to her for wise counsel. This is just what the apostle Peter tells husbands to do with their wives:

> Husbands, dwell with them according to knowledge [in an understanding way], giving honour unto the wife. (1 Peter 3:7)

Don't ever forget: Jesus is *in charge* of His church. What He says goes. But His leadership is never abusive. His greatest act of leadership was an act of supreme self-sacrifice. That's how husbands are supposed to love and lead their wives.

A Christian husband will not be looking for as many opportunities as possible to make things go his way. He will not sit permanently in his easy chair, ordering his wife around. He will be looking to do good for his wife. Husbands must be loving leaders.

FATHERS: LOVING LEADERS

Fathers, too, must be loving leaders, according to the Bible. Much of Proverbs reads like advice from a loving father to a beloved son. In fact, Solomon talks directly to his son:

> My son, give me thine heart, and let thine eyes observe my ways. (23:26)

A strong father-son relationship is full of love. The son trusts his father, and the father sets a good example for his son. (This is true for daughters as well, of course.) Young eyes observe a *lot* of the things fathers do, even when the fathers don't expect to be watched. A Christian father will love his heavenly Father enough to be able to say to his children, "Watch me. Do what I do."

A father's job is to raise his children, to bring them up—but in a specific way: "in the nurture and admonition of the Lord" (Ephesians 6:4). Fathers are to provide godly discipline and wise training for their children— that's what "nurture" and "admonition" mean. Ephesians 6:4 also says that fathers should avoid frustrating their kids: "Fathers, provoke not your children to wrath."

CASE STUDY: FAMILY FIDELITY

Keeping marriage vows may seem difficult—for richer, for poorer, in sickness and in health . . . till death do you part. Robertson McQuilkin found that what *seemed* like difficult sacrifices produced some of God's greatest blessings in his life. He retired at the height of his ministry to care for his wife through twenty-five years of battling the myriad "little deaths" of Alzheimer's. He fed and cleaned and dressed his wife, with little or no response from her for many of those years. Yet, he reflected with these words:

Life is simpler now,
No longer knitting these two
    lives
With threads of conversation,
But with the wordless
Assurances of love.
The motions of my soul
More deeply tender,
Hammered by the blows
Of adverse winds.
Love more pure, intense,
Emerges from the fire.

Life is simpler, now—
God's good gift
For two busy people
Who celebrate the past
And quietly wait
With hope.

1. What would your response be if you were the one who needed your spouse to sacrifice for you like Robertson McQuilkin did?

2. What might you be inclined to think if you were the one who needed to make the sacrifices?

3. In the midst of his sacrifices, what did McQuilkin discover, according to his poem?

4. How did McQuilkin see the sacrifices and the changes in life, according to the end of his poem?

Many, many fathers in the Western world are frustrating and provoking their children, simply by being gone. Many are *gone* gone: they've never even met their children, or they left the mothers when the kids were tiny. Many are just gone a lot of the time: they work jobs which require a lot of travel, or they always find some excuse to work in the garage or go to the golf course instead of being with their kids.

Many, many children yearn for their fathers' love and attention, and they don't get it. This can cause problems that last for years. Boys might look for acceptance from gangs or from work. Girls might look for it from boyfriends or from school. If you become a father, commit to raising your children the way the Bible instructs you to do it. Be a loving leader.

WIVES: SUITABLE HELPERS

A lot of people today, influenced by feminism, believe that husbands and wives are equal leaders in a marriage. But God describes marriage differently:

> It is not good that the man should be alone; I will make him an help meet for him. (Genesis 2:18)

A "help" that is "meet" for Adam just means a "helper" that "fits" him, or corresponds to him, or is suitable for him. A wife is a suitable helper for her husband. Proverbs 12:4 says this another way:

> A virtuous woman is a crown to her husband: but she that maketh [him] ashamed is as rottenness in his bones.

A godly wife brings glory to her husband; she makes him look good by helping him in countless ways (we talked about many in Section 6.2). And husbands need the help. They need support and encouragement and counsel. They need a wife in order to have a warm, loving home—and to be fruitful and multiply.

There once was a wife (true story) whose husband was embarking on the most important project of his career: working to bring justice to people who were oppressed. And he was given an opportunity to argue his case before some of the most powerful people in the land—in what he hoped would be a great speech. But his approach was wrong, and she knew it. He wanted to go blast those powerful people with all they were doing wrong. As he spilled out his grand plans to his wife, she listened. Then she offered a piece of advice: *You'll never accomplish all these good things if you go in with guns blazing like that. You have to be humble if you want to win them over to see that your way is better.*

He listened to his helper. He changed his approach. He rewrote his speech—and he ended up having a much greater effect than he would have had otherwise.

A good wife gives her husband what he lacks, whether it's wise advice or a healthy lunch. Together, a God-loving, married couple can do great things.

MOTHERS: INSTRUCTIVE LEADERS

The Bible doesn't give much direct instruction to mothers. It almost seems that most women naturally know what to do for their children. But the Fall has twisted motherhood too, and we need God to tell us what a good mother is. One way to find out is to listen to how people are supposed to treat their mothers. By doing that, we'll learn something about how mothers are supposed to act.

Repeatedly, the Bible tells us to honor our mothers—and not to shame or despise them.

- "Honour thy father and thy mother" (Exodus 20:12).
- "A foolish man despiseth his mother" (Proverbs 15:20).
- "The rod and reproof give wisdom: but a child left to himself bringeth his mother to shame" (Proverbs 29:15).

If the children's job is to honor and obey their mothers, not to despise and shame them, then what must be the mother's job? To lead and instruct and discipline.

Anyone who has seen a good mother has seen her doing all these things. Mothers, in order to keep the family going, have to lead the children in the right direction by giving all kinds of instructions. Sometimes it's "Put your socks on *right now!*" Sometimes it's more serious: "Are you being Christlike?" And sometimes every mother is forced to say, "Just wait till your father gets home."

And, of course, mothers can and should offer safety and wisdom. They help kids process their feelings: *When that boy said that mean thing about you, he was just trying to show off.* And they try to turn their children to God: *Do you know why you still feel guilty? It's because you're not trusting Jesus completely to take away your sin.*

Your mother knows more than you do. And she is most likely trying to lead you to love and serve God. Don't despise her, or you will bring her shame.

YOUR FUTURE

If a husband is a loving leader and a wife is a suitable helper, family life can be glorious and full of joy and love and laughter—and kids. This is what God created marriage to be.

Is this your future? What can you do now to make it more likely?

Thinking It Through 6.3

1. How are husbands and fathers supposed to be loving leaders?

2. How are wives supposed to be suitable helpers, and mothers supposed to be instructive leaders?

3. What are the blessings of a home where both the husband and the wife live biblically?

4. What can you do now to prepare to be the right kind of spouse and parent?

Act out your feelings.

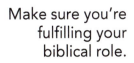

Make sure you're fulfilling your biblical role.

Blame them for your problems.

WORLDVIEW DILEMMA #23

How should I respond if Mom and Dad aren't fulfilling their biblical roles in my family

?

Discuss this with them.

Make sure you don't act like them when you grow up.

6.4 CHILDREN

What is my role in my family **?**

You are part of a family. Unless tragedy has hit your family, you have a mother and a father. You may have a brother or a sister or even several siblings.

The Bible gives you instructions about how to treat your father and mother and siblings. And if you don't already know this, one of the greatest pleasures in life is to have a loving family.

But you, by yourself, can make life miserable for your whole family. And you, working with your family, can make your home a true fortress of joy.

THE BIBLICAL RESPONSIBILITIES OF CHILDREN

You need to know from God what your role is in building such a happy life.

1. OBEYING YOUR PARENTS

There once was a college student named Lauren who wanted to spend her summer working at a Christian camp. She would be a counselor helping younger girls have a great time while learning and growing in their faith.

"No," Lauren's parents said. "We want you to stay at home this summer and work a job."

Lauren was twenty years old, and she had been living in the residence hall at her Christian college for three years. She could have said, "Mom and Dad, I don't have to obey you. I'm on my own."

But Lauren wasn't really on her own. She still had a room at home; her parents still paid for most of her needs; she was still, really, under their roof.

And Lauren was a strong Christian who believed in following her Bible. Even though Lauren was transitioning from being a child to being an adult, she wasn't completely there. So she said to her friends, who were all excited about being counselors at the camp, "I don't have to pray about God's will for my summer. I know what it is—because my parents told me what to do."

The Bible is very clear that all people of all ages must honor their fathers and their mothers. This is one of the Ten Commandments. (We'll talk about what it means to honor in a minute.)

BUT CHILDREN HAVE AN EXTRA COMMAND FROM THE LORD: OBEY.

This command is what guided Lauren. And it should be the key command guiding you as well, right up until the day when you begin to sustain yourself as an adult.

Children, obey your parents in the Lord: for this is right. Honour thy father and mother; (which is the first commandment with promise;) that it may be well with thee, and thou mayest live long on the earth. (Ephesians 6:1–3)

Parents aren't perfect. The Fall touches them too. It is possible that your parents, someday, will give you unbiblical advice. That's why you need biblical wisdom for discerning right and wrong. But unless your parents are criminals (or just non-Christians), this probably won't happen anytime soon. God's word to you is "obey."

Paul, who wrote Ephesians, echoes the same command when he wrote this to the Colossians:

Children, obey your parents in all things: for this is well pleasing unto the Lord. (Colossians 3:20)

Obey your parents—because this is right. Obey them in all things—because it pleases God. Obey your parents so that things will go well for you and so that you may live a long life. This is the reasoning of the Bible.

And the Bible observes that those who obey their parents avoid all the trouble that comes to fools. Generally speaking, the kids who obey their parents turn out to have better, happier, and even longer lives.

Lauren missed an opportunity to serve the Lord at a Christian camp that one summer. But she took the opportunity to serve the Lord in a far more important way: by obeying what He said, which was "Obey your parents."

QUICKLY, SWEETLY, AND COMPLETELY

One Christian told his kids that real obedience means three things: obeying (1) quickly, (2) sweetly, and (3) completely. Think about it: drop any one of these things, and it's not obedience.

2. HONORING YOUR PARENTS

To obey is, in one sense, a greater demand than to honor. That's because honoring your parents might not require you to obey them. Think about this situation for example: One of the closest Christian friends of the writer of this book was encouraged by his mother to try smoking marijuana in fifth grade. He obeyed, but he was doing wrong, and he knew it. Instead of obeying, the way to honor such a mother is to say, "I love you, Mom, but I cannot do what you ask because it would dishonor God."

Most of the students reading this book will never face a situation like this—having to honor without obeying. God commands you to do *both* if at all possible.

And both almost always go together. You can't obey your parents on the outside while disrespecting them on the inside: that's not really obedience. On the flip side, unless your parents offer *you* marijuana (or some other morally wrong thing), you can't honor them if you don't obey them.

Honor means "respect" or "value" or "esteem." It means to give a lot of weight to your parents' thoughts and opinions—like maybe an elephant's weight. Or a tank's. You're already old enough that your parents probably don't *only* tell you what to do. They also reason with you, counsel you, and give you ideas.

And when they do, *you should give their words weight*. Let the elephant and the tank rest heavily on your mind until they affect your thinking. Don't dismiss their words like dandelion seeds you blow into the wind. Honor your parents.

Honor starts in your heart, but soon enough the people around you will see whether you honor your parents. Or more likely, they'll hear it. They will hear whether you speak respectfully to your parents or you complain to them. They will hear whether you mock your parents behind their backs or you speak respectfully about them even when they're not around.

And God will certainly hear.

Jesus was not fooled by the Pharisees when they said, *Oh, we honor our parents! But this money that we owe them for help in their old age? Uh, we have dedicated it to God! So we can't give it to them. Sorry!*

In Matthew 15 Jesus went after this self-centered tradition the Pharisees had created to get out of honoring their parents with their money. He said, "Ye made the commandment of God of none effect by your tradition" (15:6). In other words, God commanded, "Honor your parents," and they came up with a half-clever way of emptying those words of all their power.

Honor that doesn't turn into action isn't honor. Honor your parents.

3. LOVING YOUR SIBLINGS

Not every family in the Bible is a perfect example of love between siblings—unless you're looking for perfect examples of what *not* to do.

There are basically three varieties of sinners in every family, inside the Bible and out. There are Dad sinners, Mom sinners, and kid sinners. But hopefully your family isn't as dysfunctional as Jacob's family in the Old Testament. There was one Dad sinner, four Mom sinners, twelve boy sinners, and at least one girl sinner. It was a complete mess because the sin in the family was particularly bad. Don't do what they did.

Not that Jacob had a fantastic relationship with his own parents and brother. His dad, Isaac, didn't marry multiple wives and had only two children (Jacob and Esau)—but his family became a mess too. Sin can kill family relationships, and that's what happened. Jacob cheated Esau out of his inheritance, and they became bitter and even murderous enemies. Don't do what they did.

Even Jesus' siblings thought He had gone crazy (Mark 3:21). You can see in the pages of the Bible that sin has deeply infected family relationships.

And you can see it in your life. If you have siblings, you have probably fought with them. Life with siblings is not always easy. And yet God says you owe your siblings something: love.

Biblically speaking, your sibling is your neighbor—the closest neighbor you have. A neighbor, according to the Bible, is whatever person you happen to meet as you go about your daily life. And in most families, you meet your siblings more often than anyone else in the world.

Love your neighbor as yourself. Love your sibling as yourself. Love your annoying/messy/selfish brother as much as you love yourself. Sisters too.

The Bible is triple chock-full of instructions for how you show love to others. The whole Old Testament hangs, in part, from the command to love your neighbor. Remember? But when was the last time you read any of these instructions and actually, purposefully, *obeyed* them during the lead-up to yet another fight?

Usually, fights go like this:

You: (*click*)
Sibling: Hey! I wanted to watch the Hamster Huey show!
You: That's for babies.

Sibling: MOM! He just called me a baby!
You: (*screaming*) DID NOT!
Sibling: WAAAAAAH!
Mom: GO OUTSIDE RIGHT NOW—NO MORE TV! (Or maybe your mom is a little more gentle. But Mom sinners have sometimes had it up to here, so this does happen.)

What would your family happiness level be like if you followed the basic teachings of the Bible? Don't be quick to anger (James 1:19). Don't think only of your own interests; remember that other people exist. Actually, consider them to be *more significant* than you (Philippians 2:3–4).

You: (*click*)
Sibling: Hey! I wanted to watch the Hamster Huey show!
You: Well, whose turn is it?
Sibling: It's my turn!
You: OK.
Mom: COME HERE AND GET A BIG HUG BECAUSE I AM PROUD OF YOU!

If you could get rid of one "That's not fair!" every day—and replace it with giving your sister the last popsicle—you might be shocked by what happens. Love your sibling as yourself.

A BIBLICAL WARNING TO CHILDREN

The Bible doesn't just *command*, it *warns* children to obey their parents.

The eye that mocketh at his father, and despiseth to obey his mother, the ravens of the valley shall pick it out, and the young eagles shall eat it. (Proverbs 30:17)

The warning isn't subtle. It's direct. And it's probably not talking to you—yet. It's older children, teenagers, who are usually in the most danger of ravens picking out their eyes.

Let's be clear: this verse uses a word picture. No actual ravens and eyes are involved. Honestly, the consequences of scorning your parents are *worse* than bird attacks. The Bible uses this terrible picture to show the horrendous pain that comes to people who despise their parents. It also uses the picture to get your mind imagining the worst.

Don't let this proverb be you.

LIVING LONG IN THE LAND

Instead, look for the major, serious blessings God offers to children.

> Children, obey your parents in the Lord . . . that it may be well with thee, and thou mayest live long on the earth. (Ephesians 6:1, 3)

Do you want it to be well with thee? Do you want to live long on the earth? Then purpose in your heart, relying on the grace of God, to meet your simple-to-understand responsibilities: Obey. Honor. Love.

Avoid the dangers that come from refusing your parents' commands—and their wisdom.

> My son, keep thy father's commandment, and forsake not the law of thy mother: bind them continually upon thine heart, and tie them about thy neck. . . . For the commandment is a lamp; and the law is light; and reproofs of instruction are the way of life. (Proverbs 6:20–21, 23)

Thinking It Through 6.4

1. What are the three major responsibilities of children that this section covered?

2. Suggest dangers you avoid by obeying your parents. Suggest blessings you enjoy by obeying your parents.

3. Why would fulfilling your responsibilities give you a long life?

4. Grade yourself on your current progress in fulfilling your role in your family, and explain why you gave yourself that grade.
   A: Though I'm not perfect, I really work at fulfilling my biblical role toward my parents and siblings.
   B: I want to fulfill my biblical role, but there are a few things I need to work on.
   C: I'm not great at fulfilling my family roles. It's not something I'm really working at.
   D: I mostly do what I want, though after a really big fight I might obey for a day or two.
   F: I want to do what I want, and I don't care what God says.

Why do we have to have friends ?

Girls in middle school are famous—no, infamous—for being catty. Sorry, girls in middle school. Sorry you're infamous. The capital-*D* Drama of having friends and ex-friends and former ex-friends and all that is exhausting for anybody else who is watching.

Not all girls do this, but it's painful and confusing for the many who do. Making and keeping friends is so important to a good life. Friendship is an awesome gift of God. But sometimes, because of the Fall, the gift doesn't seem like much of a gift. More of a curse, actually.

"If it be possible, as much as lieth in you, live peaceably with all men," Paul said in Romans 12:18. But sometimes it hardly seems worth the effort.

Do we *have* to have friends?

LIVING IN COMMUNITY

Yes. We were made to live in community with other people. We were designed to need one another and to give to one another. We are made in the image of a God who is one *and* three. The persons of the Trinity have always lived in community. We should too. It's not good for a person to be completely alone.

If you are alone, you can fulfill the first Great Commandment in the Bible: you can love the Lord your God with all your heart, soul, mind, and strength. But you can't fulfill the second Great Commandment: you can't love your neighbor as yourself. You were made for vertical love to God and horizontal love to other humans.

Friendship is a particular kind of horizontal love.

WHAT FRIENDSHIP IS

C. S. Lewis makes an interesting point about friendship: Friends don't stand looking at one another. They stand side-by-side looking at something else. Friendship-love is directed at objects outside the friendship. Friends unite over common loves—riding mountain bikes, painting with watercolors, reading science fiction, winning ultimate Frisbee, playing guitar, *all kinds of things.*

Lewis also makes a special point of defending same-gender friendships. It is good and right for males to sometimes prefer the company of males and for females to sometimes prefer the company of females. You already know the reason why: men and women tend to like different things.

Friendship-love between boy teammates can be quite strong as they work together to win games. The friendship-love between male soldiers in war can be extremely strong. They are focused on one common object: victory. They are also focused on the survival of their platoon. Veterans may not miss being shot at, but they regularly miss the strength of those friendships.

The friendship-love between female friends can also be extremely strong. They, too, focus on one common object. For young women, it may be common personality traits, sports, or hobbies. As they mature, they often focus on a common mission, such as raising their children.

FINDING FRIENDS

Since friends are focused on something outside the friendship, Lewis has some good advice for people who feel lonely for friends:

> People who simply "want friends" can never make any. The very condition of having Friends is that we should want something else besides Friends.

> If you didn't love mountain bikes, watercolors, guitars, or *something outside the friendship,*

> there would be nothing for the Friendship to be *about*; and Friendship must be about something, even if it were only an enthusiasm for dominoes or white mice. Those who have nothing can share nothing; those who are going nowhere can have no fellow-travellers.

If you yourself are lonely, maybe it's because you want to make a friend rather than find one the only way friends are found—by not looking for them. Instead, look for people with common interests to yours and discuss or participate in those interests with them. Your common love may develop into friendship-love.

FAITHFUL WOUNDS AND GREATER LOVE

If you do have friends, there are some things you owe them. The Bible says so.

Once, a Christian man had a long-time friend who fell far from God. We'll call them Michael and Jacob. The friendship used to be very strong; they had a common love for books, especially books about God and doctrine. Gradually, however, Jacob became different from what he used to be. Michael noticed it, and he pressed for details.

It came out that Jacob was into big trouble. He was violating the law; he was wasting his money like the prodigal son; he was ruining his life. And Michael stepped right in, even though Jacob was in another state. In Christian love he urged Jacob to repent. And when Jacob said he was too weak to turn from his sin, Michael arranged for two pastors to help him.

Proverbs 27:6 says,

Faithful are the wounds of a friend.

And it hurt for Jacob to hear the truth: his life was spiraling out of control. And yet it felt good, too, that someone loved him enough to tell him the truth in love. Jacob trusted Michael because of Michael's faithfulness over the years.

Jacob got help, and Michael was faithful to pray for him and to call him. And to call him. And to call him again. Jacob was restored, and so was his friendship with Michael.

Jesus said,

Greater love hath no man than this, that a man lay down his life for his friends. (John 15:13)

And Michael did something like this. He gave of his time, lots of it.

Not all former friends will respond as Jacob did if you lovingly warn them not to continue in sin. Some will blow you off. Many will think that their true friends are people who tell them what they want to hear. But that is not what the Bible teaches: true friends are faithful to stand in the way of friends who sin.

FRIENDSHIP FAILURES

The Bible offers some warnings about friendship. Here's one:

Make no friendship with an angry man; and with a furious man thou shalt not go; lest thou learn his ways, and get a snare to thy soul. (Proverbs 22:24–25)

God here makes a specific warning: don't make friends with someone prone to anger. But He also makes a general warning with this passage: be careful, because your friends influence you.

You can see that same general principle elsewhere in Proverbs. The very first warning in Proverbs 1 is not to fall in with a gang. Fools by themselves are bad enough; put them together in a group and they can do things that are truly terrible. Fools disregard God and follow their fallen bent to do wicked things.

And there's also this famous warning:

A companion of fools shall be destroyed. (Proverbs 13:20)

Fools can be found in all kinds of places, but there are some particular places they especially like to hang out. Bars and casinos are a good bet if you want to be a companion of fools. Many lives have been destroyed in those places.

You don't have a driver's license; the likelihood that you're going to make it to a bar or casino without being noticed is rather low. But that doesn't mean it's impossible to stumble into friendships with fools. Fools are capable of living in all climates and on all continents.

And here's the thing: if C. S. Lewis is right about what friendship is and if you find yourself a companion of fools, *the problem is with you*. The best way to avoid a friendship with fools is not to be one. If you love foolish things, you will find other people coming alongside you who love those same things.

Video games have their place (the place your parents say they should have). But there was a middle-schooler whose parents noticed he was tired all the time. They then discovered, when his conscience finally pushed him to tell them, that he'd been secretly playing video games all night, every night. He had plenty of buddies online, guys he'd chat with during the game—who themselves were staying up shooting pixels with pixels instead of getting enough sleep for school. That's foolish. This boy almost destroyed his ability to play baseball because he was so worn out during practices and games.

Beauty products also have their place (the place your parents say they should have). But there are girls who obsess so much about their appearance that they find foolish friends. They find other girls alongside of them who care only about the same thing they care about: beauty—which is something the Bible says is fleeting and vain (Proverbs 31:30). That's foolish.

Love foolish things, and you'll find friends who love those same things.

FRIENDS FOR LIFE

But love the best things (exercising your discernment), and you'll make friendships with people who help you toward wisdom.

Back to Proverbs 13:20. Yes, there's a warning: hang out with fools and you'll be destroyed. But there's another line:

He that walketh with wise men shall be wise.

Do you want wisdom? Has this book given you even a little taste of how difficult it is to get it? One of the best—and most rewarding—ways to get wisdom is to get it from godly, wise friends.

There is nothing like the joy you get when you have friends like this. To know that there are two or three friends who will always pray for you, tell you the truth, help you through conflicts, and laugh at the same jokes for years to come—it's awesome. Friendship is incredibly important for your growth in godliness and for a joyful life.

C. S. Lewis didn't just write about friendship; he was a legendary friend himself. One of life's greatest pleasures for him was to prop his feet on the fender (a low frame around a fireplace) and laugh and joke with friends. He read his Chronicles of Narnia out loud to his adult friends. Several of those friends were famous Christian writers. And one was J. R. R. Tolkien, author of *The Lord of the Rings*. Lewis wrote thousands of letters to friends and kept up with each person carefully. He invested a great deal in his friendships, and he got a great deal in return.

Thinking It Through 6.5

1. What is the most fundamental reason for having friends?

2. Name one thing you owe your friends, according to the Bible (and this section).

3. Explain the reasoning in this sentence: "If C. S. Lewis is right about what friendship is and if you find yourself a companion of fools, *the problem is with you.*"

4. What one general principle did this section draw from Proverbs 13:20?

5. What is a danger of friendship?

6. What are some blessings of godly friendship?

Be a support to them.

Love them no matter what they do.

What should I do if I have friends who choose to do wrong

?

Influence them to choose right.

Don't fight their choices and cause them stress.

The family is under attack today. It sounds silly, maybe—what's next, attacking ice cream or puppies or babies? Who really could be against the family?

But is it so strange for family to be targeted in a world in which people actually *do* attack babies—through abortion? And when you kill an unborn baby, you radically change that family. You nix that child from every future family photo.

Imagine an app that went through every photo on your mom's phone and deleted you. You no longer exist. What would your family be like?

The family is essential for a functioning society, and yet Western societies are undermining and weakening it more and more every year.

WHAT SOCIETY IS

A **society** is a web of relationships among people who depend on each other in a community. And usually when we speak of a society, we speak of a nation of people: America, Haiti, Finland, Botswana, Mongolia, South Korea. In every one of these places there are friendships, employer-employee relationships, relationships in local communities, and many other relationships. The most foundational set of relationships in every society is the family.

If you snap one little strand of a big spider web, the web remains. If you snap ten, the web remains. But at some point—at 76, maybe, or 132—the web will collapse and blow away.

So it is important to consider God's design for the family in a healthy society. Families are among the most important segments connecting us all in our big web.

Does my family matter?

COMMUNITY

FRIENDS

FAMILY

MANHOOD AND WOMANHOOD IN A FALLEN WORLD

The family began in Genesis 2. God created Adam alone, and He said this was "not good." So He made Adam a helper who fit him: Eve. Adam and Eve became a family. At the heart of every family, then, is two people: a man and a woman who are married.

Of course, God's command was for this couple to "be fruitful, and multiply." In God's design, the man and the woman at the heart of each family are at least supposed to try to have children. And that's precisely what Adam and Eve did. They quickly had sons and daughters. We know the names of three of their children: Cain, Abel, and Seth.

Because of the Fall, some children die before they can start their own families—like Abel died (at the hand of his own brother). Also because of the Fall, some married couples try to have children but cannot. But the biblical model of the family is simple: a man and a woman who marry and have children.

We've talked already about what it means to be a man and what it means to be a woman. And we've talked about some ways our culture is confused about the roles of men and women.

What this section should help you see is that this confusion amounts to an attack on the family. If nobody knows what a man is and nobody knows what a woman is, then nobody can know what a family is either—because the man and the woman are the two key members of every family.

THE CONSEQUENCES OF CONFUSION

It used to be in Western culture that men were expected to show special respect to women. Men opened doors for women; men paid for women's meals; men tipped their hats to women; men even rose from their seats when a woman entered the room. The rule was always "ladies first"—unless the situation was fighting a wild bear.

Feminism saw these traditional symbols of respect as insulting. They felt that holding the door open for a woman suggested that women aren't as strong as, or equal to, men. So a number of feminists have pushed back against these traditions. Now men and women are uncertain what's expected of them. People are confused.

And what's the result? Joseph Heath and Andrew Potter, two culture-watchers, wrote a book called *Nation of Rebels* in which they offer an answer to this question. They think many men have taken feminists' pushback "as a license [permission] to do whatever they wanted." Furthermore,

> rather than finding alternative ways of expressing concern and
> respect for women, a lot of men have simply stopped paying

any attention to the needs of women at all. For these men, equality means "I look after myself, she looks after herself."

What happens to a family when men take this warped definition of equality? Men end up looking after themselves, and women end up looking after themselves and the children too. When men fail to look after women, children end up without dads.

Births to Unmarried Mothers in 2018

- 19.2%–<26.2%
- 26.2%–<33.2%
- 33.2%–<40.2%
- 40.2%–<47.2%
- 47.2%–54.1%

This map represents both single mothers and unmarried mothers living with their partners.

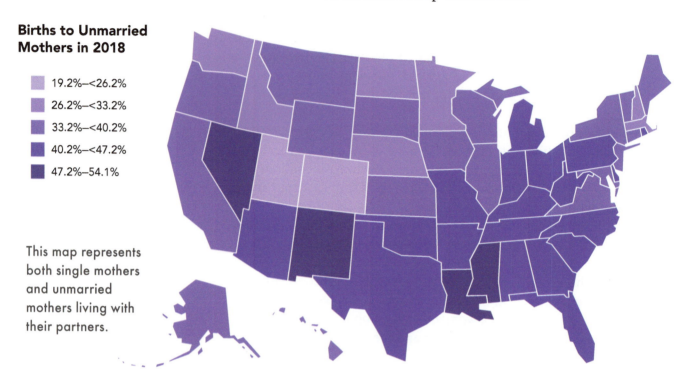

Sometimes fathers die. Sometimes fathers go into the military and are gone for long periods. Sometimes they get so terribly sick that they can no longer do most of the things dads are expected to do. But kids can understand all these circumstances.

What kids cannot understand—and should not have to understand—is a dad who leaves them. Yet this is what is happening as society moves farther and farther away from biblical gender roles.

IF YOU TREAT MEN AND WOMEN AS EQUAL IN EVERY RESPECT, YOU END UP HURTING THE FAMILY.

It is time to be alarmed. The web of society is breaking down.

WORLDVIEW QUEST: START WITH THE FAMILY

Sociologists (the people who study the relationships and changes in a society) have many different ways of describing the issues in our society—and the solutions for them. To understand the issues in society from a biblical worldview, we must start with analyzing the relationships that God created to be most important (and thus gave us the most instruction about): the family.

But the family is under attack by lots of fallen thinking. Pushing the family in a redemptive direction is one way—the biggest way—to push a society toward creational structure.

Introduction

Imagine you are volunteering for a local candidate's political campaign. He wants to understand the issues among his constituency in order to build his platform and focus the campaign. He asks for reports on the major issues the families of the district are facing. The campaign manager has tasked you and other student volunteers with putting together research on various family issues.

Task

You will develop a report detailing a specific issue among families. Then you will present it to the campaign staff and volunteers in a platform planning session.

Procedure

1. Choose one of the major issues among families to research.

2. Read articles about the issue to answer the following questions:
   a. What is the fallen thinking at the root of this issue?
   b. What are the effects of the fallen thinking on individual families?
   c. What are the effects of the fallen thinking on American society?

3. Write a report explaining the fallen thinking and the effects at the family level and the society level.

4. Present the report to your group, class, or family as you would to a campaign planning committee.

THE GRACE OF GOD IN YOUR FAMILY

You sin, your siblings sin, and your parents sin. You don't have to be fatherless to have a broken family; you might have two married parents and still live in a broken home. Sin brings brokenness. Anger, impatience, screaming, slapping, tattling, lying, stealing—these are things you may have seen in your own family. Families live together, so they see the way other family members really are.

There are many ways to deal with sin-caused brokenness in a family, but ultimately, only one works: the grace of God.

God's grace helps Christians to do good works (2 Corinthians 9:8). God's grace helps us when we have a time of need (Hebrews 4:16). If you are a Christian, these functions of grace are available to you to help you deal with the sin-caused brokenness in your family.

As you serve God and do good works by His grace, you will be an example to others in your family to allow His grace to work in them as well. If kids have no respect for parents, you be the one who starts obeying and honoring. If parents fight, you be the one to pray for them to say they're sorry. If someone hurts you, you be quick to forgive whether or not the person asks for forgiveness. If no one else wants to go to church, you set an alarm and get up and get ready—and ask for a ride from someone else if you have to.

Sin can create other kinds of broken families too—the kinds that go against God's very definition of family. Sometimes in a society, the culture responds by simply denying that it's broken. They say that a family doesn't require married parents. Or they say that there's no reason to limit a marriage to two people. Have you heard of **polygamy**?

Many TV shows imply, or even shout, that it's just fine for families to all be different—with a variety of combinations—since the family members love each other and are committed to their family.

But this isn't true. If a family isn't one husband, one wife, plus children, something is wrong. Or at least something—someone—is missing. (If a parent or even a child dies, the family is still a family. They haven't done anything wrong, but they are feeling the effects of living in a fallen world.) And broken families can't be fixed if we don't know what an *un*broken family looks like. Families do come in all sizes—depending on how many kids are in them; but the family comes in only one shape (let's see it again): one husband married to one wife, plus as many children as the Lord gives.

Human hearts are the hardest things to fix in the universe. Only the grace and power of God can fix broken families, because they are made up of human hearts. Only the sacrifice of Jesus can pay for the sins inside family members' hearts. Only the Bible's authority can correct a broken family's understanding of what a real family is.

Do you want a strong family? Look for the grace of God to fix what's broken in your current family. And shape your future family according to God's design.

POLYGAMY

Without a Bible telling us that a family includes one man and one woman together for life, people feel free to invent alternative families.

Polygamy means "having more than one spouse." This word is typically used to mean that one man is "married" to multiple women at the same time. This type of polygamy happens mostly in the developing world today.

More common in America is a kind of polygamy in which a man or woman lives with many partners outside of marriage. He or she may live with only one at a time but moves from one to another. This is not the technical definition of polygamy, but it does go against God's standard for a one-man, one-woman covenant relationship.

A STRONG WEB

What can a kid in middle school do to help society? You can protect the web of society from attack by loving your own family and helping it be strong. Do something today to strengthen the segments of the web that God gave you, the ones that connect you to your family.

The writer of this book wrote these words while sitting on the couch in his sister's home, late at night, on a sad visit. The visit was sad because that sister was in the hospital. But the writer flew across the country at a moment's notice to be with his beloved sister. That's what family does.

That little brother who annoys you so much now may, one day, cancel all his work obligations (except a few he can do while watching your toddler!) and hop on an overnight flight to come help you through a crisis. "Blood is thicker than water," people say. Family ties of love can and should be very strong. They can be a major conduit of the grace of God.

Pray to God, both now and in the future, for a strong and Christian family.

Thinking It Through 6.6

1. How does Western cultural confusion over gender roles affect the family?

2. Why do some women not want men to open the door for them or to let them go first in line at a restaurant?

3. Why are families so hard to fix when they break?

4. What can fix the brokenness that sin brings to a family?

5. What can you do to strengthen the web of society?

6.7 FRIENDSHIP AND SOCIETY

Families are important for society. They are the inner spirals of the web. Friendships are important too. They are the next spirals in the web. They aren't as central as families, but there are far more total segments.

And friendship, like the family, is under attack.

What's happening to friendship ?

THE PRESENCE OF HOMOSEXUALITY

One of the attacks on friendship in modern Western society is a sobering and difficult topic. It's a topic that you need to think about from a biblical worldview: the acceptance of homosexuality in society.

Consider this: when Abraham Lincoln was a young lawyer, he had a roommate named Joshua Speed. Speed was also his dear and close lifelong friend. And, as was common in days without electric heat, the two slept together in the same bed. They did it for four years, before Lincoln married Mary Todd.

But you can probably guess how some people in the Western world today react when they learn that the president had done this in his youth.

And consider this: to this day in Korea and in the Arab world, adult male friends commonly walk down the street holding hands or linking arms. Culture in Israel is similar: male friends use physical touch to express friendship.

But today, what would Western people do if they saw such a thing in the bread aisle at Walmart?

Everybody reading this book knows that people would snicker if they saw two boys over the age of four holding hands in public. Girls can probably get away with holding hands till they're a bit older, but the writer of this book heard those same snickers over twenty years ago when two of the sweetest, most innocent middle-school girls imaginable held hands on a hike at a Christian camp. Other girls pointed at them and laughed.

And what did they loud-whisper as they snickered? *Haha! Are they . . . gay?* The rule in American culture, at least (especially, but not only, if you are male), is that you just don't express physical affection to people of the same gender.

And why not? *Because in a society that accepts homosexuality, all same-gender friendships are under the threat of being confused with homosexuality.* This isn't completely new. C. S. Lewis was talking about the same thing in 1958 in his writing on friendship.

In Saudi Arabia, where homosexuality is absolutely forbidden by Islamic law, men can go arm in arm because there's no danger of anyone being confused. But in the West, as writer Anthony Esolen put it, homosexuals "come out of the closet, and hustle a lot of good and natural feelings back in [to it] . . . and consequently tie the tongues and chill the hearts of men, who can no longer feel what they ought, or speak what they feel."

How many men today can say what David said to his legendarily close friend Jonathan?

My brother Jonathan: very pleasant hast thou been unto me: thy love to me was wonderful, passing the love of women. (2 Samuel 1:26)

That last statement from David has gotten the modern snickerers really going. But here's the advice you should take from the friendships in the Bible: *Let them snicker—you enjoy your same-gender friendships. They are a precious gift of God.* Don't let your culture rob you of it. Girls, seek friendships with girls that are deep and lasting and rich. Boys, if you have a friend like Jonathan, be glad. You were designed to live in this kind of community.

It is *not* true to say that homosexuals can't have friends or be friends. Rosaria Butterfield, a Christian woman who used to be homosexual, has described how she learned to show hospitality and friendship from her fellow homosexual friends before her conversion. And if you have homosexual relatives or acquaintances, they by themselves are not harming your friendships.

But society's acceptance of their choices *is* harming your friendships. Homosexuality by itself can't break the web of society. But it sure can weaken it.

POLITICAL CLIQUES

Here's another threat to friendship today: political cliques. (People have a habit of siding with people who are similar to them.)

New York Times journalist David Brooks has one of the most influential jobs in the United States, and he has been working for years to unite Americans behind a shared story of what the United States is all about. He's very worried that the two major political perspectives out there will pull the country apart.

He talks about the political Right and Left, usually called "conservatives" and "liberals." Conservatives tend to see society as a fragile thing, something they wish to "conserve," or protect, by making changes slowly. Liberals tend to wish to "liberate" people, particularly those without power in society, to live the lives they want.

But now, Brooks says, the Right and Left are talking in new ways.

> The . . . right offers Tribe [a clique]. "Our" kind of people are under threat . . . . We need to erect walls, build barriers and fight.

Many people have gotten excited about telling and living out this story the Right now tells.

But the Left tells a different story:

> The left offers the idea of Social Justice. . . . The mission now is to rise up and destroy the systems of oppression.

Many people have gotten excited about telling and living out this story the Left tells.

If you ever watch or read the news, you will see that Brooks is correct. The United States used to be celebrated as a "melting pot," a place where people from all over the world were coming together as Americans. But now it's like conservatives and liberals are opposing religions, or even opposing countries. There is a great deal of hatred between them.

And friendship suffers again. When political cliques reign, people grow suspicious of everyone who doesn't agree with them. They stop talking, and that only pulls them further apart. Again, the web of society weakens.

SOCIAL MEDIA NASTYGRAMS

Hatred among cliques (not just the political ones) is especially evident in one place: social media.

Have you seen it? Have you seen people say nasty, mean, dirty things online? Things that people would never say to someone's face they say on social media—to the whole world. They scream with ALL CAPS and they curse with @#$%# words and they immediately jump to the worst possible interpretation of what someone else just said. They fight like eight-year-olds but with bigger vocabularies (or, sometimes, smaller ones).

They fill their social media feeds with hatred for whatever demonic enemies they despise, whether they are Republicans or Democrats, Cowboys fans or Patriots fans. They see no good at all in their opponents.

They lie on social media; they gossip; they spread rumors; they share fake news.

They use peer pressure on social media to get others to do and say what isn't right.

And teens and preteens use social media to tease and taunt anybody below them on the pecking order. More than one thirteen-year-old girl has committed suicide (this is absolutely true) because girls from school said such horrible, dirty, belittling things *to* her and *about* her online.

On the flip side, boys and girls (and adults too) post such perfect, airbrushed photos of themselves and their 300 percent happy lives that other people don't really get a true picture. Instead, they feel intimidated by the success, beauty, and popularity of all the "perfect" people they see on their screens. Or they feel pressured to like and do whatever everyone else likes and does. Never before in the history of the world has it been so easy to know what all the cool kids are doing.

Social media isn't all bad; a lot of it is good. It keeps some friends together who, for example, used to live near one another but now live far apart. But it also divides people, weakening or even killing friendships.

The Pew Research Center's article "Teens' Social Media Habits and Experiences" reported that these percentages of teens responded "Yes, a lot" or "Yes, a little" to these feelings about social media:

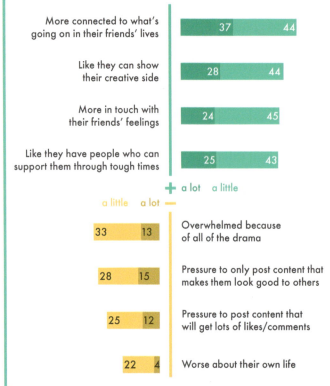

1. Do the majority of teens see social media as a good or bad thing?

2. Which listed feeling best fits with the idea that social media may divide people?

3. Which listed feeling(s) indicate(s) the negative effect on how teens view themselves?

4. Which listed feeling(s) indicate(s) the positive effect on how teens view themselves?

5. What kinds of peer pressure are evident in the listed feelings?

6. Based on the pros and cons of social media described in this section and this chart, how should you approach social media?

STRENGTHENING THE WEB

Society is created, fallen, and redeemable. In other words, God made society good; sin twists society; and one day there will be a perfect society under Christ's rule.

And one of the ways He puts it under His rule may be through *you*. Every time you, by God's grace, show love to a friend even when people laugh, you are strengthening the strands that hold society together. You are submitting one tiny part of society—one thread of the web—to Christ the King. You are overcoming evil with good (Romans 12:21).

Every time you refuse to assume what someone thinks about a controversial topic—and instead really listen to the person's explanation—you are strengthening society and honoring Christ.

Every time you use social media to build people up and give grace to them rather than tearing them down (Ephesians 4:29), you are strengthening the friendships that make for a strong society.

God's grace gives us hope that broken friendships can be mended and a broken society can be fixed—because it teaches us how to love. It teaches us to forgive by teaching us how much we have been forgiven. God's grace gives us what we need to have stable, rich, strong friendships—friendships that keep the web of society solid.

YOUR VOICE IN YOUR SOCIETY

Your voice has never been louder; technology can broadcast it to the planet in less than a second. But there have never been so many voices speaking to the planet either. And a huge number of them are saying sinful, terrible things that hurt others.

Nothing was ever *less* true than "sticks and stones may break my bones, but words can never hurt me." It's almost the opposite: hit someone with a stick, and the wound will probably heal long before they forget the mean thing you said to them.

Respond to the voices in society by strengthening your own friendships. Purpose in your heart not to speak evil of other people (James 4:11). Try to speak just one encouraging, Christian truth to a friend today. Forgive those who ask, and be extremely ready to forgive those who haven't.

Your relationships to your family, to your friends, and to the rest of your society are worth that effort.

Thinking It Through 6.7

1. How does the spider-web analogy demonstrate that friendships are important for society?

2. What negative effects have you seen social media have on friendship?

3. Have you ever seen people argue heatedly online? What did you see that was sinful in the argument?

4. When will all relationships in society—all strands of the web—ultimately be strong?

5. What is something you can do today to strengthen one key friendship?

Scripture Memory

1 Corinthians 16:13
Proverbs 31:30
Ephesians 5:22, 25
Ephesians 6:1–2
Proverbs 13:20
Joshua 24:15
Romans 12:21

Recall

1. What are two character qualities the Bible says men should have?

2. Husbands and fathers are to be what kind of leaders?

3. If children are told not to despise and shame their mothers, then a mother's job must be to lead and _____ and _____.

4. What were the three major responsibilities of children that this unit covered?

5. If your family is broken, what is the only ultimate solution?

Understand

6. What does Proverbs 31 suggest about what most women will do with their lives?

7. What does the King James Version mean when it calls Eve a "help meet" for Adam?

8. Are the consequences of scorning your parents better or worse than having a raven pick out your eyeball (Proverbs 30:17)? Explain.

9. What's the most important way you can avoid having foolish friends?

10. How does following God's design for being a family member and friend help the web of your society?

Think Critically

11. How did Jesus demonstrate biblical manhood—different from abusive, authoritarian manhood?

12. How does feminism's cry for equality seem like a good thing when it really isn't?

13. True or false: A true friend will never tell you that you are wrong. Explain with a Bible verse.

14. What are some temptations you have seen come to you or people your age through online peer pressure?

Internalize

15. What is one thing your parents or teachers have told you will make you more womanly or more manly that you know you should work on now?

16. What things will likely happen to your own children if you as their father or mother look after only yourself?

17. What if *you* are the problem in your broken friendships? What could the solution be?

HOW SHOULD I FIT INTO SOCIETY?

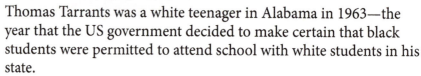

Which is more important, my community or me

Thomas Tarrants was a white teenager in Alabama in 1963—the year that the US government decided to make certain that black students were permitted to attend school with white students in his state.

He was scared by the changes around him in society. When kids in his high school told him that the white "race" was under threat from inferior people, he believed them. When they told him that the civil rights movement (efforts to make sure African Americans were given the same rights that whites enjoyed) was secretly driven by Communists, he believed them. His anger grew, and he ultimately ended up in the Mississippi branch of the White Knights of the Ku Klux Klan—a group of racist terrorists.

The KKK didn't hate just blacks; they hated Jews too. And Thomas became so radical that he actually plotted to blow up the home of a Jewish man. But before he could, he was surprised by police, who were waiting for him and his partner. Thomas' partner was killed by the gunfire, and he himself was shot. Doctors said he would die within an hour.

But he didn't.

Though Thomas can now see God's mercy in preserving his life, he didn't see God in his situation at the time. Instead, in prison, he dug deeper into his racist worldview. And then he escaped prison. When he was recaptured, yet another partner in crime was killed.

Finally Thomas ended up in solitary confinement. He read to stay sane, and eventually he read the Gospels in the Bible. He says,

> I had attended church . . . more or less regularly until my early teens, at which time I made a profession of faith and was baptized. I believed I was saved and would go to heaven when I died. Of course, the truth was just the opposite. I had only given intellectual assent to the gospel and lacked true repentance.

But Jesus' words in the Gospels opened his blind eyes. And what did he see?

> My sins came to mind, one after another. . . . I needed God's forgiveness.

Thomas confessed his sins to the one who had paid the penalty for them already. He offered his life to God. And you know what? God delivered him from his hatred. Thomas began to make friends with people in the prison whose skin color used to boil his blood.

After eight years in prison, God worked a miracle, and Thomas was allowed to get out early and go to college. He became a pastor, and then he became the president of the C. S. Lewis Institute. He wrote a book called *Consumed by Hate, Redeemed by Love: How a Violent Klansman Became a Champion of Racial Reconciliation.*

EXTREMES

Thomas was an extremist. He believed that his community—the white community within American society—was under threat. And he was willing to use violence, even murder, to protect his community. His actions, in a twisted and radical way, showed a kind of communitarian belief. Taking **communitarianism** to the extreme like this causes people's priorities to get unbalanced. People make the interests and unity of the community more important than the individual's interests and independence.

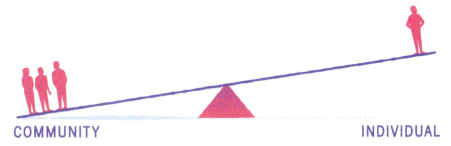

COMMUNITY   INDIVIDUAL

There are other less violent ways that people give their community too much importance. We'll look at some examples in a bit. But just take note of what Jesus said:

If any man come to me, and hate not his father, and mother, and wife, and children, and brethren, and sisters, yea, and his own life also, he cannot be my disciple. (Luke 14:26)

Your community is important, but it is not all-important. You have to be willing to "hate" even your family in order to have Christ. In other words, your love for Him is supposed to be far greater than all other loves.

But notice what else Jesus included in the list of things you must hate (compared to your love for Him). He mentioned hating your "own life also."

The other extreme is individualism: prioritizing love for your own life. **Individualism** means making the individual's interests and independence more important than the community's interests and unity. This belief is the opposite of what Thomas believed. But it's just as serious a sin.

COMMUNITY   INDIVIDUAL

American society was founded with some effort to balance the good of the nation and the freedom of the individual. But throughout its history it has leaned toward empowering and freeing the individual. Currently, the extreme in American culture is more than obvious.

Three Supreme Court justices actually said this:

> At the heart of liberty is the right to define one's own concept of existence, of meaning, of the universe, and of the mystery of human life.

To make matters worse, the justices were saying this in *Planned Parenthood v. Casey*, a case protecting women who get abortions.

That is the extreme of individualism—a society in which everybody gets to define his or her own reality, even to the point of killing unborn babies. (Though in order to do that, people have to deny that babies are individuals.)

The simple point of this section is that the individual matters, and the community matters. *But each one must be put under Christ, or else one will dominate the other.* We need to consider the individual and the community through the lenses of Creation, Fall, Redemption (CFR).

CFR: THE INDIVIDUAL

The individual matters. The individual is incredibly important—because each individual is made in the image of an infinitely important God.

The truth Thomas didn't want to accept when he was a racist was that people of all skin colors are (1) **created** in God's image—no group of people have a little more of the image than others. All are created equal in worth.

Another truth that racists have trouble accepting is that people of all skin colors, including their own, are (2) twisted by the **Fall**. And that means people of all skin colors and every ethnicity have to give an account to God of their actions.

This point from the Bible is, in fact, one way we know that the individual is important. Romans 14:12 says that "every one of us shall give account of himself to God."

And this, in turn, means that you cannot come to Christ for forgiveness as part of your family or community. You have to come alone. No one is born already a Christian. As it is said, God has no grandchildren—only children.

Many, many people don't realize these biblical facts about the individual. They think that if they were baptized as babies or if "Christian" is the box they check on paperwork or if they attended every single week of Sunday school, they're Christians.

But in order to be (3) **redeemed**, the Bible requires you to have an experience similar to Thomas's. You have to go to solitary and meet God. You have to see yourself, as an individual, as guilty of sin against Him. You must turn from your own individual sins. You must believe personally that Jesus died to take the punishment for your sins. You must believe that Jesus rose again to make it possible for God to justify you, to declare you "not guilty" in His heavenly courtroom.

And when you die, you will go alone to that courtroom. You will stand alone—unless you are in Christ. Then He will stand with you.

And here we turn to a wonderful combination of truths:

A PERSON MUST COME TO CHRIST AS AN INDIVIDUAL, BUT THOSE WHO COME TO CHRIST BECOME COLLECTIVELY THE BODY OF CHRIST.

When a person is saved, he is brought into a specific community. Yes, God saves only individuals, but His purpose is to create "a people for his name" (Acts 15:14). In other words, the church.

You're not supposed to go it alone in the Christian faith. Jesus taught us to pray, "Our Father . . . ," not "My Father . . . ." The church should always be an essential part of your life as a Christian. We'll talk more about this in Section 7.2.

CFR: THE COMMUNITY

So the community also matters. The community is incredibly important—because God has made it an essential part of life, both now and in eternity.

We've already talked in previous units about the most important little community in your life: your family. The church, too, is a massively important community you should join by trusting Christ.

And think of some of the other communities you're in. A neighborhood, a town or a city, a region, a nation—you're probably part of all of these, and more.

All of these kinds of communities are C, F, and R. They were (1) **created** good by God. They have been (2) twisted by the **Fall.** They will be (3) **redeemed** when submitted to Christ at His Second Coming (Ephesians 1:10). So you can neither ignore them nor give them too much power over you.

If you ignore the communities you're in, you are not doing your part to strengthen and help them. You are not loving the neighbors God has given you. A neighborhood where no kids go out to play with other kids because they're all inside playing video games and where no adults talk to other adults because they're all looking at screens too—that's not much of a neighborhood. That's just a collection of individualistic individuals who happen to live near one another.

On the flip side, a community can gain so much power that its members cease to have the freedom to act as individuals. Some Asian societies put extreme pressure on the young people to uphold traditions and to honor their elders. As a result, converting to Christianity is very difficult because rejecting their traditional

religion would dishonor their elders. Some religious communities we call "cults" have similar power. They instruct their members not only about what to wear and eat, but about every detail of what they are supposed to think.

There is also the powerful community sin called "peer pressure." Suddenly every person in the little community of friends has to like Pokémon® playing cards. Or has to watch a certain movie or buy a certain style of shoes. Or swear like a sailor or talk negatively about their parents! Peer pressure is an evidence of fallen community.

Seeing community through the lenses of CFR will give you a care for those around you (Matthew 22:39). And it will motivate you to push community in a redemptive direction (Matthew 5:16).

GETTING OFF THE SEESAW

So, which *is* more important, you or your community?

You're right—they're both important, and they both have an appropriate place in life.

Here are some questions to think about in your fight against extreme communitarianism and individualism. Are you focused on helping others? Do you participate in group activities for the good of the group or to advance yourself as an individual? Are you taking seriously your individual relationship with God? Are you preparing for the day when you'll stand before God without any community to help you?

Know the biblical balance between individual and community.

COMMUNITY   INDIVIDUAL

Thinking It Through 7.1

1. What is communitarianism like when it's taken to the extreme?

2. What is individualism?

3. What are two experiences described in the Bible that demonstrate that every individual is important?

4. What are two biblical reasons, given in this section, that you should participate in community?

7.2 CHURCH: THE CHRISTIAN COMMUNITY

Gooooooooooooal!

Soccer fans everywhere are electrified by that call over the loud-speaker. Soccer (or football, as it is known in most of the world) is such a popular sport that it has its own communities all over the world. Groups of people get together to talk about soccer, learn about soccer, promote soccer, and just enjoy the game.

There are teams at all levels all over the world—from the group of neighborhood kids who play against the rival neighborhood to the top national teams competing in the FIFA World Cup. Parents drive kids to practices and games. Schools take teams to compete with other schools. Fans insist their team is the best in the whole world.

People come together because of their common interest in soccer. There are school teams, recreational leagues, professional clubs, and national teams. Soccer has local communities, in which teams meet to practice and play games. But it's also a universal community. When the World Cup comes around every four years, everybody who's any kind of soccer fan is cheering on his team against everybody else's team.

Much like local soccer communities, local communities of believers also enjoy getting together (in what we usually think of as *church*). Together, they worship God, pray, learn about Christ from God's Word, and receive encouragement in their Christian walk.

And as the international soccer community is centered on, well, soccer—the church is a community centered on Jesus Christ. Joining the worldwide church happens only when someone repents of his or her sin and turns to Christ as Savior. If you think back to Unit 2, you might remember the church being described as the citizens of Christ's kingdom. They are those whom Christ the King rules. In this section, you will see other word pictures for this community belonging to Christ.

What's my community if I'm a Christian?

UNDERSTANDING THE CHURCH

The members of the church accept the gospel of Christ: He died for our sins, was buried, and rose again.

Countless people throughout the world accept and love the gospel. Just as there are former Klansmen in Alabama who accept the biblical gospel, there are former Muslims in Syria who accept it. There are former Hindus in India who accept it. There are former atheistic secularists in New York City who accept it.

Add together all the people who accept the gospel, and you get "the church." Or you get one *sense* of the word. There are two major senses:

1. The **universal church** is the collection of people throughout time since Pentecost who have believed the gospel of Christ.

2. A **local church** is a group of such believers who meet weekly to devote themselves "in the apostles' doctrine and fellowship, and in breaking of bread, and in prayers" (Acts 2:42).

Let's talk through each of these definitions.

1. UNIVERSAL CHURCH

The universal church began at Pentecost, when the Holy Spirit came and baptized the disciples into the body of Christ (Acts 1:8; 2:1–4). Jesus spoke of this community when He said,

> I will build my church; and the gates of hell shall not prevail against it. (Matthew 16:18)

Throughout time, Christ has indeed been building His church. He's doing it right now, while you read this book.

One helpful way to understand this church is through the word pictures the Bible uses to describe it.

- **Body of Christ**: Remember this one from Section 4.5? Christ is the Head (Colossians 1:18). Christians are the "members," the different parts of the body (1 Corinthians 12:12–31). Some are hands, doing practical work. Some are feet, taking the gospel to the nations. Some are eyes, looking out at the current situation and interpreting it for others.
- **Temple of God**: All the Christians in the church are like stones that God is assembling together into a temple for Him to live in (1 Peter 2:5). Christians don't go to a temple like the Jews did before Christ. We are now the temple—God lives *in us* (2 Corinthians 6:16).
- **Royal priesthood**: The church acts like priests for the Great King. They communicate His will and His presence to the nations (1 Peter 2:9).

- **God's flock:** At least since David wrote Psalm 23, believers in the one true God have been compared to sheep. It's not always a flattering comparison. Sheep are kind of dumb. They easily go astray (Isaiah 53:6). The focus of this picture is how helpless we are without our Shepherd. And that Shepherd has given the church "undershepherds": pastors (1 Peter 5:1–4). (The English word *pastor* comes from the Latin word for "shepherd.")
- **Bride of Christ**: The church is the bride and Jesus is called the bridegroom (John 3:29). He loved, and sacrificed His life for, the church as a model of how a husband is to love his wife (Ephesians 5:25, 32). At Christ's Second Coming, there will be a marriage supper for the bride (the church) and the Lamb (Christ) (Revelation 19:6–9).
- **People of God:** The ultimate promise of God is, *I will be your God, and you will be my people.* Second Corinthians 6:16 applies to the church this Old Testament promise from Leviticus 26:12 and Ezekiel 37:27. Add together all Jews and Gentiles who believe in the one true God, and you get the "people of God."

The church is an essential part of the plan of God to form a people for His name. Repent and believe the gospel, and you'll be a member of the universal church.

2. LOCAL CHURCH

But you can't stop at the universal church. The New Testament also speaks many times of particular *local* churches. When Paul wrote to the Romans, he greeted his friends Priscilla and Aquila—and "the church that is in their house" (Romans 16:5). The whole body of Christ around the planet could not have met inside one house. Paul is speaking here, as the New Testament does many times, of one local church.

Some people think that as long as they are members of the church in the global, universal sense, they don't have to be members of the church in the local sense. But you should be a member of the church in both senses. Otherwise you will miss out on one of the most important communities God gives you for your spiritual growth.

A local church will also have leadership (overseers, pastors, elders, deacons—see Titus 1:5 and Acts 6:1–6). Any random group of Christians is not a "church." Not until they do what churches are supposed to do and have the leadership that churches are supposed to have.

THE MISSION OF THE CHURCH

Once people in the church are rescued from sin, they are safe from the wrath of God. Jesus bore it for them.

BUT THEY CANNOT AND SHOULD NOT REST. THEY HAVE WORK TO DO.

They have to get the message of salvation to other people. Other people need to come into the church, the body of Christ. And the members of the body need to be active building each other up.

Christ told His disciples to make more disciples in what we call the **Great Commission**. To "commission" people is to sign them up for a special mission, to give them authority to take a special message. Here's what Jesus said:

> All power is given unto me in heaven and in earth. Go ye therefore, and teach all nations, baptizing them in the name of the Father, and of the Son, and of the Holy Ghost: teaching them to observe all things whatsoever I have commanded you: and, lo, I am with you alway, even unto the end of the world. (Matthew 28:18–20)

The mission of the church (both universal and local) is to make disciples by sharing the gospel, baptizing those who repent and believe, and teaching believers all of what Christ commanded. In addition, faithful churches will engage in all the things listed in Acts 2:42, things the earliest Christians did in church:

> And they continued stedfastly in the apostles' doctrine and fellowship, and in breaking of bread, and in prayers.

They will seek out *the apostles' teaching*—the faithful teaching of the Bible, along with singing about this truth (Colossians 3:16). They will want *fellowship*—the friendship and love that Christians are supposed to give and receive. They will practice *breaking bread* on a regular basis, which means participating in the Lord's Supper (communion). And they will engage together in *prayer*. All these centuries later, this is still what faithful churches do.

Some believers from the local church will respond to the need to go out and start more local churches where there are none. God's will is that the universal church be full of people who worship Him. Jesus said,

> The true worshippers shall worship the Father in spirit and in truth: for the Father seeketh such to worship him. (John 4:23)

And Christians join the Father in this seeking by doing what Jesus did: preaching the gospel. This is something you can do. You don't have to reach a certain age to do it. You don't have to be a Bible expert. You just have to be faithful to your Head.

PERMITTING THE LITTLE CHILDREN

Jesus allows even little children to come to Him (Mark 10:14). You aren't little anymore. You can come.

Are you part of the *universal* church? Are you part of a *local* church? The church is the most important and precious community you could ever become part of.

Thinking It Through 7.2

1. What is the difference between the universal church and a local church?

2. Who is included in the bride of Christ?

3. What are the two main places in Scripture where we find the details of the church's mission? Describe the mission.

You can watch a service on TV and still be with God.

It's better to spend time with your family since God is with you anyway.

WORLDVIEW DILEMMA #19

If God is everywhere, do I have to go to church

?

No, you can worship God better in nature.

You need other believers to help you grow in Christ.

How do I participate in the body of Christ ?

Have you ever worked out?

People know that exercise is good for their health. They also know how difficult it is to consistently do the hard work it takes to get a solid workout. Getting out of bed or up from watching TV to be active until you break a good sweat takes some real motivation.

One thing that can really help your consistency is finding workout partners. Partners can remind you that it's time to work out and you're supposed to be there. They can push you to work harder. They can be good competition to push you to do more than you might on your own.

Living the Christian life consistently is also a struggle. The world is against you if you're a believer, and your flesh is against you—kind of like the couch and the bed fighting against your workout. *You need help.* You need workout partners in the Christian life: people who can remind you what you're supposed to be doing, push you to work harder, and be good "competition" to encourage you to love God and others more than you would otherwise.

The church is the community that partners with you in this way. A local church family is made up of people who will ask how you are doing spiritually. They will check up on how motivated you are to pray and to study your Bible. They will point out areas where you have a bad attitude or where you're slipping into sin. They help you live like you're *in Christ*.

The writer of Hebrews said it this way:

> Let us hold fast the profession of our faith without wavering; (for he is faithful that promised;) and let us consider one another to provoke unto love and to good works: not forsaking the assembling of ourselves together, as the manner of some is; but exhorting one another: and so much the more, as ye see the day approaching. (10:23–25)

Let's break down this important passage. Working to hold fast the profession of our faith, the declaration of our confident hope in the gospel, is the struggle of the Christian life. God says here that believers are to think about each other "to provoke unto love and to good works." That's that good pressure from your fellow church members, who are seeking to obey the commands of the gospel.

Provoke means "to stir up to action by a challenge, to irritate." You may have heard your parent or teacher correct someone for provoking someone else. In other words, someone irritated someone into doing something—usually getting angry and acting in a way that gets them into trouble.

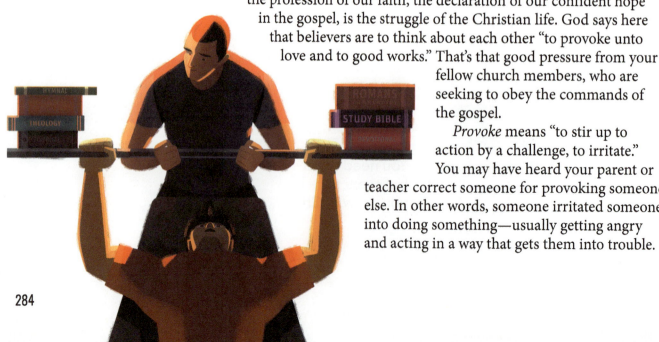

God wants believers to "irritate" other believers into doing something *good*: loving God and their neighbors better. This is the kind of provoking you ought to do.

The writer of Hebrews also encouraged believers not to neglect to assemble together. That's what a church service is—the church assembling, getting together. They exhort each other, which includes both comforting and encouraging each other.

The local church acts this way because their eyes are fixed on a promised future event. "The day approaching" for all believers is the day they stand at the Judgment Seat of Christ to receive the reward for their lives. Believers are supposed to encourage each other to keep following Christ so that they can finish well when the day of judgment comes.

Notice that God gives verses 23 through 25 as commands. There are a lot of jobs at your local church that different people do and that might be above your ability to do yet, but the basic job at church is one you *can* do. You can provoke others to love God and their neighbors better. You can exhort those who are struggling in their Christian lives. If you're a believer, you need the church and the church needs you.

Church, assemble!

CHURCH MEMBERSHIP

The way it formally assembles is through church membership. At least by the time you're an adult, you should be a church member—an official, recognized part of your local church. Your name should go on a list that other people in the church see and know.

But why?

Think of what Jesus said in Matthew 18. He said that if a brother (a fellow Christian in God's family, whether male or female) sins against you, you should go to that person and encourage him to repent (18:15). And if he doesn't listen, take one or two more people with you to help. If he still doesn't listen, Jesus said, "Tell it unto the church" (18:17). And if he doesn't listen to the church, he's supposed to be treated as an outcast. Jesus takes sin very seriously.

Here's where church membership comes in: you can't be cast out of something you were never in. And the only way to know whether someone is in or out is to have a list that people ask to be on: a membership.

People do get kicked out of churches, and even though it doesn't sound fun, it's something you should want to be possible. If you ever fall into sin, you should want people to lovingly put pressure on you to repent and obey God. You should want to be "kickoutable." And if you are sinned against, if someone isn't living like a Christian, you should want him or her to be kickoutable.

This is **church discipline**. It's the way the church puts its strongest pressure on sinners. It tells them, "We cannot consider you to be a Christian unless you repent." The goal is that the believer will sober up, take his or her sin seriously, and eventually be restored to the church.

WHAT TO LOOK FOR WHEN YOU GO TO CHURCH

Think what a church gives you: perhaps the only place on earth where you can basically trust that you will be told the hardest truths about yourself, even when you don't want to hear them. And, if someone else who claims to be a Christian sins against you, the church will tell that person hard truths about himself too.

And that's what you should be looking for when, someday, you search for a church on your own, without your parents. When you go to college or when you go out on your own for the first time, it may be up to you to choose a church. You should look for a place where they're doing what the church is supposed to do.

Remember Acts 2:42?

And they continued stedfastly in the apostles' doctrine and fellowship, and in breaking of bread, and in prayers.

1 A good church will follow the apostles' doctrine: the Bible will be central to what they're doing. Not music (though it's a good thing!), not entertainment, not the personality of the preacher; the Bible. You should come away from a sermon feeling like you just had a good meal, and what you ate was Bible.

2 A good church will have fellowship, protected by the possibility of church discipline. Only believers who show the fruit of the Spirit will truly be able to provoke others to good works. A good church will be full of people who, though certainly not perfect, strive to love their neighbors as they love themselves. They look out for one another and pray for one another. They invite each other over.

3 A good church will break bread: they will celebrate the Lord's Supper on a regular basis until Christ returns. Christ gave this practice to us as a way of helping us remember His sacrifice for our sins.

4 A good church will pray. Many churches have a prayer meeting or small-group Bible study sometime in the middle of the week. One of the major purposes of a midweek meeting is to give an opportunity for the members to learn each other's needs and pray for those needs.

WAYS YOU CAN PARTICIPATE IN CHURCH

How do *you* fit into the body of Christ?

Most churches do not permit preteens to join the official membership, because membership means voting on financial matters and other sensitive things that are mainly for adults.

But that shouldn't stop you from "owning" your local church. There are still plenty of ways for you to participate.

You can be a friend to the friendless.

You can be the one kid in Sunday school who never talks out of turn; that means a lot to teachers, actually.

You can sing in whatever choir will take you.

You can hang door hangers in a neighborhood.

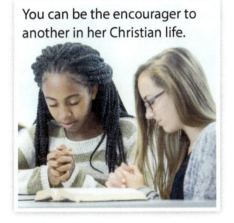

You can be the encourager to another in her Christian life.

You can help your parents at an evangelistic Bible club.

You can clean: pick up communion cups, vacuum, gather lost and found items.

You can help in the sound booth and learn some cool tech stuff in the process.

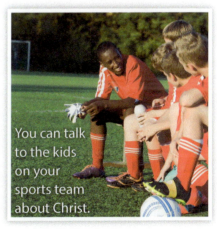

You can talk to the kids on your sports team about Christ.

And have you ever just asked a pastor or deacon, "What can I do to help?"

You can also do something that only a few middle-schoolers do: you can tell the pastor, with your face, that you are listening to and interested in God's Word as he preaches it. You can take notes on what you hear. Try to get the main points down, plus a few quotations. Preachers can tell a lot by looking at the faces in the congregation. What does yours say?

SOMEDAY THE CHURCH MAY BE YOUR MOST IMPORTANT SUPPORT IN A TIME OF TRIAL.

It will be a major source of comfort in a time of sorrow. It will be a place of wise counsel in a time of difficulty. What you get out of it then will probably have a lot to do with what you start putting into it now.

Thinking It Through 7.3

1. How exactly does the existence of church discipline imply the necessity of church membership?

2. Write out the verse that describes what you are supposed to be looking for when you look for a church.

3. What are some ways you are currently participating in your local church?

4. What are some ways you *could* participate in your local church?

We've been talking about all kinds of communities that you are or could be a part of. You *are* part of a family; you *could be* a member of a church. You *are* a citizen of a nation; you *could be* a resident of a town.

Well, you probably are a resident of a town. The number of students reading this book who live on deserted islands or in mountain caves is probably fairly low. And even they have to go to Walmart at some point. No human can survive without Walmart, as is well known.

So what is your town like? How big is it? Do you like it? Do most people who live there feel proud to live there, or embarrassed?

Do you have a beautiful view of the mountains? Or a river running by the town? Do you have any beaches? Some landmarks, some interesting buildings or parks?

Do you have any good sports teams, or do your teams always lose? How do people in your town talk? Is it different from the way people in other regions talk?

Unless you move around a lot, you probably feel like you're *from* somewhere. When someone asks you, "Where are you from?" you know what to say—and you can say more than just the name. Your hometown has an identity.

How does my local community work ?

THE BIBLE AND YOUR NEIGHBOR

What does all this talk about your hometown have to do with the Bible? Two things.

First, *you are called to love your neighbor as yourself.* That's the second Great Commandment. And who is your neighbor? Jesus was asked that question one time, and He answered with the famous story of the Good Samaritan (Luke 10:25–37). Your neighbor is whoever runs into you and needs you.

And, statistically speaking, the people who need you—and who are likely to run into you—probably live in your town. You have literal neighbors, people who live next door. And you have other "neighbors" in your town who need you too.

They need you to hold up your end of the bargain that makes for a good town. Simple things: Throwing trash in the trashcan instead of on random places on the ground. Mowing your lawn. Paying your taxes (well, your parents do that). Taking your library books back on time, in good condition.

If everybody stopped doing all these things, your town wouldn't be much of a town. More like a trash heap with people inside. In the next section we'll talk about more ways for you to give back to your community.

Second, *towns and cities aren't accidents in the plan of God.* Even if Adam and Eve had never fallen, people who were living out the Creation Mandate would have formed towns and cities.

Be fruitful and multiply and fill the earth, God said. *Subdue it and have dominion over it*, He said. And any large group who tries to do these things is going to find out that cities are required.

Yes, in the Bible you read about wicked cities like Nineveh and Babylon. But cities are not evil. The whole story of the Bible moves from a garden to a city—from the Garden of Eden in Genesis to the new Jerusalem in Revelation.

Cities are required because government, education, business, medicine, the arts, and other parts of human culture do more subduing and having dominion when all the people who interact with culture can collect their resources together.

COMMUNITY ORGANIZATIONS

A good town or city has many organizations. In other words, your community isn't just (1) government and (2) people. There are organizations *between* the government and the people. Some work alongside local government, and others are run very separately.

What would your town's identity be without the following organizations?

Without *churches*, none of the things you learned about in the last section would happen and living out the Christian life within your local community would be more difficult than it already is—nobody would be around to provoke you to love and good works!

Without *hospitals*, boy . . . let's just try not to imagine that.

Without *schools*, well, don't silently cheer for no schools. Come on, you know you need school. Without schools, a community has little hope of continuing to subdue and have dominion. It will go backward instead of forward. Fulfilling the Creation Mandate requires engineers and artists and environmental scientists and many other highly trained people. Towns in which no one can read (such as in poverty-stricken places in Haiti) are not enjoying the countless good gifts of God that come through education.

Businesses make it possible for goods (like potatoes and cars and guitars) and services (like restaurants and auto repair shops and music lessons) to move as quickly and cheaply as possible to the people who need them. When a government takes over businesses, as the Soviet Union did in the twentieth century, grocery stores end up running out of bread (and everything else).

Sports teams give people in your town the opportunity to enjoy God's great gift of refining their bodies, to push their bodies to do what they didn't know was possible. You may know the joy that comes from just running as fast as you can. And surely you know the joy of working hard with others on a team to *win*. These joys are a great gift of God, and they bring real benefits to a community. "The glory of young men is their strength" (Proverbs 20:29), and the whole community can enjoy watching them display that glory together.

Arts organizations such as ballet studios, arts councils, choirs, theaters, and symphonies bring something incredibly rich to a community too. The arts are something only humans have. Animals don't paint, and if you've ever heard cats sing, you'll know that cats actually *don't* sing. (Certain animals, such as birds of paradise, do dance—but they can't do it on purpose for creative reasons; it's just instinct.) The arts are humans at their most human. The arts are humans showing what it's like to be made in the image of a God who creates. The arts make for a community worth living in.

Libraries were built on the realization that once someone has read a book, others can profit from it too. It's hard to share houses, but it's easy to share books. A community with a library is offering resources to everyone who cares to read and learn. And when they do, the whole community benefits.

Services for the needy, *senior centers*, *fire departments*—the list of helpful organizations goes on and on. A community without organizations is an ugly and barren one. A community with them is a good gift of God, who blessed the world with the Creation Mandate for this very purpose.

CASE STUDY: THRIVING WITH COMMUNITY-BASED ORGANIZATIONS

People who study communities realize the necessity of various organizations for a community to thrive. A recent study looked at organizations that provide human services like these: healthcare, education, safety, crime prevention, and financial help. These services specifically help people through difficult times so that they can sustain themselves again.

The leaders of the study asked people to make an extra effort to strengthen human services. They thanked community-based organizations for the effort they are already making. Local organizations in America are what make the broad field of human services possible, and their "importance . . . is indisputable"—in other words, no one denies their importance.

The leaders of the study also said that 20 percent of Americans use human services. They emphasized the economic value these organizations have in their communities. Finally, they encouraged these organizations to continue working hard and being wise. Organizations can prevent even greater difficulties in their communities and help people learn to avoid difficulties in the first place. People are best served by prevention and education.

1. Why would community-based organizations be *indisputably* important to a community?

2. How would community-based organizations be vital to the economy of a community?

3. How are community-based organizations able to prevent further problems in the field of human services?

4. Where do community-based organizations fit in with the local government and the individuals of a community?

HEALTHY COMMUNITIES

Remember that society is like a web. Sever one segment within the web, and the web remains—until enough other segments have been severed, and the web collapses.

The government is like one of the largest, outermost spirals of a web. Without government ensuring justice, the web of society falls apart. This has happened in places like Somalia, and it's truly terrible. Terrible as in people in terror, people dying everywhere from hunger and endless fighting.

But the other spirals in the web of society are also important. Families and friendships, like we talked about in the last unit, are some of those spirals. They are at the center of the web. But out beyond that center are the kinds of community-based organizations that form in a healthy town or city. People in these organizations band together to do good, independently of the government.

Another true example: a mother of two small children suddenly had to go to the hospital for several days. A neighbor gathered thirty other neighbors to bring meals and provide babysitting. A neighborhood community is a very valuable thing to have when you are in need. And it's enriching to *give* to your neighborhood community too. Jesus said it's better to give than to receive (Acts 20:35).

Other independent community organizations might band together to build a park or to keep it clean. When you were a tiny kid, you probably toddled around the playground and fell flat on your face in the mulch in front of a plaque that said, "This park was built by Joseph and Loretta Somebody." And you, because you could not read (and because your face was in mulch) never gave the playground's origins a second thought. You totally took the slides and swings for granted. But at one time that playground was an untouched forest. Later it was part of a farmer's field. Somebody—a bunch of somebodies—had to get money and labor together to build that playground. If government leaders were involved, they probably didn't do it by themselves. They probably worked with independent community organizations.

Somebody had to start basketball and soccer and baseball leagues. They weren't given at Creation. Columbus did not discover them already functioning when he discovered America.

Try not taking things for granted for one week. Every time you go somewhere, see whether you can figure out how that somewhere got there, and when. You have inherited the benefits of sacrificial labor from many people who are now dead. Maybe your next class presentation can tell the story of how some of those long-gone people gave your town something it values.

A town is more than just the collection of people who live there—it also inherits countless things from people who died there. Your town has a character that goes back into the past before you were born and that may move forward into the future after you leave. And that character has a lot to do with how much people have given to their communities through independent community organizations.

If you love your neighborhood as yourself, you will give back to it. And that's what we'll talk about next.

Thinking It Through 7.4

1. List three organizations in your town from which you benefit. Give their specific names.

2. Take one of those organizations and explain how it has met needs in your family.

3. Take one of those organizations and speculate about what your community would be like if it did not exist.

7.5 GIVING BACK TO YOUR COMMUNITY

How do I participate in my local community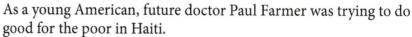

As a young American, future doctor Paul Farmer was trying to do good for the poor in Haiti.

One day he was assisting doctors in a rural clinic, and a pregnant woman was brought in. She had malaria—and five children. Things turned bad for her, dangerous. She went into a coma. The doctors said she needed a blood transfusion. But she would have to pay for it first: fifteen dollars.

She had no money. Her sister, who was with her, had no money. Paul ran around the clinic asking for donations. He rounded up fifteen dollars from other clinic workers, and the sister ran off to the city to get the blood. But then her money ran out. She couldn't afford a ride to get back to the clinic.

Her sister died, and so did the unborn baby.

The woman who had tried to save her sister just kept repeating to herself, "We're all human beings." In other words, *My sister and her baby just died because we lacked about twenty bucks. Something isn't right here.*

Farmer agreed. And he has spent the rest of his life trying to make it right for his patients. He makes every person who comes into his presence feel his focused attention—as if other people's needs don't matter right then. Here's his attitude: he knows all people in society can't be his "neighbor." Haiti—not to mention the rest of the world—is full of too much poverty and pain for him to fix. So he's just going to keep loving the people who actually come to his attention, his neighbors in his adopted community.

How are community organizations part of the Creation Mandate and the Great Commission? Many, if not most, community organizations are designed to subdue the earth and have dominion. They help to meet people's basic needs. They also have opportunity to share the gospel with those with whom they work.

Here's an example: There is an independent community organization that helps its neighbors with bicycle transportation. It has a bike shop where volunteers repair bikes for reasonable prices, give free expert advice while people repair their own bikes, and sell repaired bikes that have been donated. It offers an earn-a-bike program in exchange for community service hours. It teaches character building and bicycle repair to local kids in a six-week hands-on course. And once a month, volunteers go out into the community to do free bike-repair workshops.

1. By obeying the Creation Mandate, this organization is meeting what basic human need?

2. List the groups of people whom volunteers could make disciples of.

3. What opportunities might arise for volunteers to share the gospel?

4. List some community organizations where you could get involved to obey the Creation Mandate and the Great Commission.

BACK TO THE BASICS

Let's tie together a few major concepts, in case it's been a while since you thought about Unit 5. God first gave humans the Creation Mandate—two commands that told us to get to work but give us rich blessing when we obey. Our hard work also blesses our neighbors physically, which is the reason why obeying the Creation Mandate is one way to love your neighbors as yourself.

But later Jesus gave His church the Great Commission, a different kind of mandate—a spiritual one. We talked about this mission in Section 7.2. If you're a Christian, loving your neighbors also means caring about whether they're disciples of Jesus.

So, there are two major ways you can love your neighbors: (1) you can help their physical needs, and (2) you can help their spiritual needs. *You are called to do both.*

1. HELPING YOUR NEIGHBORS' PHYSICAL NEEDS

What you do for your neighbors' physical needs may not be as dramatic as what Paul Farmer did, but it is still a piece of God's love to your community. It will extend the blessings of the Creation Mandate to more people. You were created for this (Genesis 1:26–28).

Paul says very clearly to Titus that Christian people should give themselves to cases of urgent needs (Titus 3:14). Your neighbors are everywhere in your town, and they need your loving good works.

What can you do to love your neighbors through these organizations from the last section? And this isn't the whole list. Fulfill the Creation Mandate with the time and talent God has given *you*.

Churches: We've already talked about ways you can volunteer in your church. If you haven't yet, talk to your parents and your pastor about your options.

Sports teams: Sports are a good gift of God (as long as they don't interfere with church gatherings or important family matters). Take the gift while you can: form some memories and practice!

Hospitals: Volunteer to visit elderly patients once a week. Just chat with them and listen to their stories.

Schools: Being a dedicated student is the best way to help your school. But if there's a fundraiser, for example, get all the boys together, or all the girls, or all the redheads, and try to out-fundraise the others.

Businesses: You're getting to the age when you could possibly get a job. Your expenses are paid for by your parents, so go out there and use your competitive advantage to provide a quality service at a good price.

Senior centers: Lonely seniors would love for you to visit. You and your friends can put on a play or a concert.

Services for the needy: There's an unbelievable number of ways to help. It's best not to just give homeless people money, since they are often addicted to drugs or alcohol. So look for organizations that serve the poor in other ways, like a soup kitchen or a homeless shelter.

Libraries: You be that kid who is always asking the librarian for good books (checked by your parents, of course). Volunteer to reshelve books.

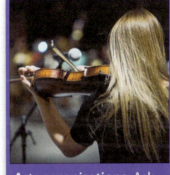

Arts organizations: Ask your parents whether you could take a few art or voice lessons or go to a classical concert.

Fire departments: Fire departments put on fire safety demonstrations; why not go and watch? Let them give you the gift of knowledge about safety. They'll enjoy giving, and one day you may be very glad you received.

2. HELPING YOUR NEIGHBORS' SPIRITUAL NEEDS

You should do good for your neighbors' physical needs because they are created in God's image, just like you are. They are brothers, not just neighbors.

You should do good for your neighbors' *spiritual* needs because you are fallen and you are redeemed—and they might be only one of those. They might not be your spiritual brothers, but they can be.

If you are a Christian, Christ has met your greatest need, greater than food, clothing, or shelter. Greater than money. He has saved you from your sin.

Most people in the world are still slaves to sin, unable to do anything that truly pleases God (Romans 8:8). Most people are "dead in sins" (Ephesians 2:5). They have "no hope, and [are] without God in the world" (Ephesians 2:12).

They need to be freed from sin, to be made alive in Christ, to be given hope. Their physical needs are important, but these spiritual needs are far more important. Physical needs last a maximum of one hundred years or so. Spiritual needs last for eternity.

You are one of God's chosen tools for meeting your neighbors' spiritual needs. Here's where the Great Commission comes in.

> Go ye therefore, and teach all nations, baptizing them in the name of the Father, and of the Son, and of the Holy Ghost: teaching them to observe all things whatsoever I have commanded you: and, lo, I am with you alway, even unto the end of the world. (Matthew 28:19–20)

That message is the gospel, or the "good news." Christians are commissioned to give this good news everywhere. Jesus said,

> Repentance and remission of sins should be preached in [my] name among all nations, beginning at Jerusalem. (Luke 24:47)

But the gospel message was not supposed to stop at Jerusalem. Jesus also said,

> Ye shall be witnesses unto me both in Jerusalem, and in all Judaea, and in Samaria, and unto the uttermost part of the earth. (Acts 1:8)

The uttermost part of the earth most certainly includes Haiti.

And what happens to the Haitian neighbors Paul Farmer saves from malaria, dysentery, and typhoid? They live longer. They live healthier lives. Perhaps Farmer helps them find rewarding work.

And in the dark of night they perform satanic voodoo ceremonies in which they offer chicken blood to spirits. If you save a Haitian woman from malaria and give her twenty more years of life, she may use that life to worship idols. Her life may be spent fearing these wicked spirits.

It's not really that different with your neighbors in your own town. Let's say you set a good example of not getting angry when a referee makes an unfair call against your team. You practice hard, and your teammates know it. These are all good things. But if you never tell your teammates the good news that Christ died for their sins, if you never tell them that God commands them to repent from their sins, their lives will be just as dark as the life of the woman in Haiti.

That darkness may be a more comfortable darkness, but poor Haitians and rich Americans are equally without Christ and without real hope. And when the day of judgment comes, Jesus says they will be separated from God forever, in a place where the worm does not die and the fire never goes out (Mark 9:48).

Your words about Christ will ring hollow to your American friends if you are *not* sportsmanlike on your sports team. They will ring hollow to Haitians on a mission trip if you aren't doing anything to feed their hungry mouths. So yes, good works are vital.

BUT *EVEN MORE* HOLLOW WILL BE YOUR GOOD WORKS FOR YOUR NEIGHBORS IF YOU DON'T GIVE THEM THE GOSPEL ALSO.

So reach out. Work with an outreach ministry at your church. Talk with your parents and pastor about starting a Bible club for kids. Ask your non-Christian neighbors what they believe about death, about the Bible, about morality. Start a conversation. Take them the good news of Christ's death for sin and His victorious resurrection. Judgment day is coming (Acts 10:42). Do the most loving community service for your neighbor that anyone can do.

Tell them the Truth.

Thinking It Through 7.5

1. What does the Creation Mandate have to do with community involvement?

2. What is the effect of caring for your neighbors' physical needs but neglecting their spiritual needs?

3. Name one organization in your town through which you could love your neighbor both physically and spiritually in the next week.

How should my government work **?**

There once was a divorced couple whose daughter was in middle school. This girl lived with her mom but would go to her dad's house every other weekend.

Only, she stopped going, and she wouldn't say why.

Her dad prided himself on being the cool dad, someone who wasn't too strict. He couldn't think of why his daughter wouldn't want to come stay with him.

He finally asked her point-blank. "Sweetie, what's wrong? Why won't you come?"

She said, "I don't feel safe at your house."

"What?" he said. "What could happen to you here?"

"It's not that, Dad."

"Then please explain!"

"Well, it's that . . . you let me do whatever I want."

Most kids reading this book probably don't have this girl's feeling. You might find yourself wishing for no rules. But truly: what if you had a life with no guardrails set by your authorities? What if you could stay out as late as you wanted, eat whatever you wanted, go wherever you wanted, watch whatever you wanted?

Maybe that sounds awesome to you, but this girl was right: it's not awesome. It's scary. Rules aren't there just to keep you away from bad stuff. They're there to keep bad stuff away from you. They're there to protect you.

WHY GOVERNMENT BEGAN

In the same way, government and its rules are there to protect citizens. Government is here, in part, because people need protection from bad stuff in society. But that's not all.

Government began for two reasons: the Fall and Creation.

THE FALL AND GOVERNMENT

If we were all perfect, if there were no sin, we wouldn't need protection. Other people wouldn't need protection from us, and we wouldn't need it from them.

But this world is fallen. And so are you. No one can fully be trusted to do what is right in all circumstances. We can't even trust ourselves. (Haven't you ever done something cruel to someone else and been surprised by your own cruelty?)

Government exists, in large part, because people sin. In Genesis 9:6, God said,

Whoso sheddeth man's blood, by man shall his blood be shed: for in the image of God made he man.

You might wonder, *Where in the world does government show up in those words?*

Here's the answer: it's reasonably obvious that if there are no authorities, the killing will never stop. Someone will murder someone, then the murdered person's relatives will murder the murderer, then the murdered murderer's relatives will murder the murderers of the murdered murderer.

It will be a never-ending mess. A blood feud. And Romans 13:4 also tells us that the government "beareth . . . the sword" (more on this in a bit). God has put the power of life and death in the hands of the government. It takes having a government to use violence in an orderly way. That's what imprisonment is too: orderly violence that removes you from your life and puts you in a box.

Because this world is fallen, some people won't stop committing crimes until they are fined or imprisoned or even killed. And God gave the government the authority to use orderly violence—it's called "coercive power," because the government can force you to do something.

CREATION AND GOVERNMENT

Government would have come to be, though, even if the Fall had never happened—because of the Creation Mandate.

Any group of people who try to live out the blessing of the Creation Mandate to fill the earth and subdue it are going to need some kind of government to ensure justice.

You might assume that unfallen people would be perfectly just. But unfallen people would still be *finite*. A farmer in one valley who puts a certain fertilizer in his crops to cause them to be more fruitful might not know that a farmer twenty miles downstream is losing fish in his now polluted fishing pond. Justice means fair use of the stream for all, but how can the first farmer know what's happening downstream? Through a local government—a place where the downstream farmer can seek justice. The government can establish policies that ensure fairness for all farmers.

A government also has the power to collect taxes and provide services for the community that no one member of the community could provide. It so happens, for example, that a good sewer system is absolutely essential to the health of a town. There are slums in Africa and India where human waste runs in little rivulets down the side of the street. It carries dangerous diseases. Running that waste

through pipes under the ground is much healthier. But it costs a lot of money to dig up the ground and put in these pipes, and it requires the combined efforts of a lot of people. This is something government can do—and something government *would* do, even if the world were unfallen.

Government is not a "necessary evil," something we could all do without if we weren't sinners. Government is a good thing that, in a very real way, was created by God. When God gave the Creation Mandate, He planted a seed that would grow into gardens and cities and governments.

PURPOSES OF GOVERNMENT

One of the purposes of government is to help those who have become unable to support themselves or their families due to loss of income.

In the Old Testament, there were laws for harvesting: the harvesters would leave the missed grain and the corners of the fields for those in poverty to glean. These laws provided a way for those who did not have the ability to provide for themselves to work for the food they needed to survive. The government should have programs to help people make it through times of poverty and find income through new job placements or new opportunities for income.

Paul's great letter to the Romans gives us more teaching about government than any other portion of Scripture, and it presents another purpose of government. Here's a paraphrase of what Paul said in chapter 13.

The public services of the government provide jobs and income.

Everyone needs to obey the top authorities, because there is no authority out there who did not get his or her job from God Himself. Whatever authority is over you, God appointed it. Whoever resists these authorities, then, resists God—and will be judged.

Your God-given rulers are not there to make you fear doing good; they are there to make you fear doing evil. Do you want to live without fear of the ruler? Then do good, and the ruler will praise you.

The government is God's servant, a servant He appointed to do you good. But if you do evil, you should be afraid—because God did not give the government its sword for no reason.

The government is God's servant, God's tool. And its job is pretty basic. What do we call punishing evil and rewarding good? We call it justice. The government exists to promote justice.

God even put a "sword" in the hand of the government to use against evil and crime in the territory under its rule. A sword is not a defensive weapon like a shield. Its purpose is to draw blood and, sometimes, to kill. If Paul had written today, he might have said that God gave government the power of the firearm.

The government is allowed to use orderly violence. Capital punishment, imprisonment, shootouts with criminals—all of these things the government can do as it works to promote public justice, safety, and order.

Most Christians throughout time have also seen another God-given power in that sword: the power of national defense. This is what the US Constitution is talking about when its preamble claims the right of the people to "provide for the common defence." Wars are usually fought between *nations*, not between families or between regions of the world. And the government has the right and duty to protect its citizens in war. God gave it a sword.

Law enforcement has authority to use physical force and weapons to punish evildoers and protect citizens.

LIMITS ON GOVERNMENT

But the government is not permitted by God to pick up its weapons against just anybody. People who are doing good should not have to fear the government; it's those who do evil who should fear.

And yet governments are touched by the Fall too. So there are governments who have tried to shove themselves into places where they don't belong—like the church. The Chinese government has torn down church buildings, even as this book was being written. This isn't ancient history; it's happening now. And the Soviet Union also famously persecuted Christians, sending many pastors to a chain of terrible labor camps called "gulags."

JUST WAR

Augustine, an early Christian theologian, formulated principles that help nations know when it is right to pick up their swords (and guns and tanks and fighter planes) against other nations in war. It's called "Just War Theory." It's a "theory" because the Bible never explicitly says these things, though they fit well with Scripture. Among the principles of the theory are that wars should only be fought by governments—by the recognized authorities. Also, war must only be a last resort, and people who are not soldiers should be kept safe if at all possible. The war itself must be for a good and just cause.

One inmate in those camps became a great writer: Aleksandr Solzhenitsyn. And in his great story about the camps, *One Day in the Life of Ivan Denisovich*, one of the characters is Alyoshka the Baptist. Solzhenitsyn created this character because Baptists were often sent to these terrible camps. You could literally go die in the frozen Siberian tundra just for believing in Christ.

Thankfully, in the modern West this kind of violent persecution has been very rare. Christians sometimes lose their jobs for their faith, but imprisonment is rare. Western governments generally agree with the ancient Roman governor Gallio.

Gallio had it right two thousand years ago when Jews took the apostle Paul to him to complain about Paul's teaching (Acts 18:12–15). Gallio told the Jews that if they were complaining about a crime, he would listen to them. "But if it be a question of words and names, and of your law, look ye to it: for I will be no judge of such matters," he concluded.

Agreeing with Roman tradition, Gallio saw that his job was to judge crimes, not sins. The line between illegal public crimes, which a government *should* take action on, and legal but "religious" sins, which are outside a government's authority, is not always an easy line to find. But Gallio was basically right.

CASE STUDY: FALLEN GOVERNMENT, BAD LAWS

Who controls the education of children? Is it their parents? Is it the government? Kimberly Yuracko, a law professor, rejects the idea of parents controlling the education of their children, especially when parents choose to educate according to a Christian worldview. She wrote a paper against unregulated home-schooling. In it she said,

> Parental control over children's basic education flows from the state (rather than vice versa). States delegate power over children's basic education to parents, and the delegation itself is necessarily subject to constitutional constraints.

Ultimately, she wants to see homeschooling regulated by laws so that homeschoolers would have to receive a minimum amount of education that the states decide. At first that doesn't sound like such a bad thing. But laws like this would make it possible for states to force children to learn worldviews that contradict their parents' Christian worldview.

1. What's wrong with Yuracko's basic assumption that the government is in charge of children's education?

2. Does the government have the authority to tell parents how to educate their children? Explain.

Government is not any of the organizations we talked about in previous sections, and it shouldn't try to be. It's not hospitals or schools or businesses or sports. Government is not the family, either. Government has a proper sphere in which it should stay, the sphere of maintaining public justice.

KING JESUS AND CAESAR

When Jews asked Jesus whether they should pay taxes to the government, Jesus told them to give to Caesar what was Caesar's and give to God what was God's (Matthew 22:20–22). He couldn't have meant that Caesar was another god and that people should obey Caesar when Caesar contradicted the one true God. No, God is God, and He rules over all caesars—the early disciples knew not to obey any authority who contradicted God (Acts 4:18–20). But when government acts within its God-given authority, it *must* be obeyed.

Thinking It Through 7.6

1. Did government begin because of Creation, Fall, or Redemption? Explain.

2. Where in Paul's letter to the Romans did he show that the government exists to promote justice? Explain.

3. What does the story of Gallio in Acts illustrate about the limits of government?

How do I honor God under my government

Most readers of this book live in a democratic republic. You live under a government that democratically elects representatives of the people, by the people, and for the people. This has been called a democracy within a republic.

Last time we checked, middle-schoolers are people. So the government is supposed to be of you, by you, and for you. In a democratic republic, the people are supposed to know and care what's going on in their government—because it's for them. The government authorities are their representatives.

As a citizen of a democratic republic, you have rights and responsibilities. But if you are a Christian, you also have another set of responsibilities.

RESPONSIBILITIES OF A CHRISTIAN CITIZEN

The Bible gives you responsibilities as a citizen, no matter where you live—in a democratic republic or a dictatorship. But the biblical responsibilities of a Christian citizen are especially important in a political system that gives you rights and responsibilities.

You should pray, participate, submit, and witness.

PRAY

Your first responsibility as a Christian citizen is to pray.

> I exhort therefore, that . . . supplications, prayers, intercessions, and giving of thanks, be made for all men; for kings, and for all that are in authority; that we may lead a quiet and peaceable life in all godliness and honesty. (1 Timothy 2:1–2)

Paul says we should pray for our government leaders. And why are we supposed to pray? So that we can lead lives that are quiet, peaceful, godly, and honest.

This instruction from Paul provides another hint about what government is for: maintaining public order. It's really hard to live a quiet and peaceful life, and even a godly life, when you live in a "failed state," a country where there is no government. There are countries in the Middle East, especially, where there is no peace. People are killed all the time when they're just going out to do their daily work.

You should thank God if your country is quiet and peaceful—and you should pray to Him to help the authorities keep it that way. This is your responsibility as a Christian citizen.

PARTICIPATE

Author Costica Bradatan recently wrote in the *New York Times* that democracy is "unnatural."

What is "natural," in his non-Christian and evolutionary view, is for us all to "assert ourselves—relentlessly, unwittingly, savagely—against others." He explains,

> We push them aside, overstep them, overthrow them, even crush them if necessary. Behind the smiling facade of human civilization, there is at work the same blind drive toward self-assertion that we find in the animal realm.

He's partly right. Civilization is a thin crust on top of barbarism. People do often crush others for selfish reasons. But we don't act like savages because we used to be animals. We do it because we used to be kings. God gave us rule over this world, and in Adam we all fell into sin instead.

It is because we are all sinners that we need democracy. C. S. Lewis has a very famous quotation in which he explains why he as a Christian believed in democracy.

> A great deal of democratic enthusiasm descends from the ideas of people . . . who believed in democracy because they thought mankind so wise and good that everyone deserved a share in the government. . . . The real reason for democracy is just the reverse. Mankind is so fallen that no man can be trusted with unchecked power over his fellows.

Lewis believed in democracy because he believed in the Fall.

This all adds up to the second biblical duty you have as a Christian citizen: participate. If democratic republics exist to make sure nobody gets absolute power, then your voice needs to be heard. Every voice in a democratic society needs to be heard. You are fallen, so not all your political ideas are right. But you are created in God's image, so not all your political ideas are wrong. Participate in your democracy if you have one.

SUBMIT

But the third responsibility of the Christian citizen is to submit, because sometimes your ideas will not win—and yet you still need to obey the government authorities God puts over you.

When you agree with your authorities, doing what they say is not submission. It isn't submitting to your parents when they say, "Finish your ice cream." That's precisely what you wanted to do. It *is* submission when they say, "Finish your brussels sprouts" and you do it cheerfully (presuming that you, like 93 percent of people under the age of ninety-three, don't like brussels sprouts and wonder why mothers keep cruelly serving them to their own offspring). The test of submission is when you disagree. This could not be clearer in the Bible:

> Let every soul be subject unto the higher powers. For there is no power but of God: the powers that be are ordained of God. Whosoever therefore resisteth the power, resisteth the ordinance of God. (Romans 13:1–2)

Submit. Be subject. Obey your government.
Unless . . .

WITNESS

Obey your government unless they tell you to do something God told you not to do, or (more likely, nowadays) they tell you not to do something God told you to do.

Daniel's three friends Hananiah, Mishael, and Azariah were willing to do a lot of submitting to the Babylonians who had captured them. They took Babylonian names: Shadrach, Meshach, and Abednego. They went through Babylonian education. But they drew the line at bowing down to a big golden statue of Nebuchadnezzar. They knew their Ten Commandments too well. God had said no idols. So, under threat of a fiery furnace, they disobeyed the government authorities. They performed the last responsibility of a Christian citizen that we'll talk about. They witnessed.

They told an angry Nebuchadnezzar, *God is able to deliver us from the fiery furnace. But if he doesn't, we still won't serve your gods or worship your statue* (Daniel 3:17–18).

Western societies today won't make you fall down and worship a statue. But by this point in this book you know: they have their own gods. When your worship of God goes against the gods of your culture, you testify to the truth. You witness. And you die if necessary. The truth is that important.

So if your government says, "Call that boy a girl or else it's the fiery furnace for you," you must witness to the truth and select door number two. You must say a loving but firm no, and (if you have the opportunity) give Christian reasons why. Witness is your responsibility as a Christian citizen.

VIRTUES OF A CHRISTIAN CITIZEN

How do you fight against falsehoods, when they're being told by your own government? How do you push for truth and for moral goodness when whole political parties made up of millions of people may be pushing the other way?

You work to develop the virtues of a Christian citizen. We've looked at four responsibilities; now we're going to look at four virtues. Virtues are excellent character qualities. They are skills. They are practices that get you from where you are to where your goal is. If your goal is to live a quiet and peaceable life in all godliness and honesty, these are the virtues that will get you there.

PRUDENCE

The first virtue is prudence. Prudence is the wisdom of knowing not just what is right, but how to get there.

The issue of abortion provides a good example. Everyone in the pro-life movement agrees that, ideally, abortion would end right now, everywhere. But American pro-lifers can't end abortion in Russia. They haven't been able to end it in America.

So instead of aiming for immediate and total victory, they have prudently fought for every piece of ground they can get. They help pass more and more restrictive laws in as many states as they can, making abortions as difficult as possible to obtain under the law. Christians have also prudently worked with their enemies when they could. This is good.

BOLDNESS WITH HUMILITY

The second virtue of a Christian citizen is boldness, but the third needs to come right along with it: humility.

Boldness is the willingness to take risks and be courageous in the face of opposition. In political life, you will get shot at if you stand for truth. But even your enemies can learn to respect you if you are boldly true to your beliefs.

Humility is recognizing that you are fallen and finite. You could be wrong on political matters where God has not spoken directly. Other people might be smarter than you.

Paul encouraged humility when he says that Christians are supposed to be considerate and courteous toward everybody (Titus 3:1–3). Why? Because, he says, we used to be "foolish, disobedient, deceived"—just like so many people we meet.

In any big group of fallen people, some problems will arise that are not easy to fix. People will disagree not only about how to fix the problems, but about what exactly the problems are. Problems in big groups of people are just not simple enough to bring forth utterly clear solutions.

Humility assumes that your political opponents may have some good ideas—and good motives.

So many Americans scream at their opponents and treat them like demons. Democrats scream at Republicans, "YOU HATE POOR PEOPLE!" Republicans scream at Democrats, "YOU HATE AMERICA!"

What may sound like boldness is actually angry arrogance. Assuming the worst motives from your political opponents is not loving and not humble. Christian citizens should be *humbly bold*.

RESPECT

The last virtue of a Christian citizen is also in Romans 13: respect. There the Bible says that you're supposed to pay the government what you owe it—and not just taxes. Pay respect to whom respect is owed (Romans 13:7).

On the internet today, it can be very difficult to find anyone who obeys these simple biblical instructions. If you dislike the current leader or leaders of your country, you still owe them respect and honor. This doesn't mean that you must respect everything they do but that you must respect their office. Bible readers have looked hard for a footnote here—*give honor to whom honor is due** [*except when the political party you don't like is in power]—but they've never found one. You're never too young to show respect or to urge others to show respect too.

Christians should develop the citizenship virtues of prudence, boldness with humility, and respect.

Thinking It Through 7.7

1. What are the responsibilities of a Christian citizen?

2. Why should you pray for your government, according to 1 Timothy 2?

3. What are the virtues of a Christian citizen?

Don't obey when the law goes against what God says.

Don't obey if you don't agree with the law.

When should I refuse to obey the law

?

Never.

Don't obey if the law puts a person's health or safety in danger.

REVIEW

Scripture Memory

Luke 14:26
Acts 2:42
Hebrews 10:24–25
Luke 10:27
Acts 20:35
Romans 13:4
Romans 13:1

Recall

1. Define *individualism*. Explain the opposite extreme of individualism.

2. What is the universal church?

3. What is the mission of the church?

4. What are the four responsibilities and the four virtues of a Christian citizen?

Understand

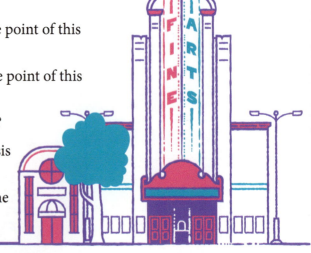

5. What is it about the Christian gospel that promotes the importance of the individual?

6. Why is the church called the body of Christ? What's the point of this word picture?

7. Why is the church called the bride of Christ? What's the point of this word picture?

8. How do businesses meet the needs of your community?

9. What connection does the Creation Mandate (in Genesis 1:26–28) have to you not littering in your town?

10. What connection does the Creation Mandate have to the existence of community organizations in your town?

Think Critically

11. Does government exist because God intended it to be part of His creation, or does it exist because mankind fell into sin? Explain.

12. Look at Romans 13. Which verse or verses tell us that government is given to us by God specifically to maintain justice?

Internalize

13. Why should you be a member of a local church?

14. How would you explain to someone the importance of the ways you serve at church, no matter how large or small they may be?

15. Describe how your church follows Acts 2:42.

16. What can you do to serve your local community this coming year?

HOW DO I RELATE TO PEOPLE WITH OTHER WORLDVIEWS?

How should I think about other worldviews **?**

When everybody around us believes something, we humans feel a lot of pressure to believe that thing too. Even little kids love to repeat what their older siblings say.

And this isn't all bad. You believe Antarctica exists, don't you? (And so does your little brother.) Well, it does exist. But do you believe this because you've traveled there by plane or boat and planted a flag on the southernmost continent of ice? Or do you believe it because everybody around you believes it?

Some Europeans think that if you roll down the window of your car while you're driving, you'll hurt your neck, make it stiffen up, and maybe send yourself to the hospital (this is not made up). What do you think of that?

You probably think it's silly. But what if you grew up with people around you believing it? What if your entire life you never rode with the windows down, and every time your fingers got close to the window button, your mom warned that you'd hurt your neck? You'd probably believe it too.

And your belief would "work." It would never let you down. You'd make it through your entire car-riding life without giving yourself a sore neck even once. Beliefs can be held by everyone you know, they can be apparently successful, and they can still be wrong.

In this final unit, we're going to talk about some of the things that people around the world believe, even to the point of basing their lives on them. And those beliefs bring them a lot of apparent success. Their worldview seems to work.

But the worldview can still be wrong.

THE MAKING OF WORLDVIEWS

Do you remember the elements of a worldview from earlier in this book? Every worldview out there, not just the Christian one, has three parts.

1 Every worldview tells a **big story** that answers questions about the world.

2 Every worldview includes **basic beliefs and assumptions driven by what a person loves**.

3 Every worldview logically leads to certain **actions** by individuals and groups, and sets of group actions make up what we see in the world as different cultures.

In this unit we are going to talk about several false worldviews. Like all worldviews, each one tells a big story about the world, includes basic beliefs driven by loves, and produces certain actions. But they are false—they don't work—because they leave out the one true God and the truths of His revelation.

Some of the false worldviews are commonly called religions (Islam and Buddhism). Some *aren't* thought of as religions. For instance, secularism isn't usually called a religion because it is a worldview that can be combined with other worldviews. Someone could hold to a certain form of Judaism, a religion, while also holding to secularism.

THE IDOLATRY OF FALSE WORLDVIEWS

Not all false worldviews may be given the title "religion." But all of them can be called idolatrous. This doesn't mean that all the people who have these worldviews bow down to statues. In fact, some of these worldviews would insist that doing so would be very wrong. Others would just say that doing so is foolish.

You learned in Section 4.6 that idolatry happens whenever worship of the true God is replaced by something else. Replacing God with something else is what all false worldviews do.

Think of some of the important worldview questions that we've considered throughout this book. The answers will show what someone's heart is ultimately worshiping.

- *Where did I come from?* A worldview that doesn't answer this question by acknowledging the God of the Bible is idolatrous. It has replaced the creator God with an idol. That idol may be a false god represented by a statue, or it may be a scientific theory. But it is an idol nonetheless.

IDOLATRY HAPPENS WHENEVER WORSHIP OF THE TRUE GOD IS REPLACED BY SOMETHING ELSE.

- *Why am I here?* The Bible teaches that humans are here to glorify God and to enjoy Him forever. But false worldviews will exchange the biblical God for a different life purpose.
- *What is wrong with the world?* There are lots of things wrong with the world, but the Bible says that the fundamental problem is human rebellion against God and His law. Notice that once again God is central to how this question is answered according to a biblical worldview.
- *How can things be made right?* An answer that offers a replacement for redemption through God the Son, Jesus Christ, is idolatrous.
- *Where am I headed?* A biblical worldview's answer still centers on God: either a person will live in the presence of God for all eternity, or he will suffer away from the presence of God for all eternity.

So in a certain sense, all false worldviews can be understood to be false religions. They are all idolatrous replacements for the true worldview, the true religion, which is taught in the Bible.

THE MAKING OF CULTURES

Often people think of religion as something private. It's something people do in their church, synagogue, mosque, or temple. It may be something people do privately at home. (These thoughts come from the false worldview of secularism.) But remember that the third element of every worldview includes group action—*culture*.

A culture is just a big group of people working out their worldview and turning it into action. Action that's quite "religious" if you consider what the group is worshiping. Think about a couple of examples.

Superstitious worldviews produce cultures in which everybody knows—and many people live by—the major superstitions. In parts of Papua New Guinea, for example, everybody just "knows" that you have to be careful not to offend your dead ancestors.

Scientific worldviews produce cultures in which everybody just "knows" that scientific studies are the most reliable way to find out the truth. Everybody believes that if rates of suicide are going up, science and technology are the only places to turn for help. Soon the TV news will be full of "A new study has shown that . . ." and "A new medication is being tested . . . ."

We've talked a lot about the three parts of a worldview: big story, beliefs driven by loves, and actions. You've seen that a group's collective understanding of these parts creates a culture. People in a given culture generally love particular things, tell a particular big story, have particular beliefs, and act in particular ways.

What this all means is that there are no "neutral" cultures. Every culture is built on a view about the way the world is. When those loves and beliefs are good and true, the culture will be successful, and even beautiful.

Cultures are also complicated things. Think about the United States. There are many things Americans have in common. Christianity has been the major religion in the United States for much of its history. So the Christian worldview has shaped American culture. But the Christian worldview has not been the only influential worldview. Secularism and Moralistic Therapeutic Deism have also had huge effects on American culture. American Christianity itself has been influenced by these false worldviews.

We'll try to keep things simple by focusing on one false worldview at a time. But you should know that sometimes worldviews influence each other, and some people buy into parts of other worldviews. People are not always consistent in the way they think.

WHY YOU SHOULD UNDERSTAND DIFFERENT WORLDVIEWS

How do you respond when you encounter a woman who is wearing a hijab (a head covering worn by Muslim women)? Do you immediately try to have a conversation with her? Do you try to share the gospel? Probably not. You may feel awkward talking with someone of another religion or worldview. You don't have to.

If you really love your neighbors as yourself, you will learn to listen to those neighbors. You will know the importance of understanding your neighbors' worldviews. How else will you figure out the real reasons for why they see a different "reality" through their worldview lenses? How will you know what Bible answers to give to their beliefs that don't match reality? How will you show Christ as the answer for their needs?

Most of all, you will try to find ways to help them respond to the creator God with whole-hearted love and worship. *You will act out the truth for them to see.*

Always be...

Gracious

Loving

humble

gentle

Christlike

HOW TO TALK TO PEOPLE WITH DIFFERENT WORLDVIEWS

This unit will try to help you know how to speak wisely and lovingly to people whose worldviews are different from yours. But there will be common themes in that advice, no matter what worldview you are dealing with.

Always it will be right to be gracious and loving toward deceived people who hold false worldviews (2 Timothy 2:24–26). You should love these neighbors who have been trapped by Satan's lies—enough to show them the same love and grace that God has shown you.

Always it will be right for you to be humble, because if you know the truth of Christ, you don't know it because you deserve to know it. This knowledge has been given to you as a gift (1 Corinthians 4:7).

Always it will be right to be like Jesus, who saved His harsh words for teachers who knew better and were leading others astray (Matthew 23). Jesus was much more gentle with the average people who were being led astray (Matthew 9:36).

You can't live in the modern world and avoid running into people who see life through different worldviews. You will find out through experience that not everybody agrees about the way the world ought to be, or about what counts as a good human life. But lovingly sharing what God has revealed about His world through the Bible will always be a good response.

Thinking It Through 8.1

1. What are the elements of any worldview?

2. Some worldviews believe that people should be free to think and do as they please, without ever being confronted with another worldview. How are these worldviews idolatrous?

3. Why is it impossible to have a culture without a worldview?

4. Should a Christian be excited to see multiple cultures represented in his church? Explain.

5. Why is it important to take time to understand people with other worldviews?

Stop talking
to her.

Pray for her.

WORLDVIEW DILEMMA #219

How do I respond when my Muslim friend says that Jesus didn't really die on the cross

?

Ask her, "Do you know why
Christians believe Jesus
had to die on the cross?"

SECTION
8.2 ISLAM

Is belief in monotheism enough?

One of the most influential religions in the world—claiming the allegiance of over 1.5 billion people—is Islam. It is at the heart of many cultures around the world.

Islam means "submission"—submission to Allah, the god of Islam. Someone who submits to Allah is called a Muslim. One person in every five on the entire planet is a Muslim.

ALLAH

English speakers typically call the god of Islam "Allah" to distinguish him from the Christian God. The word *Allah* is Arabic for "the God." *Al* in Arabic means "the"; *'ilah* means "God" or "god." (The English words *algebra* and *algorithm* come from Arabic. You can see *al*—the article *the*—at the beginning of each one.)

But it isn't precisely true to say that Allah is the name of Islam's god. Arabic-speaking Christians refer to the God of the Bible using the same word. In the same way, English uses one word to refer both to the true God and to false gods. Keep reading to find out how we know the Christian God and the Islamic god are different.

THE HISTORY OF ISLAM

Islam began in AD 610 in what is now Saudi Arabia. A man named Muhammad claimed to receive revelation from Allah through the angel Gabriel. Because Muhammad could not read or write, others wrote down his recitations in a holy book. It is called the Qur'an, which means "recitation." This book is the basis for Islamic beliefs.

Muhammad lived in a city called Mecca, and he began to gain followers. But all did not go well for him. In 622 Muhammad was forced to flee to a city called Yathrib. He soon renamed it "the city of the prophet" (namely himself), or just "Medina." To this day, Mecca and Medina are two of the most important cities in Islam.

Jerusalem is the other important city, which explains many of the headlines in newspapers to this day. Muslim tradition says that Muhammad was transported there by the angel Gabriel to pray with Abraham, Moses, and Jesus. Then, Muslims believe, Muhammad ascended to heaven. The spot where all this happened just so happens to be the Jewish Temple Mount. An Islamic shrine built there has led to great tension between Muslims and Jews.

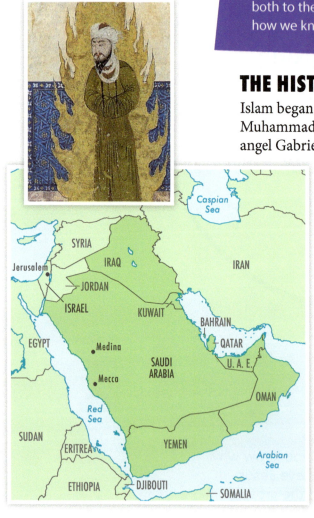

THE STORY, BELIEFS, AND PRACTICES OF ISLAM

Islam has developed an alternate big story about the world. That story starts and ends with one God, so it has similarities to the biblical story. But at absolutely essential points it is massively different. And these differences lead to a set of beliefs and practices quite opposite from Christianity.

CREATION

In both the Bible and the Qur'an, God is outside of creation. He is transcendent. In both, He created the world, with mankind as His highest creation.

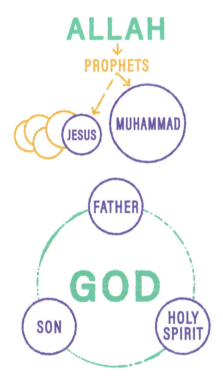

But think about who this Creator is. There is a key difference here: Allah is definitely *not* a trinity. The very first stated belief of Islam is that there is only one God and that he has no Son. Jesus is referred to nearly one hundred times in the Qur'an, but He is treated as a prophet and not as divine. The Bible, however, demands the Trinity. There is one God in three persons: Father, Son, and Spirit. Muslims and Christians do not worship the same God.

Allah could not have created the world for the reason the God of the Bible did—as an overflow of the love between the three persons of the Trinity. Allah famously has ninety-nine names. He is "the Most Merciful," "the Judge," and "the Subduer." But the Qur'an never gives the key description the Bible gives of God: "God is love." How could Allah be love when he existed by himself, with no one to love?

FALL

In both the Bible and the Qur'an, Adam and Eve fell into sin after being tempted by Satan. But here's another massively important difference: in the Qur'an, Adam and Eve did not pass their sin nature on to their children. They were forgiven. There is no original sin (sin nature) in Islam. Mankind is *not* fallen at the core.

Mankind is, however, weak and forgetful. So Muslims believe people do sin. People must be forgiven by Allah if they hope to reach heaven and avoid hell.

REDEMPTION

Having different beliefs about sin means that Christians and Muslims have different views of redemption. Muslims do not believe their relationship with Allah has been severed. Instead, there are only particular sins to be forgiven. They do not see salvation as restoring a relationship with Allah but as escaping punishment for their sins.

Muslims believe that Allah is merciful, but they don't believe forgiveness will come to them by grace through Jesus' payment for their sin. Christ's death on the cross is actually mentioned in the

Qur'an, but Islam typically teaches that Jesus was replaced on the cross by someone else who was made to look like Him. Muslims believe that Jesus, who was not God's Son, never died for human sin. If there were no just punishment for sin, though, Allah can't be called both just and merciful. His mercy would excuse sin.

"Redemption" in Islam, then, doesn't actually exist. You achieve salvation mostly by doing good works. This is also massively different from the Christian reason for doing good works.

THE FIVE PILLARS

And here are the good works faithful Muslims must do. They obey the Five Pillars in hopes of entering paradise when they die.

1

Shahadah
To become a Muslim, someone must sincerely recite these words: "There is no God but Allah, and Muhammad is the prophet of Allah."

2

Salat
Pray up to five times a day facing Mecca.

3

Zakat
Give charity to the poor.

4

Sawm
Go without food or water from sunrise to sunset for the whole month of Ramadan.

5

Hajj
Make a pilgrimage to Mecca (if physically and financially able).

DIFFERENT GROUPS IN ISLAM

Islam as a religion is not united. There are two major (and many minor) divisions within it. The two major groups are the Sunnis and the Shiites. They trace their split all the way back to the early years after Muhammad's death. The two groups fought over the proper successor to Muhammad. To this day, Sunnis and Shiites hold different views about Islamic leadership. They commit acts of violence against one another.

After Osama bin Laden's attacks on New York's Twin Towers on September 11, 2001, acts of violence are what Muslims are most known for. Anytime there is an act of terrorism—intentional violence against civilians during peacetime—many people will assume Muslims are involved.

And that *is* fair and *isn't* fair at the same time.

Moderates in Islam do exist. Many Muslims reject the terrorism of the extremists. It isn't fair to say "Islam is a violent religion" when so many Muslims—from Indonesia to Michigan (where a large Muslim population lives)—are just as peaceful as you.

But it also isn't fair to say what US President George W. Bush said right after the September 11 attacks:

> The face of terror is not the true faith of Islam. That's not what Islam is all about. Islam is peace.

Think about what Bush was doing. He was defining people's religion for them. Plenty of Muslims—from Syria and Palestine to sub-Saharan Africa—disagree. Who's to say that the violent version of Islam is the wrong one, just because Americans happen to like the peaceful brand?

CASE STUDY: ISLAM'S UNANSWERABLE QUESTION

Islam teaches that Allah designed the world to be a place of temporary testing. Those who are faithful even while they suffer will be rewarded in the afterlife. Their suffering will also allow good to happen for other people and bring unity to a community.

Suffering can also be the consequence of disobeying the moral and natural laws set up by Allah. Muslims look to faithfully follow this balance to avoid suffering:

> And the heaven He raised and imposed the balance that you not transgress within the balance. And establish weight in justice and do not make deficient the balance. (Qur'an 55:7–9)

A believer might even suffer so that other believers would be tested. It reveals who will remain committed to charity. Muhammad reportedly said,

> Allah . . . would say on the Day of Res- urrection: O son of Adam, I was sick but you did not visit Me. He would say, O my Lord; how could I visit Thee whereas Thou art the Lord of the worlds? There-

upon He would say: Didn't you know that such and such servant of Mine was sick but you did not visit him and were you not aware of this that if you had visited him, you would have found Me by him? (Sahih Muslim 2569)

Scholar Mohammad Elshinawy summarizes, "One of the most foundational concepts . . . is that pure evil does not exist." There is always some reason for evil in the wisdom of Allah.

1. Which of the five worldview questions does Elshinawy seek to answer?

2. How does the Islamic answer fail to make sense of evils like child abuse?

3. How does the Bible explain these kinds of evils?

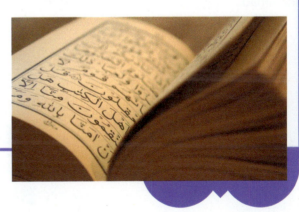

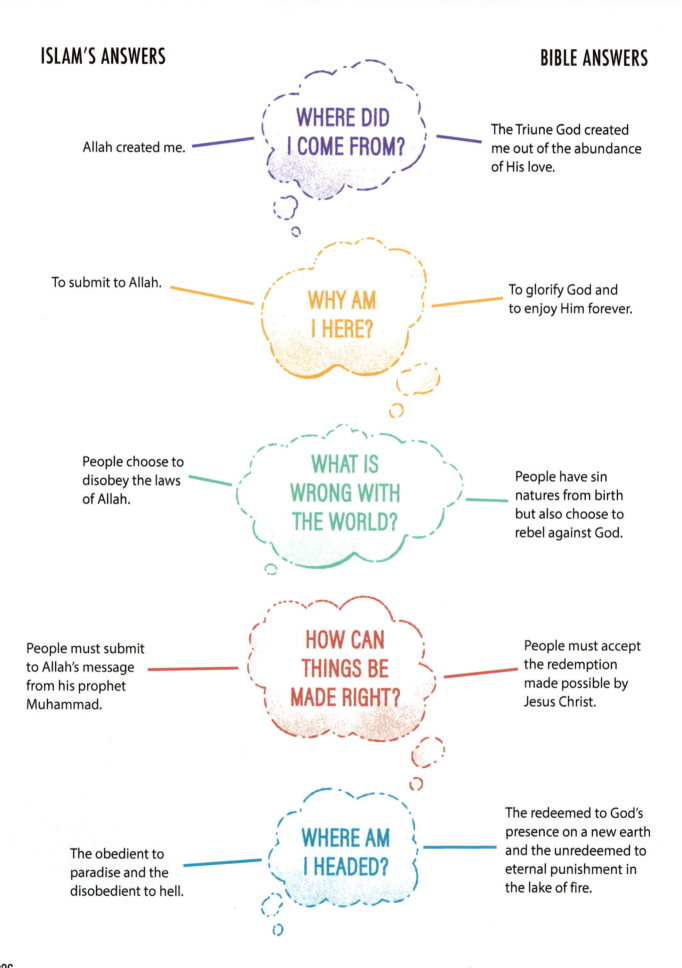

WHERE DID I COME FROM?

Allah created me.

The Triune God created me out of the abundance of His love.

WHY AM I HERE?

To submit to Allah.

To glorify God and to enjoy Him forever.

WHAT IS WRONG WITH THE WORLD?

People choose to disobey the laws of Allah.

People have sin natures from birth but also choose to rebel against God.

HOW CAN THINGS BE MADE RIGHT?

People must submit to Allah's message from his prophet Muhammad.

People must accept the redemption made possible by Jesus Christ.

WHERE AM I HEADED?

The obedient to paradise and the disobedient to hell.

The redeemed to God's presence on a new earth and the unredeemed to eternal punishment in the lake of fire.

There are statements in the Qur'an that do lead to violence. The Qur'an commands violence against disobedient wives.

> Those [wives] from whom you fear arrogance—[first] advise them; [then if they persist], forsake them in bed; and [finally], strike them. (4:34)

And it commands violence against unbelievers.

> Kill the polytheists wherever you find them and capture them and besiege them and sit in wait for them at every place of ambush. (9:5)

Some Muslims interpret verses like these in ways that limit how they are applied to modern time. Others obey them literally.

If the Qur'an were a true revelation from God, we could expect its statements to fit together. But the Qur'an is not from the true God. We can expect that some readers will get violence out of it and others will get peace at the same time.

BIBLE ANSWERS TO MUSLIM BELIEFS

Islam denies the one doctrine of the Christian faith that, as G. K. Chesterton said, is "the only part of Christian theology which can really be proved." What Chesterton is saying is that you can't have your eyes open and deny that something is wrong at the heart of each human on the planet.

And yet Islam does deny this. And by downgrading its definition of sin, it downgrades our need for a Savior. There is no Savior in Islam. You do your best to follow the Five Pillars and hope Allah will be merciful to you.

Islam offers its followers no sure hope of salvation because it doesn't have the power of Christ's New Covenant. Only biblical Christianity offers heart change from the inside out.

Christ the Son is the only way to the Father.

Thinking It Through 8.2

1. How did Islam become a religion?

2. Do Muslims and Christians worship the same God? Explain.

3. What are the Five Pillars of Islam?

4. Which Muslims are true Muslims—the peaceful ones, the violent ones, or both? Explain.

5. How does Islam leave people with unanswered questions? How does biblical Christianity provide answers?

8.3 BUDDHISM

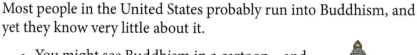

Is belief in a remedy for suffering enough **?**

Most people in the United States probably run into Buddhism, and yet they know very little about it.

- You might see Buddhism in a cartoon—and you might not even know that's what you're seeing. Have you ever seen a cartoon in which somebody sits cross-legged with his eyes closed and chants, "Ommmmmm"? That's referring to Buddhism (though a few other religions chant that word too).
- Have you ever seen a little statue that looks like this at a Chinese restaurant? That's a statue of Buddha.
- Have you ever heard about a bad person who had a terrible accident, and an adult commented, "That's karma"? Or have you seen someone do something nice and heard someone else say, "That's good karma"? *Karma* is a word found in Buddhism (borrowed from Hinduism).
- Have you ever heard the word *nirvana*? It showed up in *Toy Story*® when the squeaky alien toy thought it was reaching the ultimate reality by arriving at Sid's house, but the word also pops up in English in other ways. *Nirvana* is a word that comes from Buddhism.

For about 500 million people—more than the population of the United States and Canada combined—Buddhism has a massive impact. Buddhism is especially popular in eastern and southeast Asia: China, Japan, South Korea, Myanmar, Thailand, Laos, Cambodia. Buddhism greatly affects the cultures of these countries and many of their neighboring countries.

Some Buddhist beliefs have become noticeable in certain parts of American culture. Buddhism gives people an opportunity to be "spiritual" without believing in a god.

THE HISTORY OF BUDDHISM

Buddhism—like Judaism, Christianity, and Islam—has a definite historical beginning. But we don't really know for sure when that was. And that says something about Buddhism. This religion doesn't tie itself to history the way other religions do.

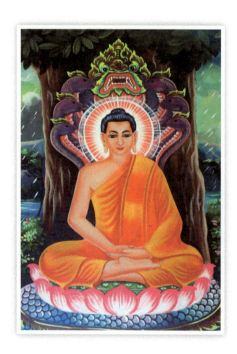

All the same, the history of Buddhism is important for understanding this religion. Buddhism was founded by Siddhartha Gautama. He was born at least five hundred years before Christ on what is now the border of India and Nepal. His father was a chieftain in the warrior caste.

The details of his life are not certain. But the general story is that Gautama was wealthy. He grew up, got married, and had a child. But once he really saw the suffering in the world, he decided to be an ascetic, someone who purposefully lives a life of severe self-discipline, without the comforts and pleasures others have. When he believed he had succeeded in full asceticism, he took on the name Buddha, "Enlightened One." He began to teach others the principles of his religion.

THE STORY, BELIEFS, AND PRACTICES OF BUDDHISM

Buddhism is known for connecting itself to principles: Four Noble Truths. These truths actually form something like a story—a big story, even—but one that is very different from the Christian story.

FOUR NOBLE TRUTHS

1 Stress (or Suffering): Buddhists are not united about where we all came from, but they do agree about what life is like: all life is stress. It's not just that times of suffering and disappointment happen; it's that having existence is itself stress. ▶

2 Desire (or Thirst): The reason people are so stressed is that they desire things. They want stuff; they want friends; they want food; they want to keep existing. If they didn't desire, they wouldn't have stress. ▶

3 Cessation: If they could cease desiring, all the stress would go away. They would achieve nirvana— liberation from desire. They could end the cycle of death and rebirth, which brings so many desires. The illusion of personhood would end, and they'd have no more stress. ▶

4 The path: The way to achieve this cessation, and eventual nirvana, is to practice the path. This path contains eight practices. Following the Eightfold Path is good karma, which helps people be reborn closer and closer to enlightenment. ▼

THE EIGHTFOLD PATH

8 Right concentration: Through meditation, train the mind to be rid of all desires and feelings.

7 Right mindfulness: Be aware of what's going on inside the mind in order to change bad habits or embrace positive thoughts.

6 Right effort: Think and act positively; then prevent evil in the world.

1 Right understanding: See the world through the teachings of the Four Noble Truths.

2 Right intention: Commit to letting go of desire or ill will.

3 Right speech: Don't tell lies or gossip or say harsh things.

4 Right action: Don't cheat or steal. Live in harmony with others.

5 Right livelihood: Don't make a living through bringing harm to others. Instead, work a job that will help people.

The story Buddhism tells doesn't focus on Creation. It doesn't have a Fall—but it has something similar. It has stress, or suffering. There's no Redemption, at least not exactly. No one is restored to the state God intended for them. Instead they escape into nirvana.

THE PROBLEM WITH DESIRE

It is common for people to look at something God created good and to blame that thing for all the trouble in this world. That's what Buddhism does: it looks at desire and says that desire is to blame for our troubles.

But the Bible does not teach that desire is wrong. Desire is a good thing, created by God. It is something God Himself has. In a way, it is something God Himself *is*.

To understand this, you need to see the connection between desire and love. The two are almost the same thing. To desire something is to love it; to love it is to desire it. Love is your heart going out to something. (Remember that definition from Section 3.5?)

You see the horse on the first day of camp, see it shake its mane, see its beauty—and your heart responds with love. Your heart sings about horses. You desire to taste the joys of caring for a horse, to enjoy the thrill of galloping on a horse! None of this is bad; it is good. God made horses in part so that humans would admire their beauty and desire the joys that only horse-riding can bring.

OK, maybe you don't love horses. Let's try another example.

You see the needs of the world. They need hope; they need help; they need Christ. And your heart responds with love. Your heart sings about bringing the gospel of Christ to the nations. You desire to prepare yourself and then dedicate yourself to the God-given joys of loving and serving others. None of this is bad; it is good. God made us to desire to see others find true joy.

God has desires. God has loves. And to say those two things is basically to say the same thing twice. He loved His creation when it was first made (Genesis 1:31). He loves His own glory (Isaiah 42:8). He loves the world (John 3:16). *God is love* (1 John 4:8).

The problem with humans, according to the Bible, is not that they have desires and loves. It's that they desire and love the wrong things. They don't love God first and their neighbor next. They desire things they're not supposed to have: wicked and twisted things.

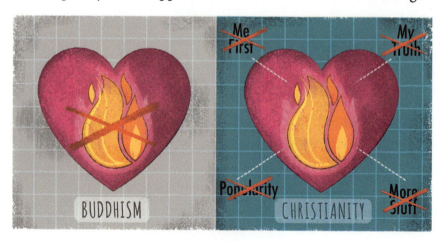

In the Christian story, stress and suffering happen not because of desire but because of sin. The answer is to see creation restored. And one of the things that will be restored is desire. In the new earth, the redeemed will desire only good. No more sin or curse.

BIBLE ANSWERS TO BUDDHIST BELIEFS

The Buddhist wonders how to rid himself of desire so that he can rid himself of stress.

The Bible says that our desires are not something to get rid of; they are something to purify. Our desires are a clue that the ultimate object of our desires *does* exist—and we should seek Him.

No one ever said this better than C. S. Lewis in *Mere Christianity*. Lewis actually made an argument for the existence of God that was based on human desires. He said,

> Creatures are not born with desires unless satisfaction for those desires exists. A baby feels hunger: well, there is such a thing as food. A duckling wants to swim: well, there is such a thing as water.

OK, so far so good. But what about when all your physical desires are met, and yet you still desire something more? Well, Lewis said,

> If I find in myself a desire which no experience in this world can satisfy, the most probable explanation is that I was made for another world. . . . Probably earthly pleasures were never meant to satisfy it, but only to arouse it, to suggest the real thing.

Yes, our desires are a clue. The endless search for satisfaction that humans are always on is a clue. *Something endless exists to satisfy us.* Someone endless invites us into that satisfaction. That someone is God, your Creator.

There are desires that need to be killed. Sinful desires. But desire itself is good. We should *not* try to quench our desires; we should try to stoke them—if they are good.

The Bible does offer an escape from stress and suffering. It offers rest—rest in that day when our desires will be fulfilled.

DESIRE EXISTS BECAUSE HEAVEN DOES. DESIRE EXISTS BECAUSE GOD DOES.

This is the good news the Buddhist needs to hear.

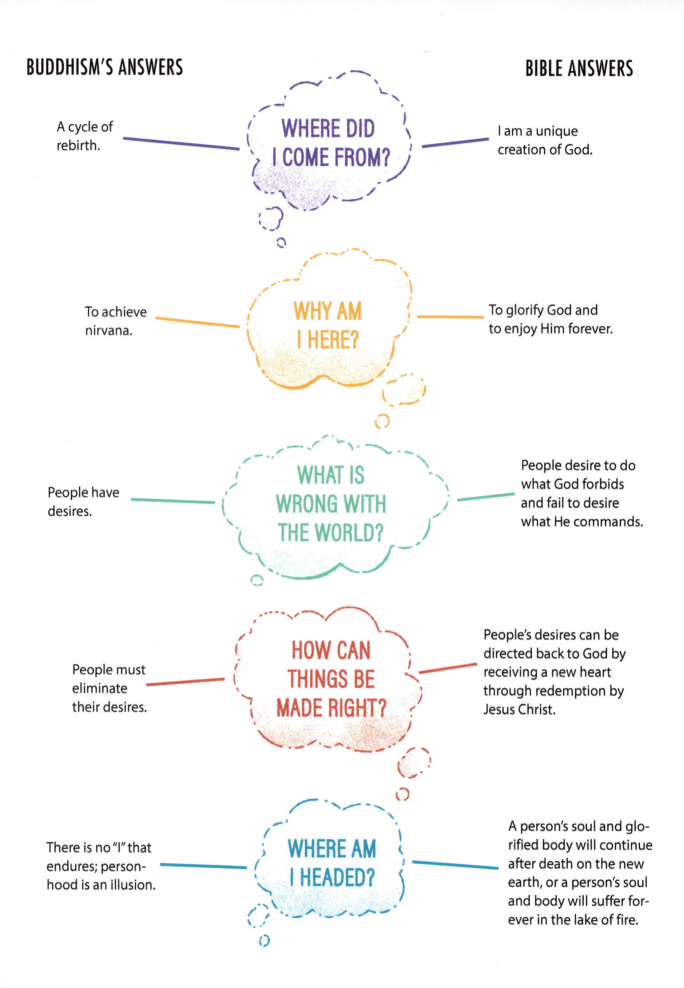

BUDDHISM'S ANSWERS

BIBLE ANSWERS

A cycle of rebirth.

WHERE DID I COME FROM?

I am a unique creation of God.

To achieve nirvana.

WHY AM I HERE?

To glorify God and to enjoy Him forever.

People have desires.

WHAT IS WRONG WITH THE WORLD?

People desire to do what God forbids and fail to desire what He commands.

People must eliminate their desires.

HOW CAN THINGS BE MADE RIGHT?

People's desires can be directed back to God by receiving a new heart through redemption by Jesus Christ.

There is no "I" that endures; personhood is an illusion.

WHERE AM I HEADED?

A person's soul and glorified body will continue after death on the new earth, or a person's soul and body will suffer forever in the lake of fire.

CASE STUDY: BUDDHISM'S UNANSWERABLE QUESTION

Nirvana doesn't actually mean living eternally in some state. Buddhists do not believe in a permanent self. Author Carl Olson explains nirvana this way:

> In a literal sense, nibbāna [nirvana] means the blowing out or extinction of a fire or the flame of a candle. From the Buddhist perspective, this does not mean that the flame is utterly annihilated. It rather persists in an unseen state. According to the predominant classical Sanskrit viewpoint, to blow out a candle is not to destroy the light but is rather to transform its mode of existence from visible to invisible. Similarly, . . . what are extinguished finally by the realization of nibbāna are the fires of greed, hatred, and delusion [what we think of as self].

Nirvana is the ultimate reality for a Buddhist. But because Buddhists believe it's impossible for someone who has not experienced nirvana to understand it, not much is written about it.

1. How do Buddhists view the concept of an eternal soul?

2. What worldview question does Buddhism try to answer with this view?

3. How does Buddhism fail to make sense of our desires for something greater after this life?

4. How does the Bible answer this worldview question?

Thinking It Through 8.3

1. How did Buddhism become a religion?

2. What is the Eightfold Path?

3. How does the Eightfold Path relate to the Four Noble Truths?

4. What does the Buddhist think we should do with our desires? What does the Christian think?

5. Where does Buddhism teach that people are headed? Where does the Bible teach that people are headed?

Is living a good life and seeking peace with others enough

There were two non-Christian men, Bradley and Thomas (these are true stories). Both seemed successful in the world. Each had a wife and children. Each of them was *not* religious.

Each was more than happy to believe that there is no God, that all that exists is matter and energy. Each was happy to believe that life came from non-life, and that humans are the result of billions of years of evolution. Their unbelief came from an alternative big story about the world and its beginning.

But each had Christian friends.

Bradley mocked Christians. He thought that believing in a supernatural being was for weak minds who inexplicably rejected science.

Thomas was a super nice guy; he didn't mock Christians, but he did argue with them good-naturedly on the internet.

Thomas's Christian friend Mike asked, "How can you live without any meaning for your life? If matter and energy are all that exists, then one day everything we do will be completely forgotten. There won't be anyone left to remember it." But Thomas was happy, he said, to create his meaning for himself. He lived his life with his family without a single thought for God.

Bradley was different. His Christian friend Tracy had a constant joy. He couldn't help noticing it. So he had a question for her: "How can you be joyful in this terrible world?"

Her answer was Jesus.

This rocked Bradley's world. Clearly, Tracy had something he didn't have. Her worldview was working for her in a way that his wasn't working for him. Bradley thought regularly about killing himself. Even getting married and having a good job didn't give meaning to his life.

Bradley started looking for Jesus.

THE HISTORY OF THE NONES

Many people are unbelievers like Thomas and Bradley. And even some people who check the "Christian" box in polls aren't really believers.

Christianity, though not always *biblical* Christianity, has been the most popular religion in the United States since its founding. But precisely because it has been so popular, a lot of people have always called themselves Christians even when their connection to a church was rather weak. Maybe they went on Easter and Christmas. These are called "nominal" Christians, because they are Christians in name only.

But beginning in 2010, the Pew Research Center, which polls the American population, noticed a trend. More of these nominal Christians were marking a different box when asked about their religion: *None.*

They claim to have no religion. So researchers began to call them the "Nones."

The Pew Research Center reported the trend in the article "In U.S., Decline of Christianity Continues at Rapid Pace." Between 2009 and 2019, the percentage of people in the United States who called themselves Christians dropped from 77 percent to 65 percent. The number of Nones went from 17 percent to 26 percent. Young people are far more likely to be Nones than older people.

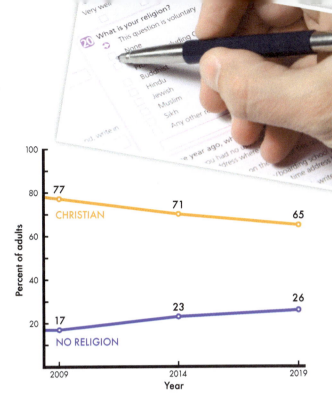

Now in one sense, nobody is a None. You've already learned that everybody worships at least something. And, in fact, some Nones still believe in some kind of higher power. They just aren't connected to any organized religion like Christianity, Judaism, or Islam. They sometimes call themselves "spiritual, but not religious."

No holy book, no rituals, no *official* beliefs.

UNBELIEF'S DIFFERENT BELIEF

But *nobody doesn't believe*. You can't not believe. We made this point back in Section 4.6: you can't *not* worship, any more than you can't *not* breathe. And like breathing, it's so normal that people don't even realize they're doing it. Being a "None" is itself a religious viewpoint.

We know this because the Bible says it. According to Romans 1:18–23, a passage we've talked about a few times, all people know this truth: the God of eternal power and divine nature exists. But many suppress that truth.

And what happens when they suppress the truth? Think about this famous saying that came from some of G. K. Chesterton's ideas:

When men choose not to believe in God, they do not thereafter believe in nothing, they then become capable of believing in anything.

When people deny what is obvious—that God made the world—Romans 1 says they have "changed the truth of God into a lie, and worshipped and served the creature more than the Creator" (1:25).

Everybody worships. If they don't worship the Creator, they pick something He created and worship it instead. It might be freedom and equality. It might be human rights. Or progress. Or self-help.

NONES DO WORSHIP. THEY DO BELIEVE.

Nones don't like to hear this. They generally like to think that, instead of beliefs, they have logical reasoning and common sense.

But even famous non-Christian thinker Stanley Fish says that Nones and Christians are *not* having a fight between reason and faith. He says, "It would be more accurate to frame it as a struggle between two different theologies." Yes, two very different responses to God.

Even Nones, says Fish, have "basic and inviolable assumptions"—just another way of saying "basic beliefs"—which they build on. ("Inviolable" means something can't be violated or denied, because it is considered authoritative.)

One side, the Christian side, believes that "true authority" for saying what is true and good comes from outside of nature—from God. The other side, the side the Nones are on, believes that the rules we have are all made up by humans—because there is no God. It takes strong faith to believe that everything we see comes from nothing and no one. Fish says that "each position is a theology." Each viewpoint is based on faith.

THE STORY, BELIEFS, AND PRACTICES OF UNBELIEF

Nones actually have *lots* of faith. And some hard-core beliefs.

Their creed (a formal statement of beliefs) might just be what Beatles star John Lennon sang in his world-famous song "Imagine." He encouraged his listeners to imagine that heaven and hell don't exist. Instead of thinking about the future, they could all just live in the moment.

In the worldview of the Nones, people kind of *have* to live in the moment because there are no moments after they die. They don't go up to heaven or down to hell, as the Bible says. They just go *piff*.

CASE STUDY: THE NONES' UNANSWERABLE QUESTION

Some Nones believe that people are ultimately on their own. Humans can achieve a good, successful life by their own power.

These Nones do not recognize any real brokenness in the world. Instead, they believe there are natural obstacles humans face. They also believe that private ownership and profit have inadequately met people's needs. As an alternative, they propose cooperation among everyone for the common good and sharing the resources of the world.

1. What seems good about these ideas?
2. What worldview question do these ideas fail to answer?
3. What is the biblical worldview answer to that question?
4. What does the biblical answer indicate about the proposed solution of sharing everything?
5. Give an example demonstrating the problem with the proposed solution.

Lennon asked people to imagine that there were no nations and no religion. These two things have repeatedly brought war—the Nones (like Lennon) are right about this. But the Nones think that if they take nations and religions away, war will go *piff* too, and we'll all have peace.

Truly, great is the faith of the Nones. They are able to maintain their faith despite powerful counter-evidence. It was, in fact, the two nations who tried to get rid of religion who ended up doing the most killing in the twentieth century. The Marxist Soviet Union and Communist China killed tens of millions of their own citizens. And then there are nations that lost nationhood—like Somalia, whose government simply failed. These non-nations all descended into bloody, never-ending warfare.

Lennon also invited people to imagine that no one has personal property but that people share what they have like loving, unified brothers. He failed to mention that (in the Nones' worldview) after the world is united, all dreamers will go *piff* too.

The big story of the world told by the Nones starts with nothing and ends with nothing. And yet Nones don't seem to mind.

BIBLE ANSWERS TO NONES' BELIEFS

Nones often don't want to talk about religion. And it's hard to give them Bible answers when they already think their worldview makes logical sense. But one way to initiate a conversation about their beliefs is to ask *them* questions. Ask them, *Do the things you love really match with your worldview?*

Think of some examples. Nones love the idea that people should peacefully coexist. But is that what they should expect if humans are the result of millions of years of evolution? Evolution is all about the survival of the fittest. It's red teeth and claws everywhere, because the animals who aren't fit *die*. The fittest people, the fittest nations will survive. The people and nations who don't make the cut . . . well, sorry. Their dreams go *piff*.

Some Nones look at the evil and suffering in the world and say that there can't be a God. They love the ideas of fighting evil with peace, of healing people's suffering through sharing. But only if there is a God judging human sin at the end of history is there a possibility that evil won't win. And only a God sharing His beloved Son will bring ultimate healing to people suffering physically—and spiritually.

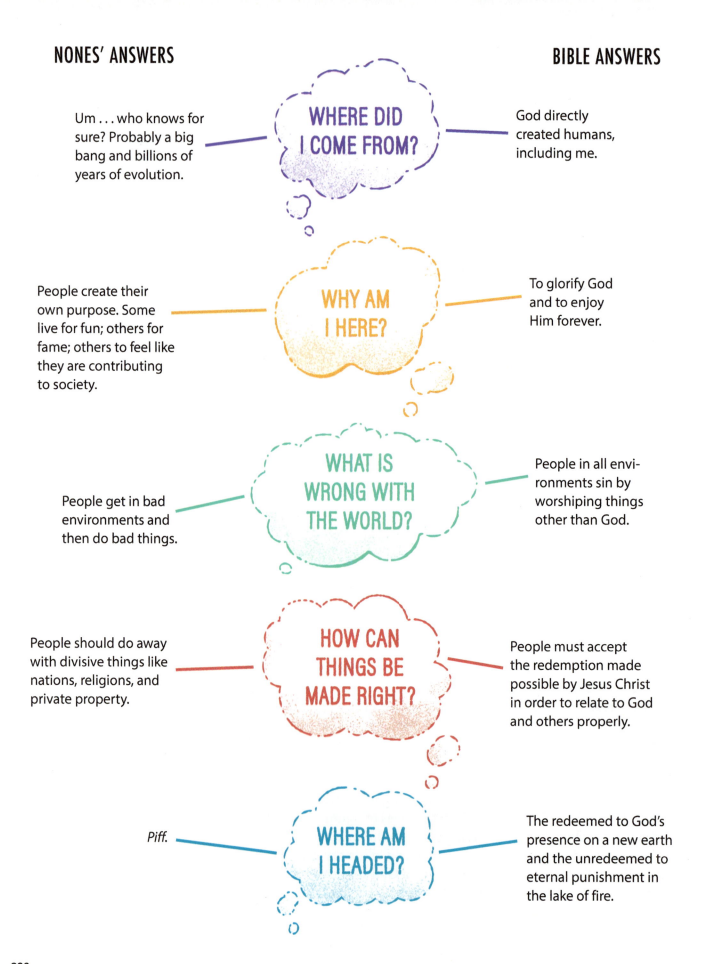

Um . . . who knows for sure? Probably a big bang and billions of years of evolution.

WHERE DID I COME FROM?

God directly created humans, including me.

People create their own purpose. Some live for fun; others for fame; others to feel like they are contributing to society.

WHY AM I HERE?

To glorify God and to enjoy Him forever.

WHAT IS WRONG WITH THE WORLD?

People in all environments sin by worshiping things other than God.

People get in bad environments and then do bad things.

People should do away with divisive things like nations, religions, and private property.

HOW CAN THINGS BE MADE RIGHT?

People must accept the redemption made possible by Jesus Christ in order to relate to God and others properly.

Piff.

WHERE AM I HEADED?

The redeemed to God's presence on a new earth and the unredeemed to eternal punishment in the lake of fire.

The Bible tells us that all people, including Nones, have consciences. They know that some of their own thoughts and feelings and actions are wrong, truly wrong. But Nones can't be forgiven unless a God takes the punishment of human sin on Himself. Otherwise they will still be feeling guilty when they finally go *piff*.

Actually, quite a number of things are difficult to explain without a God:

- the origin of the laws of nature
- the reason the universe can support life
- the origin of self-consciousness

The Nones often can't be bothered with these topics. But remember: the Bible tells you that, somewhere in their hearts, there is a knowledge of God and His moral laws. They might be suppressing these things, but they're there. Someday your questions and your truth-telling may get through to them.

They got through to Bradley, the former None. Bradley hadn't been looking for Jesus, and then suddenly he was. How did this happen? Surely Jesus had something to do with it.

Jesus reached out to Bradley through questions he couldn't answer. He wasn't satisfied with a life that would one day go *piff*. He knew he was made for more. So, share what you've learned from the Bible with unbelievers. God uses His Word to produce faith in the truth.

"SCIENCE CANNOT DO ANYTHING TO RELIEVE THE GUILT WEIGHING DOWN OUR SOULS, A WEIGHT TO WHICH IT HAS ADDED . . . , PRECISELY BY RENDERING US ABLE TO BE IN CONTROL OF, AND THEREFORE ACCOUNTABLE FOR, MORE AND MORE ELEMENTS IN OUR LIVES."

—WILFRED MCCLAY

Thinking It Through 8.4

1. What is a major difference between when Islam and Buddhism started and when the unbelief of the Nones started?

2. How does the big story told by the Nones start and end?

3. Which of the following statements would be made by Christians? Which would be made by Nones?
   "I go to church only for the community connection."
   "Everyone worships someone or something."
   "I can be joyful when things go wrong."
   "I believe only what science proves."
   "I want to help people."

4. How do the Nones fail to answer how things will be made right? How does biblical Christianity answer this question?

SECTION
8.5 SECULARISM

Is practicing religion only in church enough?

It's about time we talked about the worldview that runs the West: secularism. You've been seeing glimpses of it since Unit 1.

The word *secular* has been used by Christians through much of history. In Latin it referred to the "world." And the world that this word pointed to was the world of work—the world of butchers, bakers, and candlestick makers—rather than the sacred realm of the church and worship. The Roman Catholic Church at the time had what they called "secular" clergy. These were priests whose job was to live in the "real world." It was only monks who had the privilege of avoiding it.

There *are* differences between the world of daily work and the world of theology and worship. Seeing a difference between work and worship is a *Christian* idea. As Jesus taught Mary and busy Martha long ago, worship of Christ is the center of life (Luke 10:38–42). Worship is more important than doing dishes.

But it is a massive mistake to think that God doesn't care about doing dishes, or (worse) to kick Him out of the kitchen. Secularism today says that God, if He exists at all, doesn't rule over the "secular" world. In fact, He doesn't belong there at all.

At this point you should be having flashbacks to a really important concept you learned in Section 1.6: the two-story view. The Bible teaches that God rules over all His creation (Daniel 4:35). He rules over farming and banking and education and healthcare just as much as He rules over preaching and giving the gospel. God is God over all. And He belongs in all—not just in a religious, church-like story of the house.

Yet the Western world, beginning especially with the so-called Enlightenment in the 1700s, has been trying to push God into private places only (church and home).

They have told their Creator, like they would a dog, "Sit. Stay!"

"No—I said, STAY!"

That is secularism. Secularism is often boiled down to the idea that no theological ideas are allowed in public places like schools and government buildings. But secularism is actually a complete worldview, a lens through which many people—even people who follow an established religion—see the world.

That's right. Nones, Muslims, Jews, Buddhists, Hindus, Christians—anyone has the ability to be a secularist. The heart response of each one to God is this: *You can offer me (or just other people) some insight for my personal life, but that's as far as You can go.*

A secular person will have an odd two-sided worldview. Half for personal beliefs about God, or at least tolerance of others' personal beliefs. Half for decision-making in the public "real world." Secularism believes that only "neutral," "rational," "non-religious" viewpoints should be allowed in public.

AN EXAMPLE OF SECULARISM

Kim Davis was the county clerk for Rowan County, Kentucky. One of her jobs was to issue marriage licenses, official state permission slips for couples to get married. That job changed when the US Supreme Court made homosexual marriage legal in all fifty states.

Davis was a Christian who believed that there is no such thing as a homosexual marriage, any more than there are square circles or three-wheeled bicycles. When homosexual couples came to her office for licenses, Davis refused to sign the forms. She wasn't opposed to others issuing licenses as long as her name was not on the forms. But the Kentucky government would not fulfill her request.

Soon one homosexual couple was back with a large crowd and multiple cameras to video the event. One of the men demanded that Kim Davis give him a license to marry.

She politely refused.

He angrily said, "Under whose authority are you doing this?"

She calmly (but a little shakily because of all the angry eyes staring at her) replied, "Under God's authority." She walked back into her office and shut the door.

You might anticipate the reply that immediately rushed to the minds of every secular person who watched this video: *Kim Davis is imposing her religion on other people!*

You may have had the same thought.

But wait. The First Amendment to the US Constitution says that the government is not allowed to make laws "prohibiting the free exercise" of religion. That doesn't mean religious people get to go to the gym for free. It means they get to "work out" their religion in real life, and the government can't stop them.

This freedom, guaranteed by the US Constitution, runs smack into secularism. Secularism wants religious viewpoints *out* of public spaces like marriage licensing offices.

THE HISTORY OF SECULARISM

Secularists actually have historical reasons for their worldview. The history of secularism goes like this:

It used to be that the Western world was pretty well united under one institution, the Roman Catholic Church.

When the Protestant Reformation came along (1517), Europe was split.

Split Europe began to fight: Protestants against Catholics.

Enlightenment thinkers (late 1600s–1700s) said that nothing can be known with certainty about God. They figured that if they subtracted religion—especially Christianity—from European culture, they'd be left with no fights.

Their conclusion: we should all put our religion aside when we come into the public square. ("The public square" is a metaphor for all public spaces.) This secular worldview is *not* shared by all Americans. But it is massively influential among the recognized leaders in American culture, from politics to academics to the arts.

And it all makes a certain amount of sense. The Bible does teach that no one can be forced to believe. Salvation is a gift from God that must be received (Ephesians 2:8–9). So it's understandable that European societies ended up thinking that religion ought to be kept private.

CASE STUDY: SECULARISM AND VIOLENT RELIGION

Jean-Jacques Rousseau began the push toward a secular society during the Enlightenment. He claimed that religions are violent and practice large-scale killing when allowed into the public square. He made several other claims specifically about Christians: They were trying to set up a spiritual kingdom on earth. They wanted to divide power between the government and the church so that they could rule others. Meanwhile, they showed only fake respect for the established government. According to Rousseau, when Christianity did come into power,

> what the pagans had feared took place. Then everything changed its aspect: the humble Christians changed their language, and soon this so-called kingdom of the other world turned, under a

visible leader, into the most violent of earthly despotisms [dictatorships].

1. What assumption did Rousseau make about Christians who live under a non-Christian government?

2. What biblical principle demonstrates that biblical Christianity does not match Rousseau's assumption?

3. In what way did Rousseau apply a single historical example to all Christianity?

4. What biblical principles prove this example to be ultimately non-Christian?

THE MYTH OF SECULAR NEUTRALITY

The problem is that it doesn't work. Nobody can keep all theological assumptions out of the public square. Nobody can be neutral about important things like marriage. Every law imposes someone's moral views on someone else.

Back to Kim Davis.

Her secular critics often said precisely what the judge in charge of her court case said. Read this very carefully, because secularism is far more likely to tempt you (or crush you) than Islam or Buddhism is. The judge wrote,

> The State is not asking her [Davis] to condone [homosexual] unions on moral or religious grounds, nor is it restricting her from engaging in a variety of religious activities. . . . She is even free to believe that marriage is a union between one man and one woman . . . . However, her religious convictions cannot excuse her from performing the duties that she took an oath to perform as Rowan County Clerk.

The judge is saying that Davis is free to practice her religion *as long as her religion doesn't tell her to practice her religion in public spaces.* ("Sit. STAY!")

And yet the judge himself was unable to keep his own theological beliefs out of the case. He wrote a long opinion (a formal legal judgment). And in that opinion he couldn't stay neutral on the question at the heart of the case: *What is marriage?*

Science and reason alone can't tell you what marriage is. Only your true or false religion can tell you. Either you believe that marriage is a divine creation, or you believe it's a human creation. There is no neutrality on this question—or on any moral question.

YOU CANNOT SERVE GOD AND SECULARISM.

The judge wrote that homosexual couples have "a fundamental right to marry." Hidden in that little word *marry* are a number of beliefs that are *not* neutral or scientific. If anything, science would point in the opposite direction.

The judge used words like "equal" to argue that homosexual couples can marry just like opposite gender couples can. He said that to stop two men from marrying is to cause them "harm," which could not be undone.

Secularism loves to appear neutral. Who wants to be against equality? Who's in favor of harm? But the judge smuggled in his own (false) ideas of what counts as "equal" and "harm."

Christianity says that people *do* have an equal right to marry anyone as long as it is according to God's structural design for marriage. And Christianity says that real harm comes to them when we encourage them to define marriage their own way. We are giving them a license to risk their immortal souls. Remember Section 4.7: Paul said that homosexuals "shall not inherit the kingdom of God" (1 Corinthians 6:9). *There is no worse harm imaginable.*

The judge wrote that Davis "promote[d] her own religious convictions at the expenses of others." But that is precisely what he was doing to Davis.

THERE IS NO ULTIMATE NEUTRALITY. SOMEONE'S VIEW IS GOING TO WIN. AND SOMEONE'S IS GOING TO LOSE.

The judge then quoted the just-as-secular governor of Kentucky. The governor said that if clerks (like Kim Davis) couldn't in good conscience sign marriage licenses for homosexual couples, they should "resign and let someone else step in." *Leave the public square.*

That is not neutrality.

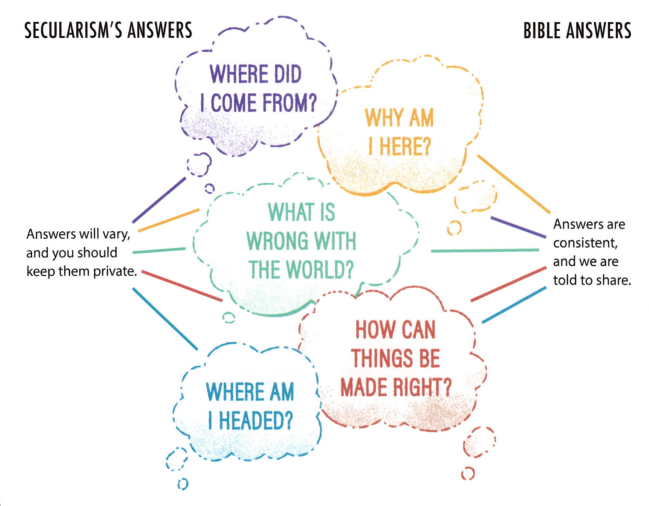

SECULARISM'S ANSWERS

BIBLE ANSWERS

WHERE DID I COME FROM?

WHY AM I HERE?

WHAT IS WRONG WITH THE WORLD?

HOW CAN THINGS BE MADE RIGHT?

WHERE AM I HEADED?

Answers will vary, and you should keep them private.

Answers are consistent, and we are told to share.

BIBLE ANSWERS TO THE SECULAR SOLUTION

Secularism seeks the solution to this question: "If religions cause such deep disagreements, how can we make a peaceful society (still keeping individual religious rights, of course)?"

And the Bible answers, in a way, "We can't." There's no guarantee in Scripture that a bunch of rebels against their Creator can form prosperous and peaceful societies.

But God is good, and God is love. He sends rain on both righteous and unrighteous people (Matthew 5:45). He even showed concern for the welfare of wicked Babylon while His people were captives there. He told His people to work toward the well-being of that city, and to pray for it, because in its peace they would find peace (Jeremiah 29:7). When God told Christians to devote themselves to good works (Titus 3:14), He was giving them basically the same advice He gave ancient Jews.

God blessed mankind to be fruitful, fill the earth, subdue it, and have dominion over it (Genesis 1:26–28). And God has blessed all societies to do these things for all time. It is their sin that has brought them trouble, not their merciful God.

Secularism asks Christians to check their faith at the door to all public spaces. But Christians cannot, *must* not, give in. We never get to have a break from the rule of our Creator, a vacation on an island He's not King of. And why would we want to?

Thinking It Through 8.5

1. Define *secularism*.

2. Briefly explain the history of secularism.

3. Give an example of secularism that you have personally seen.

4. How do secularists answer the question "What is wrong with the world?" How does this contrast with the way biblical Christianity answers this question?

God loves you too much to worry about a little lie.

Always be nice.

WORLDVIEW DILEMMA #99

What if telling the truth will hurt my friend's feelings

?

As long as you mostly tell the truth, a little lie isn't too bad.

Lie if you have to.

MORALISTIC THERAPEUTIC DEISM

Three big words. Add them together, and they are the name of one of the most powerful (but false) religions in North America. It's a hidden religion you've never heard of but is in plain sight everywhere. It's a religion that's hard to distinguish from the two-story view; they're fraternal twins. And it's a parasite that is sucking blood from Christianity.

(Gross, right? But true.)

Here are the three words that name this religion: Moralistic Therapeutic Deism (MTD for short). Now, what do they mean?

Is belief in God enough?

Moralistic means that this religion is focused on being nice. Be nice, and you'll have a happy life.

Therapeutic means "able to heal." This religion is centered on you, and thus on making you feel better.

Deism means an absent god—though MTD makes this god come back when you want a little of his magic pixie dust.

THE STORY, BELIEFS, AND PRACTICES OF MTD

"Moralistic Therapeutic Deism" is a term invented by a professor named Christian Smith, who interviewed hundreds of American teenagers a few years back. He asked them all kinds of questions about their religious lives. And he wrote a book called *Soul Searching* about what they said.

Most American teens have a pretty positive view of religions, but they are extremely bad at explaining theirs. For example, an eighteen-year-old Catholic girl that Smith talked to described the beliefs of Catholics this way:

> Like, you, you live better, like you, um, you have like a standard for yourself that's higher than like other people. Uh, I don't know.

(For what it's worth, that's not an accurate summary of Catholic doctrine.)

There were some—especially Mormons and Bible-believers—who were much better at explaining what they believe. But many teens who attended Catholic or very liberal churches (churches that don't believe the Bible is really true) had no idea what they believed.

Yet they *did* believe. By asking them lots and lots of questions, Smith discovered their beliefs—and he found a hidden religion that has been taking over Christianity in America: MTD. He called it the "dominant religion among contemporary U.S. teenagers."

The teens didn't hold any cohesive big story—more like personal stories of how religion helped them. Yet they made sense of their world with a set of beliefs that Smith summarized like this:

1. A God exists who created and orders the world and watches over human life on earth.
2. God wants people to be good, nice, and fair to each other, as taught in the Bible and by most world religions.
3. The central goal of life is to be happy and to feel good about oneself.
4. God does not need to be particularly involved in one's life except when God is needed to resolve a problem.
5. Good people go to heaven when they die.

What do you think of these beliefs?

CHRISTIANITY AND MTD

And what does the Bible say about them? Let's evaluate them one by one.

1. A God exists who created and orders the world and watches over human life on earth.

Well, yes. That's all biblical. MTD sucked these beliefs out of Christianity. People who follow MTD may actually think they *are* Christians because they hold beliefs like these. But the lowercase-*g* god of MTD never seems to get described beyond this. He's like a hazy cloud. The harder you look and the closer you get, the more he fades away into nothing.

"It doesn't matter which religious faith [people have]," one teen told Smith, "as long as they believe in God." But the true God is neither nebulous nor all-inclusive.

By contrast, the God of the Bible has a Son who died for human sin and rose again to give people new life. The God of the Bible commands all people everywhere to repent from their sins and believe in that Son. He created, yes, but He also commands.

2. God wants people to be good, nice, and fair to each other, as taught in the Bible and by most world religions.

Another American teen told Smith, "That's one way that someone can try to be a better person, through organized religion." One religion isn't more right than another, as long as whichever you follow is helping you be good.

In MTD, "good" and "nice" mean you don't tell other people that what they're doing is wrong. If MTD had its own version of a Bible, it would delete all verses but this one: "Judge not, that ye be not judged" (Matthew 7:1).

And things get tricky here. Yes, the God of Scripture wants people to be good and nice and fair. But once again we've got a place where MTD resists defining its terms.

In the real Bible, being good means being like God (Luke 18:19). And being like God means standing against people when they do wrong. Even the apostle Paul did that to the apostle Peter (read Galatians 2:11–14). Christians are called to be kind and tenderhearted and quick to forgive (Ephesians 4:32). But Christians are not supposed to be so "nice" that they fail to tell people the truth. That actually *isn't* nice. People need to hear the truth, even if it hurts them at first.

3. The central goal of life is to be happy and to feel good about oneself.

Another teen said to Smith, "If people without religion are happy, that's okay for them. But if they start feeling like there's something missing, then I think they should believe in something." In other words, you don't exist for MTD's god. He exists for you. If you want him. Religion is just a tool to help you be happy.

The Bible does *not* teach that the goal of life is to be happy. The Bible is the true story of what God is doing *to glorify Himself* by redeeming His fallen creation. "Of him, and through him, and to him, are all things: to whom be glory for ever" (Romans 11:36). You are one of those things that is from God and to God.

Now, loving God and trusting Him and obeying Him *will* make your life better. It will sometimes make you feel good about yourself—though it will also regularly make you feel bad about yourself because it will show you your sin. And Jesus does promise happiness to those who meekly follow Him (Matthew 5:1–12).

But the central goal of the Christian life is to glorify God and enjoy Him forever, not to glorify and enjoy yourself.

4. God does not need to be particularly involved in one's life except when God is needed to resolve a problem.

Okay, it wasn't fair to say that MTD's version of the Bible would have only one verse in it. Actually, it would keep twice that many verses. Here's the other one it wouldn't throw out:

"I know the plans I have for you," says the Lord, "plans to prosper you, not to harm you, to give you a future and a hope." (Jeremiah 29:11)

One American teen said to Smith, "It's important that people take religion as their own and interpret it as it helps them." In MTD, you can take or leave god. Mainly he's nice to have around when you need a good luck charm. When you're hoping that Target hasn't run out of those cool shoes, you can pray a quick prayer. When you're lonely, god will come listen to you complain. And then when you feel a little better and decide you'd rather watch a movie, he'll go away again and wait for the next time you need him. ("Sit! STAY!")

But read the Bible, and you'll see that the biblical God isn't like an outdoor cat, happy for you to pet it as you walk by and just as happy to do its own thing (which is mostly to sleep in the sun). God is not a pet you can sort of control—He's more like a lion. He is the King of the jungle (and the whole rest of the planet).

God isn't just available; He's always present. He's always ruling, directing, guiding. Your job is to fit into His story, not to fit Him into yours.

5. Good people go to heaven when they die.

One teen said to Smith, "To go to heaven you don't have to go to church." Another told him, "If you do the right thing and don't do anything bad, I mean nothing really bad, you know you'll go to heaven."

Go to a funeral and listen to people who aren't Christians speak. What will you hear? A lot of stuff that is sort of vaguely Christian but not really. The writer of this book just heard these words at a funeral: "I believe that Katie's spirit is here with us now. And someday I'll meet her again up in the sky in a big party. I will only say nice things about her here because, you know, I don't want her ghost to haunt me!"

CASE STUDY: CHURCH AND MTD

In a sequel called *Souls in Transition*, Christian Smith interviewed young adults, ages eighteen through twenty-three, about their religious beliefs. He found that Moralistic Therapeutic Deism "continues to be the faith of very many emerging adults." Here is what one of them said about church.

> Religion is not made for young people. Look at the entertainment aspect: even education, the average elementary school all the way through college, it's so oriented around movies, video games, entertainment, fun books. Why on earth would young people go to church if it doesn't offer anything personal as a reward, especially when church just tells them what they're doing wrong? . . . To youth, it's boring. I myself didn't like going to church when I was younger, and sometimes still don't when I feel lectured at. . . . It really doesn't give comfort when kids are doing all these things wrong in their lives.

1. Which of the three words in MTD's name does this quotation demonstrate?

2. Is this view of church wrong? Explain.

3. How should believers view church?

4. How do you view church?

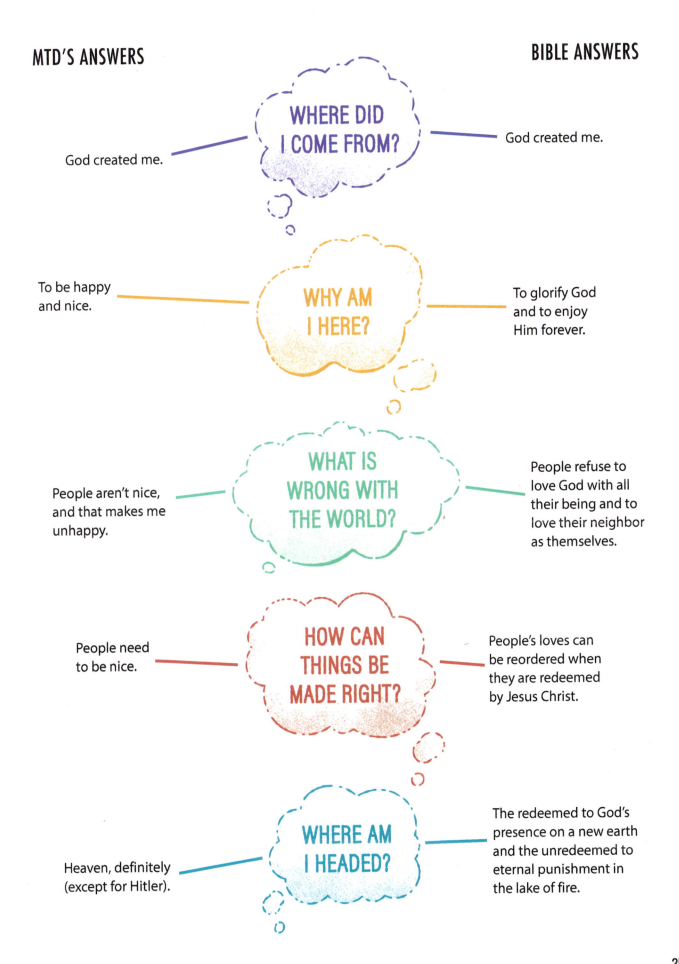

WHERE DID I COME FROM?

God created me.

God created me.

WHY AM I HERE?

To be happy and nice.

To glorify God and to enjoy Him forever.

WHAT IS WRONG WITH THE WORLD?

People aren't nice, and that makes me unhappy.

People refuse to love God with all their being and to love their neighbor as themselves.

HOW CAN THINGS BE MADE RIGHT?

People need to be nice.

People's loves can be reordered when they are redeemed by Jesus Christ.

WHERE AM I HEADED?

Heaven, definitely (except for Hitler).

The redeemed to God's presence on a new earth and the unredeemed to eternal punishment in the lake of fire.

Every follower of MTD thinks he or she is going to heaven. The idea that good, nice, and fair people like them might be left out . . . well, never occurs to them.

The Bible offers eternal life only to those who will repent and trust Christ. There is no one good enough for heaven without receiving God's righteousness *in Christ*.

BIBLE ANSWERS TO MTD'S BELIEFS

You've now read pretty much an entire book teaching a biblical worldview. Can *you* explain in basic terms what you believe and how it fits into your life? Can you explain how biblical worldview lenses help you see reality?

There are many people who have gone through books like this and chosen not to believe God's words. They have become believers in Moralistic Therapeutic Deism (or total secularists or Nones).

There's one huge question, though, that MTD cannot really answer, but you should be able to now. It's the question of every human conscience: *What do I do with my guilt?*

MTD offers no hope. If you're not happy and you don't feel good about yourself, MTD says, "Be good and nice!" That's not an answer. There's no hope there because far too often, if we're honest with ourselves, we are neither good nor nice.

The Bible tells Christians to "be ready always to give an answer to every man that asketh you a reason of the hope that is in you" (1 Peter 3:15). Here's the reason: Jesus died to pay the penalty for all the times you were bad and mean. Even one sin would have been enough for you to need a Savior. Jesus rose again and offers you new life *in Him*. There's actual relief from your nagging, guilty conscience now and the promise of full redemption from your body of sin when you die.

That is reason for hope.

Thinking It Through 8.6

1. List the five beliefs of Moralistic Therapeutic Deism.

2. Which of the five beliefs of MTD have you heard people say in real life?

3. Which of the five beliefs of MTD is most similar to biblical Christianity?

4. What answer does MTD have for human guilt? How does biblical Christianity answer human guilt?

The Bible is the true story of what God is doing to glorify Himself by redeeming His fallen creation. You can say it in your sleep now:

CREATION, FALL, REDEMPTION.

God created; mankind fell; Christ is redeeming and restoring fallen people and the whole universe to be what they were created to be.

This book has tried to show that this big story is the only one that makes sense of all the little stories out there, including all the stories that make up your life.

This book has tried to show that who God is, how you spend your time, how you relate to others, how you discern your place in the world, and how you view other worldviews all has to be fit into the story of the Bible.

So let's end this book with four stories. Each will demonstrate a truth essential to using your biblical worldview in real life:

What should I do now ?

1 God gave me a good world as a gift to enjoy. (That's **Creation**.)

2 The world I live in demands that I be discerning. (That's **Fall**.)

3 I can thrive in this world with God's help. (That's **Redemption** of people.)

4 I can live with hope that Christ will make everything right again. (That's **Redemption** of the universe.)

1. GOD GAVE ME A GOOD WORLD AS A GIFT TO ENJOY.

Ransom Poythress is the son of a theologian and Bible professor. Ransom himself is a teacher of science.

But for a while in his life, he fell out of love with science. "Droning professors, stuffy classrooms, and inane [meaningless] paperwork" just about snuffed out the sparkle science used to have for him. He felt that the "thrill of discovery" had to be there somewhere still, but it was covered up, hidden.

But then he went to seminary to study the Bible, and in those studies and in that Bible, he rediscovered his love for God's creation.

This is how it happened. His father, the seminary professor, was giving a lecture on science and faith to an audience at a major university. Ransom had to introduce his father to the crowd, and he was nervous.

But as his dad's talk went on, something special happened in that room. People fell silent, whether they were Christians or not. Was Ransom's father a spellbinding orator? Was he a stand-up comedian?

No, just the opposite. Neither his words nor his appearance were anywhere close to extraordinary. Ransom wondered why the audience was listening so intently.

Then it hit him:

My father was overjoyed with what he was saying. He didn't just think intellectually that God was revealed in all creation; he felt it. In his talk, he actively worshiped God for the beautiful harmonies revealed in creation. He glorified God for the way he revealed himself. Here was a man with two PhDs enamored [captivated] and animated, rocking back and forth, hardly able to contain his giddy enthusiasm! He was full of child-like amazement, and it was infectious. We all wanted that.

God created this world to be full of good things for you to study, taste, experience, hear, and see. Will you immerse yourself in those good things? Will you put in the time to study and experience those things with gratitude to your good Creator?

God gave you a good world as a gift to enjoy.

2. THE WORLD I LIVE IN DEMANDS THAT I BE DISCERNING.

This is a short story, but it gets repeated so, so often that it is a very important story. It goes like this:

> Person wakes up and goes to work or school for the day. Person comes home and turns on TV or some other screen. At some point, person gets some food (screen stays on). Six hours of screen time later, person goes to bed. Repeat.

Great writer David Foster Wallace was not a Christian. In that five-point story above, he saw hopelessness, and he decided to write an essay about it. He knew that people claimed to need to "unwind" every day with the help of television, but why six hours a day?

Wallace wrote that what TV *really* does is sell dreams, dreams of a life that rises above the boredom and pointlessness people feel in their actual lives.

The stuff on TV, Wallace said, is larger than life. It's "shoot-outs and car wrecks." It's "the rapid-fire 'collage' of commercials, news, and music videos." It's "the 'hysteria' of prime-time soap [opera] and sitcom." And it all says, "Life is quicker, denser, more interesting, more . . . well, *lively*" than the lives we actually have.

He summed up the TV's message: "There's a world where life is lively, where nobody spends six hours a day unwinding before a piece of furniture." But then it says, ironically, "Your best and only access to this world is TV."

A small amount of entertainment is part of the good world that God gave you as a gift to enjoy. But it seems many people can't limit themselves to small doses.

Your parents may determine the boundary for you between appropriate and inappropriate amounts of screen time. But the day is coming, if it hasn't already, when it will be up to you. Will you go with the flow of pixels and binge-watch some random TV show? Or will you embrace the exciting but demanding calling of God to fill the earth, subdue it, and have dominion over it (and use screens discerningly to do it)? Will you invest your life in the Great Commission of Christ to take the gospel to the nations?

Life presents you with innumerable choices. You have to choose where you'll store your treasures (Matthew 6:19–21).

The world you live in demands that you be discerning.

3. I CAN THRIVE IN THIS WORLD WITH GOD'S HELP.

Ernest Gordon lay expecting to die in what the prisoners of war called the Death House. Though this was supposed to be the prisoners' hospital, most men who entered it did not leave it alive. The physical conditions were more awful than your brain could imagine. The smells—even worse.

These prisoners had been forced to build a railroad by hand through the jungles of Thailand on a starvation diet. Ernest explained,

> As conditions steadily worsened, as starvation, exhaustion, and disease took an ever-growing toll, the atmosphere in which we lived was increasingly poisoned by selfishness, hatred, and fear.

As he lay in that house of death with multiple diseases ravaging his body, Ernest saw something different—something he couldn't explain. Another prisoner named Dusty Miller came up to him and asked whether he could bathe the wounds on Ernest's legs.

Dusty was a Christian who lived out his faith in the prison camp. His selfless actions moved Ernest to seek out what Jesus was really like. Ernest started as a skeptic, but as he studied and talked through the Gospels with other believers in the camp, he discovered the new life Jesus offered, which surpassed all that he knew in the camp. He followed Christ, and his life began to change.

God was working in other lives as well. Ernest said,

> Death was still with us—no doubt about that. But we were being slowly freed from its destructive grip. . . . Selfishness, hatred, jealousy, and greed were all anti-life. Love, self-sacrifice, mercy, and creative faith, on the other hand, were the essence of life, turning mere existence into living in its truest sense.

The prisoners of war began to live more fully than their free captors. Their thriving was evident even when they were liberated. Soldiers, who saw their suffering, were about to take revenge on the captors, but the prisoners stopped them. God's forgiveness of their own sins had helped them forgive the sins done against them.

Will you return good for evil in the world around you? Will you push back on fallen direction with grace and faith? Will you make the most of the life God has given you?

You can thrive in this world with God's help.

4. I CAN LIVE WITH HOPE THAT CHRIST WILL MAKE EVERYTHING RIGHT AGAIN.

Rebecca McLaughlin is the mother of an eight-year-old girl. Like all mothers, Rebecca has words of praise for her daughter: "Her vocabulary is broad, her imagination is wild."

"But," says her own mother, "her stories are dull." Poor kid. What makes this girl's stories so uninteresting? Her mom explains,

> [It's] because she strives for happiness throughout. Without suffering, her characters cannot develop. Without fellowship in suffering, they cannot truly bond.

Ah. Now that makes sense. Think of some of the world's most popular stories, from *Grimm's Fairy Tales* to *The Secret Garden*. In classic stories, the characters suffer. In *The Secret Garden*, Mary loses both of her parents and must move to a new place; Colin loses his mother and is rarely cared for by his father. Dickon faithfully puts up with their faults in order to teach them kindness.

And the characters bond. Classic stories bring us some of literature's greatest friendships, like Mary, Colin, and Dickon. Suffering binds them together, as it binds us in real life. You are young. But some of you have really suffered. And all of you will, someday in some way. Seek friends like these who will suffer alongside you.

But classic stories don't end with suffering, because the real world doesn't. And your life doesn't have to either. Suffering is the path to salvation in the good stories.

Rebecca explains how this works in the best story of all,

> The Bible begins and ends with happiness, but the meat [the middle] of the story is raw. Christians are promised that one day, God "will wipe away every tear from their eyes, and death shall be no more, neither shall there be mourning, nor crying, nor pain anymore" (Rev. 21:4). But we are not promised that God will not allow us to cry in the first place. What end could possibly be worth all this pain? Jesus says he is.

Will you embrace suffering on the road to glorification? Will you surround yourself with people who will claim God's promise of Redemption with you?

You can live with hope that Christ will make everything right again.

WORLDVIEW QUEST: MY WORLDVIEW PLAN

Introduction

Few people think about their worldview as a whole. This book has confronted you with both a biblical worldview and alternate worldviews. And it prompted you to think through your own worldview as you worked your way through each unit.

While few people take much time to think through their worldview, fewer still take the time to actively shape their worldview with a focused plan of action. Finishing this book without planning some actions in response would be missing a valuable opportunity.

Task

Section 8.7 has given you four truths about life based on a biblical worldview. These four truths were developed based on the biblical answers to these five worldview questions.

1. Where did I come from?
2. Why am I here?
3. What is wrong with the world?
4. How can things be made right?
5. Where am I headed?

Using these four truths and the answers you've learned for the five worldview questions, you will create a personal plan of action that you will explain in a video presented to your family or your class.

Procedure

Your plan of action will include three parts: values, goals, and tasks. Your values should be based on the four truths. Your goals should be based on your values. Your tasks should break down your goals into steps that can be accomplished in daily actions.

1. Develop values, goals, and tasks from each of the four truths. You should have at least one value for each truth, at least one goal for each value, and at least two tasks for each goal.

   a. Your values should be things you hold as important based on the truth and a biblical worldview. For instance, "beauty" might be a value based on the first truth. Your values may be stated as single words, phrases, or sentences. "I value beauty in God's creational order" might be a value sentence.

   b. Your goals should be based on your values and should be measurable and attainable. "I will value beauty in art" is not a measurable goal. "I will be able to describe the beauty of art based on the recognized standards for great art" is both measurable and attainable.

   c. Your tasks simply break down your goals into steps. "Check out and read a book about art" is a task that will move you toward your goal.

2. After developing your plan, create a script for your video. This script should be written with the audience of your family or class in mind. The purpose of the script is to explain your plan to this audience.

3. Use the script as you shoot your video. Edit your video as needed.

4. Present this video to your family or class.

Scripture Memory

Romans 1:21
John 1:1, 14
Philippians 3:20–21
Psalm 10:4
1 Corinthians 10:31
Luke 9:23
1 Peter 3:15

Recall

1. What is a worldview?

2. In what century and in what country (give the modern-day name) did Muhammad begin the religion of Islam?

3. When and where was Buddha (Siddhartha Gautama) born?

4. What conclusion did the Enlightenment secularists make from all the religious wars happening in Europe?

5. What is the one belief of Moralistic Therapeutic Deism that is most similar to biblical Christianity?

6. Which religion from this unit tries to eliminate desire as the way to eliminate suffering?

Understand

7. Do worldviews make cultures, or do cultures make worldviews? Explain.

8. What is the major difference between the Christian view of God and the Muslim view of God?

9. Describe the Five Pillars of Islam.

10. If, as John Lennon imagined in a famous song, there were no heaven, no hell, no nations, and no religion, do you think people would live in peace? Explain.

Think Critically

11. What does Islam say to a Muslim who asks, "How can I know that I will be with God when I die?" What does biblical Christianity say to that same Muslim?

12. Many Nones say they are spiritual but not religious. Based on the elements of a worldview, what is the problem with their statement?

13. How would you describe the god of a religious secularist?

14. Is Moralistic Therapeutic Deism watered-down Christianity or a different religion altogether? Explain.

Internalize

15. How does understanding someone else's worldview help you help them? How does it help you help yourself?

16. How often is it appropriate to use harsh language with those with whom you disagree? When is it appropriate?

17. Which non-Christian worldview is most likely to tempt you?

NOTES

UNIT 1

1.3

Excerpts from MERE CHRISTIANITY by C. S. Lewis copyright © C.S. Lewis Pte. Ltd. 1942, 1943, 1944, 1952. Reprinted by permission.

Andrew Sullivan, "America's New Religions," Intelligencer, *New York Magazine*, December 7, 2018, http://nymag.com /intelligencer/2018/12/andrew-sullivan-americas-new -religions.html.

1.4

C. S. Lewis, *The Lion, the Witch and the Wardrobe*, in The Chronicles of Narnia (New York: HarperCollins, 1950), 131.

Excerpts from MERE CHRISTIANITY by C. S. Lewis copyright © C.S. Lewis Pte. Ltd. 1942, 1943, 1944, 1952. Reprinted by permission.

Richard Dawkins, "Richard Dawkins: You Ask the Questions Special," *Independent*, December 4, 2006, https://www .independent.co.uk/news/people/profiles/richard-dawkins -you-ask-the-questions-special-427003.html.

1.5

Floyd Cochran, interview by Terry Gross, *Fresh Air*, WHYY-FM Philadelphia radio broadcast, March 21, 1994, Audible® audio, June 13, 2001, https://www.audible.com/pd/Fresh-Air-Floyd -Cochran-Audiobook/B002VE7KWO.

1.6

John F. Kennedy, "Address to the Houston Ministers Conference" (speech, September 12, 1960), transcript, https://www .jfklibrary.org/learn/about-jfk/historic-speeches/address -to-the-greater-houston-ministerial-association.

Stephen Jay Gould, *Leonardo's Mountain of Clams and the Diet of Worms: Essays on Natural History* (Cambridge, MA: Belknap Press of Harvard University Press, 2011), 282.

1.7

Piet van den Berg and Tim W. Fawcett, "Evolution and Bad Boyfriends," *New York Times*, October 11, 2013, https://www .nytimes.com/2013/10/13/opinion/sunday/evolution-and -bad-boyfriends.html.

Marilynne Robinson, "Humanism," in *The Givenness of Things: Essays* (New York: Farrar, Straus and Giroux, 2015), 7.

UNIT 2

2.2

J. R. R. Tolkien, *The Return of the King*, in *The Lord of the Rings* (New York: Houghton Mifflin, 1966), 1007.

C. S. Lewis, *The Last Battle*, in The Chronicles of Narnia (New York: HarperCollins, 1956), 767.

2.3

Total Fertility Rate (TFR) vs. GDP per capita chart adapted from original chart created by Gregor Hagedorn, "CIA WFB TotFertilityRate-GDP-Population - Complete 2016.png," Wikimedia Commons, June 1, 2017, CC by SA, https://commons .wikimedia.org/wiki/File:CIA_WFB_TotFertilityRate-GDP -Population_-_Complete_2016.png.

2.4

Steve Jobs, commencement address at Stanford University (June 12, 2005), prepared text and video, *Stanford Report*, June 14, 2005, https://news.stanford.edu/2005/06/14/jobs -061505.

2.5

Julie Rose, "'Violins of Hope': Instruments from the Holocaust," WFAE 90.7 Charlotte radio broadcast, aired on *All Things Considered*, NPR, April 15, 2012, https://www.npr.org/2012 /04/15/150645417/violins-of-hope-instruments-from-the -holocaust.

"Violins of Hope: Strings of the Holocaust," directed and produced by Lance K. Shultz, aired on February 8, 2016, on WVIZ / PBS Ideastream Specials, https://www.pbs.org/video/wviz -pbs-ideastream-specials-violins-hope-strings-holocaust.

2.6

Albert M. Wolters, *Creation Regained*, 2nd ed. (Grand Rapids, MI: Eerdmans, 2005), 45–46.

2.7

C. S. Lewis, *Christian Reflections* (1967; Grand Rapids, MI: Eerdmans, 2014), 41.

UNIT 3

3.1

Amazon Viners, Reddit community "r/amazon," https://www .reddit.com/r/amazon/comments/8lfq7c/amazon_vine_11 _years_thanks_and_good_bye/.

J. I. Packer, *Knowing God* (Downers Grove, IL: InterVarsity, 1973), 19.

3.3

Frederick Douglass, *My Bondage and My Freedom* (New York: Miller, Orton & Mulligan, 1855), 90.

Richard Dawkins, *River Out of Eden: A Darwinian View of Life* (New York: Basic Books, 1995), 133.

3.4

Dana Gioia, "Beauty's Place in the Christian Vision" (chapel message, February 8, 2012), Biola University, La Mirada, CA, video, https://www.youtube.com/watch?v=xmEbg36_IDY (accessed June 2019; video made private by March 2020).

3.5

Jonathan Edwards, *Ethical Writings*, ed. Paul Ramsey, vol. 8 of *The Works of Jonathan Edwards*, ed. John E. Smith (New Haven, CT: Yale University Press, 1989), 369.

C. S. Lewis, *The Four Loves* (New York: Harcourt, Brace, 1960), 127.

3.6

Jonathan Edwards, *Ethical Writings*, ed. Paul Ramsey, vol. 8 of *The Works of Jonathan Edwards*, ed. John E. Smith (New Haven, CT: Yale University Press, 1989), 414 [first quotation], 467 [second quotation].

Isabelle Dances into the Spotlight, American Girl®, directed by Vince Marcello (2014).

UNIT 4

4.1

Rosaria Champagne Butterfield, *Openness Unhindered* (Pittsburgh: Crown & Covenant, 2015), 31.

C. S. Lewis, *Prince Caspian*, in The Chronicles of Narnia (New York: HarperCollins, 1951), 416.

4.2

United Nations General Assembly, Resolution 217 A, "Universal Declaration of Human Rights," December 10, 1948, https://www.un.org/en/universal-declaration-human-rights/index.html.

Cornelius Van Til, *The Defense of the Faith*, 4th ed., ed. K. Scott Oliphint (Phillipsburg, NJ: P&R, 2008), 34.

4.3

Mildred D. Taylor, *Roll of Thunder, Hear My Cry* (New York: Dial Books, 1976), 114 [first and second quotations], 126 [third quotation].

Stephen Jay Gould, quoted in David Friend and the editors of *Life*, *The Meaning of Life: Reflections in Words and Pictures on Why We Are Here* (Boston: Little, Brown, 1991), 33.

4.6

Molly Worthen, "The Anti-College Is on the Rise," *New York Times* online, June 8, 2019, https://www.nytimes.com/2019/06/08/opinion/sunday/college-anti-college-mainstream-universities.html.

David Foster Wallace, "This Is Water," commencement address at Kenyon College (May 21, 2005), http://bulletin-archive.kenyon.edu/x4280.html.

4.7

Kevin Vanhoozer, *Hearers and Doers: A Pastor's Guide to Making Disciples through Scripture and Doctrine* (Bellingham, WA: Lexham, 2019), 63.

Alastair Roberts, "Why We Should Jettison the 'Strong Female Character,'" Mere Orthodoxy (website), April 18, 2016, https://mereorthodoxy.com/why-we-should-jettison-the-strong-female-character/, citing William D. Lassek and Steven J. C. Gaulin, "Costs and Benefits of Fat-Free Muscle Mass in Men: Relationship to Mating Success, Dietary Requirements, and Native Immunity," *Evolution and Human Behavior* 30 (2009): 322–28.

UNIT 5

5.2

Tests for discerning among choices drawn from Mark Minnick, "Making Mature Choices, Part 2," sermon at Mount Calvary Baptist Church (September 19, 2007), audio, https://www.mountcalvarybaptist.org/Pages/Sermons/Default.aspx?SeriesID=282.

5.3

The Chick-fil-A® Corporate Purpose is property of CFA Properties, Inc. All Rights Reserved. The views and opinions expressed in this book are those of the authors and do not necessarily reflect the official policy or position of Chick-fil-A, Inc. or any of its affiliates. [used by permission]

S. Truett Cathy, *Eat Mor Chikin: Inspire More People* (Decatur, GA: Looking Glass Books, 2002), 11 [first quotation], 46 [second quotation], 48 [third quotation].

5.4

Kurt Eichenwald, "The Bible: So Misunderstood It's a Sin," *Newsweek* online, December 23, 2014, https://www.newsweek.com/2015/01/02/thats-not-what-bible-says-294018.html.

Molly Worthen, "The Anti-College Is on the Rise," *New York Times* online, June 8, 2019, https://www.nytimes.com/2019/06/08/opinion/sunday/college-anti-college-mainstream-universities.html.

5.5

Andy Crouch, "Gestures and Postures," chap. 5 in *Culture Making: Recovering Our Creative Calling* (Downers Grove, IL: IVP Books, 2008).

Chris Williams, "Goodbye, Family Christian Stores," *Chrisicisms* (blog), February 25, 2017, https://www.patheos.com/blogs/chrisicisms/2017/02/25/goodbye-family-christian-stores/.

5.6

Andy Crouch, *Culture Making: Recovering Our Creative Calling* (Downers Grove, IL: IVP Books, 2008), 67.

Makoto Fujimura, "How to 'See' My Painting," February 12, 2015, https://www.makotofujimura.com/writings/how-to-see-my-painting/. [used by permission] In quotations where there are bracketed and unbracketed ellipses, bracketed ellipses indicate intentional omissions from the source text, usually for brevity; unbracketed ellipses are suspension points present in the original.

UNIT 6

6.1

Bill Watterson, *Calvin and Hobbes,* October 10, 1986 [first quotation], February 6, 1994 [second quotation], August 2, 1993 [third quotation]. [used by permission]

William D. Lassek and Steven J. C. Gaulin, "Costs and Benefits of Fat-Free Muscle Mass in Men: Relationship to Mating Success, Dietary Requirements, and Native Immunity," *Evolution and Human Behavior* 30 (2009): 322.

6.2

Alastair Roberts, "Why We Should Jettison the 'Strong Female Character,'" Mere Orthodoxy (website), April 18, 2016, https:// mereorthodoxy.com/why-we-should-jettison-the-strong -female-character/.

James Damore, "Google's Ideological Echo Chamber," July 2017, https://www.dhillonlaw.com/wp-content/uploads /2018/01/Damore-Google-Manifesto.pdf, 3 [first quotation], 5 [second quotation, italics added], 6 [third quotation].

Jayme L. Sophir on behalf of the National Labor Relations Board to Valerie Hardy-Maloney, Advice Memorandum, January 16, 2018, concerning case 32-CA-205351, https://www .nlrb.gov/case/32-CA-205351.

Alastair Roberts, "Questions and Answers on my 'Strong Female Character' Trope Article," *Alastair's Adversaria* (blog), January 1, 2018, https://alastairadversaria.com/2018/01/01 /questions-and-answers-on-my-strong-female-character -trope-article/.

6.3

Leo Tolstoy, *Anna Karenina*, trans. Rosamund Bartlett (Oxford: Oxford University Press, 2014), 3.

Some content taken from pages 64 [first quotation] and 39-40 [second quotation] of *A PROMISE KEPT,* by Robertson McQuilkin. Copyright © 1998. Used by permission of Tyndale House Publishers, a Division of Tyndale House Ministries. All rights reserved. To order book, please visit www.tyndale.com.

6.5

C. S. Lewis, *The Four Loves* (New York: Harcourt, Brace, 1960), 66 [first quotation], 66–67 [second quotation].

6.6

Joseph Heath and Andrew Potter, *Nation of Rebels: Why Counterculture Became Consumer Culture* (New York: HarperCollins, 2004), 80.

"Percentage of Births to Unmarried Mothers by State," 2018, Centers for Disease Control and Prevention, https://www.cdc .gov/nchs/pressroom/sosmap/unmarried/unmarried.htm.

6.7

Anthony Esolen, "A Requiem for Friendship: Why Boys Will Not Be Boys and Other Consequences of the Sexual Revolution," *Touchstone*, September 2005, https://www .touchstonemag.com/archives/article.php?id=18-07-021-f.

David Brooks, "An Agenda for Moderates," *New York Times* online, February 25, 2019, https://www.nytimes.com/2019 /02/25/opinion/moderate-politics.html.

Chart adapted from "Most Teens Say Social Media Better Connects Them to Their Friends' Lives and Feelings, but Some Also Feel Overwhelmed by the Drama on These Sites," from "Teens' Social Media Habits and Experiences." Pew Research Center, Washington, D. C. (November 28, 2018) https://www.pewresearch.org/internet/2018/11/28/teens -social-media-habits-and-experiences/. Pew Research Center bears no responsibility for the analyses or interpretations of the data presented here. The opinions expressed herein, including any implications for policy, are those of the author and not of Pew Research Center.

UNIT 7

7.1

Thomas Tarrants, "God's Mercy to a Klansman," *Christianity Today*, September 2019, 79.

Planned Parenthood of Southeastern Pa. v. Casey, 505 U. S. 833 (1992) at 851.

7.4

Independent Sector, "The Importance of Community-Based Organizations in Human Services," January 23, 2018, https:// independentsector.org/news-post/the-importance-of -community-based-organizations-in-human-services/.

7.5

Story of Paul Farmer taken from Tracy Kidder, *Mountains Beyond Mountains* (New York: Random House Trade Paperbacks, 2009), 80.

7.6

Kimberly A. Yuracko, "Education off the Grid: Constitutional Constraints on Homeschooling," *California Law Review* 96, no. 1 (2008): 132, doi:10.15779/Z38MH6D.

7.7

Costica Bradatan, "Democracy Is for the Gods," *New York Times* online, July 5, 2019, https://www.nytimes.com/2019 /07/05/opinion/why-democracies-fail.html.

C. S. Lewis, "Equality," in *Present Concerns*, ed. Walter Hooper (San Diego: Harvest Books, 1986), 17.

UNIT 8

8.2

George W. Bush, remarks at Islamic Center of Washington, DC (September 17, 2001), transcript and video, The American Presidency Project, https://www.presidency.ucsb.edu /documents/remarks-the-islamic-center-washington.

Qur'an 55:7–9 (Sahih International).

Sahih Muslim, trans. Abdul Hamid Siddiqui, https://sunnah .com/muslim/45/54.

Mohammad Elshinawy, "Why Do People Suffer?: God's Existence and the Problem of Evil," Yaqeen Institute for Islamic Research, July 2, 2018, https://yaqeeninstitute.org/mohammad-elshinawy/why-do-people-suffer-gods-existence-the-problem-of-evil/.

Qur'an 4:34; 9:5 (Sahih International). Brackets are in the original.

G. K. Chesterton, *Orthodoxy* (Peabody, MA: Hendrickson, 2006), 10.

8.3

Excerpts from MERE CHRISTIANITY by C. S. Lewis copyright © C.S. Lewis Pte. Ltd. 1942, 1943, 1944, 1952. Reprinted by permission.

Carl Olson, *The Different Paths of Buddhism: A Narrative-Historical Introduction* (New Brunswick, NJ: Rutgers University Press, 2005), 65.

8.4

Chart modified from "In U.S., Smaller Share of Adults Identify as Christians, While Religious 'Nones' Have Grown," from "In U.S., Decline of Christianity Continues at Rapid Pace." Pew Research Center, Washington, D.C. (October 17, 2019) https://www.pewforum.org/2019/10/17/in-u-s-decline-of-christianity-continues-at-rapid-pace/. Pew Research Center bears no responsibility for the analyses or interpretations of the data presented here. The opinions expressed herein, including any implications for policy, are those of the author and not of Pew Research Center.

Stanley Fish, *The First: How to Think about Hate Speech, Campus Speech, Religious Speech, Fake News, Post-Truth, and Donald Trump* (New York: One Signal, 2019), 147.

Wilfred M. McClay, "The Strange Persistence of Guilt," *The Hedgehog Review* 19, no. 1 (Spring 2017), https://hedgehogreview.com/issues/the-post-modern-self/articles/the-strange-persistence-of-guilt.

8.5

"Kentucky Clerk Kim Davis Denies Same-Sex Marriage License [*sic*]," ABC News, September 1, 2015, https://www.youtube.com/watch?v=_Xg1Dh2xhXg.

Jean-Jacques Rousseau, *The Social Contract* (New York: E. P. Dutton, 1913), 115.

Miller et al. v. Davis et al., No. 0:2015cv00044 - Document 43 (E. D. Ky. 2015), at 27–28 [first quotation], 2 [second quotation], 10 [third quotation], 16 [fourth quotation], 15 [fifth quotation], 6 [sixth quotation].

8.6

Christian Smith, *Soul Searching: The Religious and Spiritual Lives of American Teenagers*, with Melinda Lundquist Denton (Oxford: Oxford University Press, 2005), 132 [first quotation], 162 [second quotation], 162–63 [third quotation], 127 [fourth quotation], 126 [fifth, sixth, and seventh quotations], 127 [eighth quotation], 136 [ninth quotation].

Christian Smith, *Souls in Transition: The Religious and Spiritual Lives of Emerging Adults*, with Patricia Snell (Oxford: Oxford University Press, 2009), 155 [first quotation], 30–31 [second quotation].

8.7

Taken from "Redeeming Science: A Father-Son Tale," chap. 1 in *Redeeming the Life of the Mind: Essays in Honor of Vern Poythress* by Ransom Poythress, © 2017, 30 [first and second quotations], 32 [third quotation]. Used by permission of Crossway, a publishing ministry of Good News Publishers, Wheaton, IL 60187, www.crossway.org.

David Foster Wallace, "E Unibus Pluram: Television and U.S. Fiction," chap. 2 in *A Supposedly Fun Thing I'll Never Do Again: Essays and Arguments* (Boston: Back Bay Books, 1998), 39.

Ernest Gordon, *Through the Valley of the Kwai* (New York: Harper, 1962), 74 [first quotation], 109 [second quotation].

Taken from *Confronting Christianity: 12 Hard Questions for the World's Largest Religion* by Rebecca McLaughlin, © 2019, 206. Used by permission of Crossway, a publishing ministry of Good News Publishers, Wheaton, IL 60187, www.crossway.org.

GLOSSARY

A

adoption A word picture for salvation that describes a person's being brought into God's family and made an heir with Christ, being responsible to live as a child of God, and ultimately bearing the family resemblance perfectly in a glorified body.

assumption An idea that people believe without trying to prove or without knowing they have it.

B

basic beliefs Things that people believe but probably never think about; things that can't always be proven but are used to prove other beliefs.

biblical theism Belief in God and in His revelation in the Bible.

biblical wisdom Believers fearing the Lord so that they read His Word and His creation in such a way that they end up knowing and loving and doing what is truly best in each situation of life.

big story A worldview's story that seeks to explain where the world came from, why it's here, what is wrong with it, how it can be made right, and where it's going.

body of Christ A word picture for the church as variously gifted, individual members of Christ's body, with Christ as the Head.

bride of Christ A word picture for the church as those whom Christ loved and gave Himself for (as a model for husbands and wives) and as those who await a marriage supper at Christ's Second Coming.

C

church All the people Christ has rescued from the kingdom of darkness and brought into His kingdom; kingdom citizens, who have the responsibility to submit to Jesus as King and bring others to the rescue and rule of Christ.

church discipline The local church removing from its membership someone who is living unrepentantly in sin, with the hope that the disciplined person will repent and be restored to the church.

communitarianism The belief that the interests and good of the community should not be neglected because of too much emphasis on an individual's interests and independence.

conscience The understanding of right and wrong that God writes on every person's heart.

covenant An agreement between two or more people with certain requirements and promises.

Creation The act of God to create the heavens and the earth in six literal days and in agreement with His perfect character and order.

Creation Mandate The command given by God to mankind to have children and to fill and rule over the earth; also known as the "Cultural Mandate" because living out the Creation Mandate results in culture.

culture The result of people living out the Creation Mandate, building on the traditions passed down to them and then creating new things; a group's actions that logically come from their common worldview.

D

dualism The belief that there are two equal gods, one good and one evil.

E

eternal Above time; having no beginning or end, no past or future.

F

Fall The breaking of God's law by Adam and Eve with the consequence of sin for them, all creation, and all their descendants.

fallen direction The bending of something away from creational structure because of the Fall.

fear of the Lord The emotion of a loved child toward a powerful, holy God.

feminism The belief that social structures like marriage, family, and work are oppressing women and need to be changed or abolished in order to make women free and equal to men.

folk culture Local activities that developed in isolation from mass media.

G

gender Male or female according to birth and according to God's design for each person He creates.

general revelation God's communication of Himself to mankind through the natural world.

God's flock A word picture for the church as sheep who need their Shepherd and undershepherds (pastors).

good works Actions that God has called believers to do for the purpose of representing Him in the world and showing their adoption into God's family, not for the purpose of earning salvation.

Great Commandments The summary of all the law: to love God with all your being and to love your neighbor as yourself.

Great Commission The last command of Jesus to His followers to make disciples by sharing the gospel, baptizing those who repent and believe, and teaching believers all of what He commanded.

H

high culture The arts performed at their most advanced levels.

homosexuality The desire of men or women to engage in marriage-like relationships with those of the same gender, contrary to God's design and commands.

I

image of God The quality that God created humans with, giving them worth above all other creatures; the whole person being like God in the characteristics appropriate for humans to have; being a mirror of God's glory.

immanence God's active, intimate involvement with His creation.

incarnation The act of God the Son to take on human nature in order to be born on the earth as Jesus, to die as a perfect human sacrifice, and to rise from the dead and live forever in a glorified body, just as believers will.

individualism The belief that the individual's interests and independence are more important than the community's interests and unity.

inspiration (of Scripture) The work of God to breathe out all Scripture through the Holy Spirit.

J

justification A word picture for salvation that describes a person's being declared not guilty for his sins and receiving Christ's perfect record instead.

L

local church A group of believers who meet weekly to devote themselves "in the apostles' doctrine and fellowship, and in breaking of bread, and in prayers" (Acts 2:42).

M

morality Beliefs about what is right and what is wrong.

N

New Covenant The covenant that was promised in the Old Testament and established by Jesus in the New Testament, giving God's people new hearts with His law written on them.

O

omnipotent All-powerful.

omnipresent Present everywhere.

omniscient All-knowing.

P

people of God An all-inclusive term for both Old Testament believers and the church as those who belong to God.

polygamy Having more than one spouse at the same time.

pop culture The set of movies, shows, books, albums, online videos, sports teams, Broadway shows, and other kinds of entertainment that are made popular at a given time through mass media.

R

Redemption God's restoration of sinners to a right relationship with Him through the death and resurrection of Jesus Christ, culminating in their eternal life with Him and in the complete restoration of the creation from the effects of the Fall.

redemptive direction The pushing of something that has been bent from the Fall back toward its creational structure and the final redemption that Christ will bring.

royal priesthood A word picture for the church as priests communicating the will and the presence of the Great King to the nations.

S

sanctification The process by which God restores believers from their fallen state to be more and more like the image of His Son.

Second Adam A title given to Jesus because He accomplished perfectly what the first Adam failed to do.

secularism The worldview controlled by the two-story view, allowing religious activities and convictions to be practiced in private places but demanding that they not be brought into public places.

seed Offspring; a theme throughout the Bible to track the promised offspring who would fulfill the covenants; used as singular to mean one person or used as plural to refer to a group.

society A web of relationships among people who depend on each other in a community.

special revelation God's communication of Himself to mankind through His Word, the Bible.

structure The way God's creation is supposed to work, in agreement with His purpose and plan.

T

temple of God A word picture for the church as living stones that God is assembling together into a temple for Him to live in.

transcendence God's complete separation from and superiority to His creation.

transgender People who were born male or female but who reject their God-given gender and opt to talk, act, and dress like the opposite gender.

Trinity The word used to describe God as three persons (Father, Son, and Spirit) in one God.

two-story view A dualistic view of life as two separate levels with two different authorities: (1) real life on the lower level ruled by self or science and (2) the church or religion on the upper level ruled by God.

U

union with Christ A word picture for salvation that describes a person's being made one with Christ in order to receive all the benefits of His death and resurrection.

universal church The collection of people throughout time since Pentecost who have believed the gospel of Christ.

W

worldview The way a person makes sense of the world through a big story, which is the foundation for his basic beliefs and loves, which in turn shape his actions as an individual and within his culture.

SCRIPTURE MEMORY

SCRIPTURE INDEX

VERSE	PAGES
46:9	33, 98
46:9–10	56, 58
48:9, 11	118
53:6	280
55:8–9	128
57:15	57, 131

JEREMIAH

VERSE	PAGES
9:23	136
9:23–24	142
17:9	115, 149
23:23–24	131
29:7	345
29:11	349

EZEKIEL

VERSE	PAGES
36:26	77, 119
37:27	280

DANIEL

VERSE	PAGES
3:17–18	308
4:30	33
4:35	34, 128, 340

MATTHEW

VERSE	PAGES
1:21	106
4:17	79
5:1–12	349
5:11–12	196
5:13–16	196–97
5:16	221, 277
5:45	345
6:2	185
6:8	106
6:19–21	355
6:25–33	58
6:33	94
7:1	348
9:36	320
10:30	97, 106
15	246

VERSE	PAGES
15:6	246
16:18	279
18:15	285
18:17	285
19:4	139
20:28	238
22:20–22	305
22:37–39	31
22:37–40	40, 115
22:39	277
23	320
28:18–20	81, 281
28:19	98
28:19–20	298

MARK

VERSE	PAGES
3:21	247
7:21–23	149
9:48	299
10:14	282

LUKE

VERSE	PAGES
4	176
9:23	347
10:25–37	289
10:27	289
10:38–42	340
11:42–43	117
12:15	29
14:26	272, 273
18:19	106, 349
19:10	53
24:47	298

JOHN

VERSE	PAGES
1:1	98
1:1, 14	129, 322
3:16	4, 97, 106, 115, 330
3:19	150
3:29	280
4:23	282

VERSE	PAGES
4:24	120
5:39	53
5:39–40	16
8:42	154
8:44	154
10:35	102
13:1	115
13:13–14	238
14:6	100
14:15	165
15:1, 4–5	161
15:13	115, 252
15:20	196
17:6	119
17:11, 15	175
17:14–16	211
17:17	102
17:24	118, 124
20:21	53

ACTS

VERSE	PAGES
1:8	279, 298
2:1–4	279
2:42	82, 278, 279, 281, 286
4:18–20	305
6:1–6	281
9:36, 39	219
10:42	299
15:14	118, 275
18:12–15	304
20:35	293, 294

ROMANS

VERSE	PAGES
1:18	101
1:18–23	335
1:20	25
1:21	316
1:23	146
1:25	335
1:32	103
2:14–15	101, 104, 108

TOPICAL INDEX

PHOTO CREDITS

COVER

Front drbimages/iStock/Getty Images Plus/Getty Images; **Back** Mix and Match Studio/Shutterstock.com

UNIT 1

3 shapecharge/iStock/Getty Images Plus/Getty Images; **7** "Poiuyt .svg" by AnonMoos/Wikimedia Commons/Public Domain; **16** Aflo Co. Ltd./Alamy Stock Photo; **23** Adobe Stock/tab62; **27**tl filipefrazao /iStock/Getty Images Plus/Getty Images; **27**tr FG Trade/E+/Getty Images; **27**b AnnaNahabed/iStock/Getty Images Plus; **32** FatCamera /E+/Getty Images; **35** Library of Congress/Archive Photos/Getty Images

UNIT 2

49 PeopleImages/iStock/Getty Images Plus; **52**t monkeybusiness images/iStock/Getty Images Plus/Getty Images; **52**ct Oksana_Alex /iStock/Getty Images Plus/Getty Images; **52**cbl images by Tang Ming Tung/Moment/Getty Images; **52**cbr Caiaimage/Sam Edwards/Getty Images; **52**bl Jcomp/iStock/Getty Images Plus/Getty Images; **52**br Courtney Hale/iStock/Getty Images Plus/Getty Images; **53**tl SDI Productions/E+/Getty Images; **53**bl Monkey Business Images /Shutterstock.com; **53**tr Courtney Hale/iStock/Getty Images Plus /Getty Images; **53**ct Hero Images/Getty Images; **53**cb Imgorthand /E+/Getty Images; **53**b Caiaimage/Paul Bradbury/Getty Images; **55**tl SDI Productions/E+/Getty Images; **55**tr Compassionate Eye Foundation/Robert Kent/Digital Vision/Getty Images; **55**bl Juanmonino /iStock/Getty Images Plus/Getty Images; **55**br Photo by Gerardo Marrufo on Unsplash; **66** Library of Congress/Corbis Historical/Getty Images; **67** Davel5957/iStock/Getty Images Plus/Getty Images; **71** (poverty) Robert Alexander/Archive Photos/Getty Images; **71** (cancer) napocska/Shutterstock.com; **71** (frustration) Phil Boorman /Cultura/Getty Images; **71** (gossip) FatCamera/E+/Getty Images; **71** (conflict) Image Source/Getty Images; **71** (lying) dorioconnell/E+ /Getty Images; **71** (music) Andrew Chin/Getty Images Entertainment/Getty Images; **71** (idol) Mint Images/Mint Images RF/Getty Images; **71** (anger) skynesher/E+/Getty Images; **72**t Justin Sullivan /Getty Images News/Getty Images; **72**bl SKrow/iStock Unreleased /Getty Images; **72**bc © iStockphoto.com/Roberto A Sanchez; **72**br iCreate Magazine/Future/Getty Images; **74** angintaravichian/iStock /Getty Images Plus/Getty Images; **82**tl PeopleImages/E+/Getty Images; **82**tr P Maxwell Photography/Shutterstock.com; **82**bl Nicholas Castro/Lightstock; **82**br FatCamera/E+/Getty Images; **88** Rischgitz/Hulton Archive/Getty Images

UNIT 3

93 Compassionate Eye Foundation/DigitalVision/Getty Images; **94**t Nattawut Lakjit/EyeEm/Getty Images; **94**ctl CSA Images/Getty Images; **94**ctr ET-ARTWORKS/Getty Images; **94**cbl TatianaMironenko /iStock/Getty Images Plus/Getty Images; **94**cbr Mark Collinson /Alamy Stock Photo; **94**bl Pilith/Shutterstock.com; **94**br agrobacter /iStock/Getty Images Plus/Getty Images; **95** Michael Prince/The Forbes Collection/Contour RA/Getty Images; **102** Library of Congress, Public Domain; **123**t TCD/Prod.DB/Alamy Stock Photo; **123**c Clive Mason/Getty Images Sport/Getty Images; **123**b Clive Mason /Getty Images Sport/Getty Images; **124–25**bg blyjak/iStock/Getty Images Plus/Getty Images; **124–25**ti NASA, ESA/Hubble and the Hubble Heritage Team/Public Domain; **124–25**ci Art Wager/E+/Getty Images; **124**bli mikroman6/Moment/Getty Images; **124**bri taratata /iStock/Getty Images Plus/Getty Images; **125**ti aLittleSilhouetto /iStock/Getty Images Plus/Getty Images; **125**ci Ridofranz/iStock /Getty Images Plus/Getty Images; **125**bi Martin Harvey/Getty Images; **126**tl Gilbert Rondilla Photography/Moment/Getty Images; **126**tr Granger Wootz/Getty Images; **126**bl Courtney Hale/iStock /Getty Images Plus/Getty Images; **126**br monkeybusinessimages /iStock/Getty Images Plus/Getty Images

UNIT 4

135 Catherine Delahaye/Stone/Getty Images; **136** Chris Bennett /Getty Images; **139** DA4554/iStock/Getty Images Plus/Getty Images; **142**l DOMINIC LIPINSKI/AFP/Getty Images; **142**c AFP Contributor /AFP/Getty Images; **142**r Image Broker/Media Bakery; **144**tl UEye Ubiquitous/Universal Images Group/Getty Images; **144**tc Jose Luis Pelaez Inc/DigitalVision/Getty Images; **144**tr MoMo Productions /DigitalVision/Getty Images; **144**bl Arctic-Images/The Image Bank Unreleased/Getty Images; **144**bc PeopleImages/E+/Getty Images; **144**br mihailomilovanovic/E+/Getty Images; **145**tl Jorge Fernández /LightRocket/Getty Images; **145**tc Cavan Images/Getty Images; **145**tr Stefano Montesi - Corbis/Corbis News/Getty Images; **145**bl Westend61/Getty Images; **145**bc Klaus Vedfelt/Digital Vision/Getty Images; **145**r MoMo Productions/Digital Vision/Getty Images; **159**tl fizkes/iStock/Getty Images Plus/Getty Images; **159**tr Wavebreakmedia/iStock/Getty Images Plus/Getty Images; **159**bl Andersen Ross Photography Inc/DigitalVision/Getty Images; **159**bc Juanmonino/E+/Getty Images; **159**br Photo by Janko Ferlič on Unsplash; **163** Kittiphan Teerawattanakul/EyeEm/Getty Images; **173**tl HRAUN/E+/Getty Images; **173**tc PeopleImages/E+/Getty Images; **173**tr Wavebreakmedia/iStock/Getty Images Plus/Getty Images; **173**bl anthurren/iStock/Getty Images Plus/Getty Images; **173**br Ridofranz/iStock/Getty Images Plus/Getty Images; **176** artisteer/iStock/Getty Images Plus/Getty Images; **177** xavierarnau /E+/Getty Images

UNIT 5

183 Ridofranz/iStock/Getty Images Plus/Getty Images; **186** (pueblo home) Susan Vineyard/iStock/Getty Images Plus/Getty Images; **186** (Kazakh music) Avalon/Universal Images Group/Getty Images; **186** (Italian food) Pinkybird/E+/Getty Images; **186** (Yoruba art) Metropolitan Art Museum, New York, Gift of Mr. and Mrs. Klaus G. Perls, 1991, www.metmuseum.org; **186** (Russian choir) Ferenc Szelepcsenyi /Alamy Stock Photo; **186** (Japanese greeting) stockstudioX/E+/Getty Images; **186** (Quechua dance) © Barna Tanko | Dreamstime.com; **187** (Kamean home) Tyler Olson/Shutterstock.com; **187** (Armenian music) imageBROKER/Alamy Stock Photo; **187** (Chinese art) "Song of the Lute" by Ding Yunpeng/Wikimedia Commons/Public Domain; **187** (French food) elena_hramowa/iStock/Getty Images Plus /Getty Images; **187** (Kiwi choir) paul kennedy/Alamy Stock Photo; **187** (Brazilian greeting) skynesher/E+/Getty Images; **187** (Maasai dance) Wolfgang Kaehler/LightRocket/Getty Images; **195**tl monkeybusinessimages/iStock/Getty Images Plus/Getty Images; **195**tr monkeybusinessimages/iStock/Getty Images Plus/Getty Images; **195**bl imtmphoto/iStock/Getty Images Plus/Getty Images; **195**br Westend61/Getty Images; **198**t FatCamera/E+/Getty Images; **198**b RossHelen/iStock/Getty Images Plus/Getty Images; **199**t Monty Rakusen/Cultura RF/Getty Images; **199**c Monty Rakusen /Cultura RF/Getty Images; **199**b ZUMA Press, Inc./Alamy Stock Photo; **206**tl Granger Wootz/Getty Images; **206**tr damircudic/E+/Getty Images; **206**bl Yasser Chalid/Moment/Getty Images; **206**br Caia